Wat

Christopher Hibbert was an acclaimed English author, historian and biographer. He has been called 'probably the most widely-read popular historian of our time' and was the author of over fifty works of history.

WATERLOO

CHRISTOPHER
HIBBERT

First published in the United Kingdom in 1998 by Wordsworth Editions Limited

This edition published in the United Kingdom in 2021 by

Canelo
Unit 9, 5th Floor
Cargo Works, 1-2 Hatfields
London, SE1 9PG
United Kingdom

A CIP catalogue record for this book is available from the British Library.

Print ISBN 978 1 80032 597 5
Ebook ISBN 978 1 80032 596 8

Look for more great books at www.canelo.co

Printed and bound in Great Britain by Clays Ltd, Elcograf S.p.A.

1

For James Leasor

Introduction

The French Revolution: Its Impact and Influence

"On this day, at this place," said Goethe, "a new era opens in the history of the world."

The day was September 20, 1792; the place, Valmy. Here, through the thin patches of a drifting mist, Goethe had seen the well-trained Prussian army of Frederick William II, officered by veterans of the King's uncle, Frederick the Great, falter, halt, and turn aside, demoralized before the massed forces of the Revolution.

Goethe was right; a new era had opened at Valmy; and although that era seemed to close twenty-three years later at Waterloo, in fact it was never to close. The French Revolution, by its early military success, succeeded in imposing its view on the civilized world; and by the methods used to achieve that success it imposed on the civilized world the barbarism of total war.

On the day after Valmy, the French National Convention declared that the monarchy was abolished; and a few hours later, on September 22, there dawned the first day of Year One of the Republic. Before Year One was out, the head of Louis XVI was held up by Sanson to the crowds at the foot of the guillotine.

The Prussian commander, the Duke of Brunswick, had threatened to destroy Paris should any harm come to the

King; but now that Louis was dead, the threat was turned. "The kings in alliance try to intimidate us," Danton called back defiantly. "We hurl at their feet, as a gage of battle, the French king's head."

The reaction of Europe to this fierce provocation was immediate. Within less than a fortnight France found herself at war not only with Prussia and Piedmont but also with Spain, Holland, England, and the Austrian Empire.

Out of this threat to Republican France – besieged by the armies of Europe, impugned by plotting émigrés, and torn apart from within by political and religious forces unsympathetic to the spirit of the Revolution – was born the Terror.

But while Terror reigned in France, while in Paris alone well over two thousand heads fell into the guillotine's basket, the French Republic, dominated for one cataclysmic year by Robespierre, astonished the world by its military success. Between July 28, 1793, when the thin, precise, incorruptible, fanatical lawyer from Arras entered the *Comité de Salut Public* in his immaculate sea-green coat, and July 28, 1794, when the guillotine's blade cut through his neck already blood-smeared from a shattered jaw, the forces at the Jacobins' command achieved a series of triumphs that rocked every throne in Europe.

For the war that was fought for the life of the Republic was a war fought, too, for France. The Revolutionary troops marched into battle, singing the *Marseillaise*, a hymn not only of freedom but an exultation in "*le jour de gloire.*" Patriotism surged in a country where, for the first time in her history, the common people felt a common cause, where *liberté, égalité, fraternité* were words of new meaning, at once an inspiration and a source of pride. And with this nascent pride, this reorientated patriotism came ambition and the desire to conquer. *Fraternité* began to be forgotten; *victoire* took its place. Where, the ruling dynasties asked each other in concern, would the Revolution end?

By the beginning of 1795 the Republic seemed safe, even invincible, and the way was prepared for expansion. The worst of the royalist uprisings had been suppressed; Toulon, which had surrendered to the English the year before, had been recaptured; the Hanoverians had been defeated at Hondschoote, and the Duke of York forced to retreat to Furnes, abandoning the siege of Dunkirk; the Piedmontese had been driven back from Aigueville on to the Mont Cenis Pass. Lazare Hoche had forced Wurmser back across the Rhine; at Fleurus, Jean-Baptiste Jourdan had overwhelmed the Austrians and driven them back through Liège; Belgium had been reconquered, and the way prepared for Charles Pichegru to overrun Holland.

They were young these Revolutionary generals, inexperienced, impromptu and *roturier*: Pichegru, the son of a laborer, was thirty-three; Jourdan, a peacetime silk mercer, was thirty-two; Hoche, who had once been a groom in the royal stables and a private in the *Gardes françaises*, was twenty-six. Yet within three years they had defeated Europe.

This had not been done by the vital spirit of the Revolution alone, nor yet by virtue of their own considerable talents. They had been helped by the veterans of the old royal army, by the officers of the less aristocratic and more scientific corps of artillery and engineers, who had stayed with their regiments, accepting the Revolution, while noble officers were deserting in protest against it. They had been helped, too, by the relatively good standard of their firearms – the 1777 model of the flintlock musket remained unchanged until 1840, while their light and simple field guns, though smoothbore and muzzle-loading, were the best in Europe. But above all, these young generals owed their success to the *levée en masse*, universal conscription that could bring into the field well over a million men, and to the brilliant soldier who had shown that this unwieldy and callow host could overcome the more carefully drilled and far more experienced armies of the old European powers.

–

Lazare Nicolas Marguerite Carnot was born in Burgundy in 1753. When the Revolutionary Wars broke out he was a captain in the engineers. In 1794 he was still a captain; but as the member of the *Comité de Salut Public*, charged with the direction of military affairs, he had become the inspiration of the national defense, the organizer of victory.

His achievements, eclipsed today by the fame of the man whose rise to supreme power depended on them, were indeed astonishing.

When the Revolution began, the French army – considerably smaller than the Austrian, slightly larger than the Prussian – had a wartime strength of 295,000 men, including 76,000 militia and 23 regiments of foreigners, all recruited by voluntary enlistment. Pay was meager (six *sous* a day); food was often inedible; the hospitals were primitive; and accommodation in the barracks was so limited that soldiers frequently had to sleep three in a bed. No one could be surprised that the type of man enlisted was, as often as not, undesirable, nor that an average of 20,000 men were lost each year through disease and desertion. Discipline was maintained by means of various degrading forms of punishment on the Prussian model.

Regimental officers were drawn from the families of the lesser nobility, and promotion from the ranks was virtually impossible.

There were, however, strong compensatory influences, which saved the army from disintegration when the Revolution brought such severe strains to bear upon its loyalty: despite his conditions the French infantryman and cavalry soldier remained cheerful and lively, respecting and trusting his skilled and experienced noncommissioned officers; the artillery was universally recognized as being better than that in any other army; while the engineers, for whose guidance Captain Carnot had written various papers and manuals, were also unsurpassed in knowledge, ability, and self-respect.

When war came these virtues in the French army were not by themselves enough, of course, to withstand the shock of a Europe roused in arms against the Republic. In August of 1791 the Assembly was compelled to call for volunteers sufficient to form 169 new battalions; but although men all over France rushed to enroll themselves, the early enthusiasm was soon dispelled, and eventually only 60 disorderly battalions took to the road. Two years later, after the execution of the King had brought the enemies of the Republic across its frontiers, far more drastic measures were required – and required immediately – to drive them back.

On August 23, 1793, the Convention, by a decree of incalculable significance, called out the entire population of the country to fight for the life of the government. A whole nation was put in arms at the service of the State. The "armed horde" had been given the seal of official sanction.

Conscription, as Carnot was well aware, could not but revolutionize the whole system of warfare. Since the Thirty Years' War had ended, in 1648, leaving Central Europe in ruins above the bodies of its 8,000,000 dead, warfare had become limited in its scope and purpose, and had been conducted by professional and fiercely disciplined standing armies mainly to settle quarrels that were dynastic rather than ideological.

The aim of a military commander was no longer to destroy the enemy, but to exhaust him, to outmaneuver him rather than to bring him to battle. Even Marshal Saxe, that most original of eighteenth-century military writers, insisted that battles should only be sought when "you have all imaginable reason to expect the victory." Otherwise the ideal was to force your opponent to sue for peace by occupying his territory, striking at his lines of communication, besieging his fortresses, and consuming his supplies. It became frequent, Daniel Defoe, himself a soldier, observed, "to have armies of 50,000 men of a side stand at bay within view on one another, and spend a whole campaign in dodging, or, as it is genteelly called, observing one another, and then march off into winter quarters."

These prolonged maneuvers were, of course, dictated by the military conditions of warfare as much as by the predilections and prejudices of the commanders involved. The lack of good roads made rapid movement impossible; the difficulties of supply in the field made reliance on a chain of magazines essential; the proliferation of strong fortresses hampered the approach to a battlefield, weakened armies which were compelled to detach forces to invest them, and hindered the exploitation of victory. Above all, the traditional order of battle that armies adopted made them incapable of forcing battle upon an unwilling enemy.

> The idea that an army should be drawn up in rigid line of battle, normally with the infantry massed in the centre and the cavalry on the wings, had become fixed by the custom of centuries [Sir Basil Liddell Hart has written]. In the days when shock weapons predominated, this rigid formation had the virtue of solidity. But like most military practices it persisted long after its value had declined and its handicaps had increased. So long as it persisted it meant that an army was a limbless body, or, at its best, a trunk with short stumps... [It] was a single piece on the chessboard of war. And the comparison with chess may help us to realize the difficulty of cornering an opponent when only two pieces exist on the board.[1]

Dictated by such conditions and such antecedents, this eighteenth-century form of restricted warfare had one supreme advantage. It left the civilian population largely undisturbed. It was, in Guglielmo Ferrero's opinion, one of the greatest achievements of the eighteenth century. It was lost as a result of the French Revolution, and the Convention's decree of August 1793:

> From this moment until our enemies shall have been driven from the territory of the Republic, all Frenchmen are permanently requisitioned for service in the armies. The

> young men shall fight; the married men shall forge weapons and transport supplies; the women will make clothes and serve in the hospitals; the children will make up old linen into lint; the old men will have themselves carried into the public squares to rouse the courage of the fighting men, to preach the unity of the Republic and hatred against kings.

In the past soldiers had been expensive, now they were made cheap; losses suffered in battle could be made up from an almost limitless store. Blood could flow for victory without fear of the army's death. The triumph of Napoleon was made possible.

But before these triumphs could be achieved, a whole new concept of warfare had to be devised. The new conscript was generally more intelligent if less amenable to discipline than the old professional soldier, so many of the shoulder-to-shoulder tactical procedures, which the royal army had practiced on the drill square, had to be abandoned in favor of a looser organization that made more allowance for individual initiative: also, the increased size of the Republic's armies made transport and supply a problem that could only be resolved by discarding tents in favor of the bivouac, the wagons of the commissariat in favor of compulsory requisitioning, foraging, and plunder.

Carnot's quick and receptive mind immediately grasped the advantages that could be derived from these necessary alterations in the organization of armies and the conduct of war. The precise, choreographic techniques of eighteenth-century maneuvering and counter-maneuvering had to be abandoned; but their place could be taken by a far more effective, more ruthless style. Carnot understood the character of the men at his disposal; he knew what they could be made to do. He knew that they could not and would not be made to parade; but he was equally aware of how well they could fight and how much they would endure. They were capable, he discovered, of carrying into practice the war of swift movement regardless of seasons, the war of surprise and quick concentrated attacks that were to bring them to victory.

This new style of warfare was not invented by Carnot. He was the unflaggingly energetic organizer of victory, the commander in whose highly capable hands all power lay, from whom all decisions emanated. But he was not so much evolving new theories as bringing the theories of others to bear on the solution of new problems.

These theories, which Carnot adapted to his purposes, had been dominating military thought in France for almost half a century, sweeping into the background the classical influence of the Greek and Roman masters that had pervaded the ideas of Gustavus Adolphus and those other skilled practitioners of seventeenth-century warfare.

Marshal Saxe's insistence on the necessity for mobility and vigorous pursuit, his views on fortifications and armored cavalry, on organization and supply all ran counter to the conventional military ideas of his time, but they had all had great influence in France. Pierre de Bourcet and the Comte de Guibert had both followed his *Mes Rêveries* with important and revolutionary works of their own.

De Bourcet's perception of the true theory of concentration, his grasp of the advantages of dispersing an enemy's forces, his belief that "a plan must have several branches," at once contain echoes of Saxe's teaching and foreshadow the maxims of Napoleon. So does Guibert's profoundly influential *Essai général de tactique*, which, published in 1770, laid renewed emphasis on mobility, fluidity, and adaptability as the secrets of success. So even do the Chevalier du Teil's and Jean Baptiste de Gribeauval's works on the proper uses of modern artillery.

Carnot was not the only soldier of genius to perceive how these theories might be put to the test by means of the great *levée en masse* and so transform the map of Europe.

In 1800, when Carnot entered upon his duties as Minister of War, another, younger officer consolidated an already formidable reputation on the battlefield of Marengo – an officer who was to epitomize the hungry power of the Revolution, and so eventually become the victim of its ambition.

1

Napoleon: The Man and the Soldier

Napoleon was born on August 15, 1769, at Ajaccio in Corsica. He was at first a sickly child, for his mother had spent the last months of her pregnancy as a refugee, wandering about in the mountains where General Paoli, the champion of Corsican independence, was soon to be defeated by the French.

Napoleon's father, Carlo Buonaparte, a charming, weak-willed lawyer, had been one of Paoli's lieutenants; but he did not follow his leader into exile, preferring to make his peace with the French and to profit by his submission. He was an extravagant man and his beautiful wife, whom he had married when she was only fourteen, was to bear him thirteen children, of whom eight survived their infancy.

The importance of Napoleon's Corsican origin and background has often been exaggerated; but, viewed in retrospect, it combines certain factors which laid the foundations of his career. First of all, there was the influence of his mother in his childhood. At St. Helena he reflected that, "I was very well brought up by my mother. I owe her a great deal. She instilled into me pride and taught me good sense." He used to recount with a mixture of admiration and indignation how his mother gave him a birching for mimicking his grandmother. He might have added that it was his parents' friendship with de Marbeuf, the French Governor of Corsica, that gave him the chance of the best professional education for a military career. Thirdly, it was in the minute but complicated and hard-hitting school of Corsican politics that he acquired his political apprenticeship.[2]

Through the influence of de Marbeuf, Napoleon was given a place at Brienne, a school founded by St. Germain, Louis XVI's Minister of War, for the sons of nobles.

One of his fellow pupils has provided a revealing glimpse of him at this time:

Bonaparte and I were eight years of age when our friendship began. It speedily became very intimate, for there was a certain sympathy of heart between us. I was one among those of his youthful comrades who could best accommodate themselves to his stern character. His natural reserve, his disposition to meditate on the conquest of Corsica, and the impressions he had received in childhood respecting the misfortunes of his country and his family, led him to seek retirement, and rendered his general demeanour, though in appearance only, somewhat unpleasing. Our equality of age brought us together in the classes of the mathematics and *belles lettres*. His ardent wish to acquire knowledge was remarkable from the very commencement of his studies. When he first came to the college he spoke only the Corsican dialect, and the vice-principal gave him instructions in the French language. In this he made such rapid progress that in a short time he commenced the first rudiments of Latin. But to this study he evinced such a repugnance that at the age of fifteen he was not out of the fourth class. There I left him very speedily; but I could never get before him in the mathematical class, in which he was undoubtedly the cleverest lad at the college. I used sometimes to help him with his Latin themes and versions in return for the aid he afforded me in the solution of problems, at which he evinced a degree of readiness and facility which perfectly astonished me.

When at Brienne, Bonaparte was remarkable for the dark colour of his complexion (which, subsequently, the climate of France somewhat changed), for his piercing and scrutinising glance, and for the style of his conversation both with his masters and comrades. His conversation almost always bore the appearance of ill-humour, and he was certainly not very amiable. This I attribute to the misfortunes his family had sustained and the impressions made on his mind by the conquest of his country.

The pupils were invited by turns to dine with Father Berton, the head of the school. One day, it being Bonaparte's turn to enjoy this indulgence, some of the professors who were at table designedly made some disrespectful remarks on Paoli, of whom they knew the young Corsican was an enthusiastic admirer. "Paoli," observed Bonaparte, "was a great man; he loved his country; and I will never forgive my father, who was his adjutant, for having concurred in the union of Corsica with France. He ought to have followed Paoli's fortune, and have fallen with him."

Generally speaking, Bonaparte was not much liked by his comrades at Brienne. He was not social with them, and rarely took part in their amusements. His country's recent submission to France always caused in his mind a painful feeling, which estranged him from his schoolfellows. I, however, was almost his constant companion. During play-hours he used to withdraw to the library, where he read with deep interest works of history. I often went off to play with my comrades, and left him by himself in the library.

The temper of the young Corsican was not improved by the teasing he frequently experienced from his comrades, who were fond of ridiculing him about his Christian name Napoleon and his country. He often said to me, "I will do these French all the mischief I can."[3]

As a recent biographer, Felix Markham, has written:

To his school-fellows he was an obvious object for mild ragging because of his foreign accent and his passionate Corsican patriotism, though this did not prevent him from making a few close friends. His odd Corsican name "Napoleone" was corrupted into the nickname of *Paille-au-Nez* (Straw-nose). Was his pose of the persecuted Corsican patriot a form of defence against his foreign accent and poverty, or was it even a form of subconscious jealousy of his mother's friendship with his patron, de Marbeuf? His parents had, after all, thrown in their lot with the French, and a more ordinary boy would have conformed to the French background in which he found himself.

Even as a small child he was noted for his enthusiasm in organizing fierce and elaborate mock-battles. An English fellow-pupil of Napoleon recalled in 1797 the cold winter of 1783 when fierce battles raged among the snow fortifications designed by Napoleon.

The school inspector reported that Napoleon's aptitude for mathematics would make him suitable for the navy, but eventually it was decided that he should try for the artillery, where advancement by merit and mathematical skill was much more open than in the infantry. In 1784 he was nominated, in a patent signed by Louis XVI, to a place at the *École Militaire* in Paris.

This French Sandhurst had been founded in 1751, largely at the instance of Madame de Pompadour, to remedy the lamentable lack of education of gentlemen-cadets. It contained both paying pupils and King's scholars and, despite St. Germain's reforms, it reflected the social standards of the *haute noblesse*, who affected to despise the poor scholars. Napoleon here encountered the "cascade of disdain" which was one of the most important psychological causes of the Revolution. Laura Permon, later wife of General Junot, Duc d'Abrantès, whose mother was a friend of Letizia Buonaparte and befriended Napoleon in Paris, recollects that Napoleon ranted violently against the snobbery of the *École Militaire*. Napoleon said, "We were fed and served magnificently," and as First Consul he made the *École Militaire* considerably more austere. But even before the Revolution its staff of teachers was of high quality.

Napoleon took the passing-out examination in one year, instead of the normal two or three years, and was placed forty-second in the national list. His performance was so good that he jumped the intermediate grades and was commissioned as Lieutenant to the *Régiment de la Fère* at Valence, together with his greatest friend de Mazis. When Napoleon and de Mazis visited the Permons to show off their new uniforms Napoleon looked so thin and small that Laura and her sister instantly gave him the nickname of "Puss-in-Boots." This was too much for Napoleon's sense of humour, and for many years Laura was greeted by Napoleon as "little pest." As a schoolboy

Napoleon was certainly a youth with a considerable chip on his shoulder. Like so many of the products of the *École Militaire*, de Mazis emigrated during the Revolution. When he returned to Paris in 1802 under the amnesty for the *émigrés*, he was warmly welcomed by Napoleon; as Keeper of the Wardrobe he remained one of his court officials till the end of the Empire.

The artillery *Régiment de la Fère* had a reputation as one of the smartest and most efficient in the French Army. The significance of the professional and practical training Napoleon received there between 1785 and 1788, and at the artillery school of Auxonne, commanded by Maréchal du Teil, in the year 1788–9, will become apparent later at Toulon and in the Italian campaigns.[4]

At Auxonne the lessons of Gribeauval and Guibert, of Bourcet and Carnot had long been understood and assimilated; and Maréchal du Theil, the commandant of the school, was one of their main exponents, teaching the idea of the blitzkrieg, *the swift concentration at a given point followed by a vigorous surprise attack and an energetic pursuit, emphasizing the need for technical development and a more scientific approach to the theory of war, particularly in the use of mobile artillery. The young Buonaparte became du Theil's favorite pupil.*

It has been shown that Bonaparte learned warfare in the first place by learning principles, and not by mysterious intuition; though, far from following the manner of mediocre men who learn principles by rote, he showed his genius by his way of powerfully apprehending them. He seized upon the principles that were elemental and directed them to the complex and moving problems that a strategist has to face; doing this with versatility and precision, and with masterly control of the super-abundant details... So, though it was Bourcet, for example, who taught that a military plan should be mobile and multiple in character – admitting of alternative courses of action in response to whichever of the various possible moves the enemy might make – it was Bonaparte who, as a strategist in politics and war, had a mind so to speak congested with alternatives, and possessed the elasticity that enabled him to suspend the final choice and withhold his decision until events should have given him his cue.[5]

Napoleon was away from Paris during the early months of the Reign of Terror; but his friendship with the Robespierres had led to a short term of imprisonment. In 1795, however, he saved the new regime in Paris by firing on the mob on the steps of the church of Saint-Roch. And Barras, chief of the Thermidorians,

rewarded the Corsican with the hand of a discarded mistress, Josephine de Beauharnais, one of the merry widows of the Thermidorian carnival. The penniless, uncouth, provincial officer fell madly in love with the aristocratic demimondaine, his senior by six years. The command of the Italian expedition was a handsome wedding gift.[6]

But Napoleon did not owe his command wholly to influence. Emigration and the guillotine had bequeathed to the army an acute shortage of professionally trained officers of proved talent.

If he survived the guillotine or the hazards of battle, a man with Napoleon's qualifications was not unlikely to get high command at an unusually early age.

One of the first of the Napoleonic myths is the picture of the young, small, insignificant General being greeted with derision by the veteran officers of the Army of

Italy. In fact, he was known to them through his staff work for the Army in 1794–5, and even the Piedmontese commander was aware of his reputation as "a brilliant theorist and strategist". Yet he was young and untried as a commander in the field. Masséna recalled his first meeting with Napoleon: "They imagined from the way he carried about his wife's portrait, and showed it to everyone, and still more from his extreme youth, that he owed his appointment to yet another bit of intrigue." "But in a minute or two he put on his General's hat and seemed two feet taller." General Augereau went about saying, "I can't understand why this little b… has so frightened me." Napoleon reported, in more conventional language, to the Directory the day after he assumed command: "I have been received by the Army with signs of pleasure and the confidence owed to one who was known to have merited your trust." Henceforth he was to sign his name "Bonaparte" instead of the Italian "Buonaparte".[7]

As Professor Wilkinson has suggested, the first campaign

contained the germ, and more than the germ, of all his future exploits. It exemplified all his principles: the original distribution of the troops into three groups or camps about twelve miles distant from one another; their swift concentration by a forward march begun before dawn; the seizure of a central position from which to strike the separated portions of the enemy; the aim of the enemy's communications; the spreading of the divisions like a net to enclose the enemy's flanks; the drawing in of the net to envelop the enemy; the combination of a frontal attack with a surprise attack on the flank; the use of a river to mask a movement against the enemy's rear; the collection on the battlefield of a superior force; above all the unprecedented rapidity of movement and the incessant, never-resting energy of the action…

The great principle on which Napoleon at St. Helena constantly insisted was: "Tenir son armée réunie," which he rightly considers as the principle of all the great captains. It is one of Guibert's leading ideas. It received a peculiar application in Bourcet's treatise on mountain warfare. "In a mountainous country," said Bourcet, "it is constantly necessary to split up your army into small parcels. This constitutes the science of mountain warfare provided the general who employs it always has the means of reuniting his forces when it becomes necessary." This is in a nutshell the best description of the Napoleonic method of handling an army.[8]

The triumphs of the Italian campaign made Bonaparte one of the most famous names in the world and gave the Republican troops a reputation for invincibility. Propaganda presented the men and their leader as though they were a combination of genius and élan *suddenly created by the magical impetus of the Revolution. And although the origins of their success were to be found in roots both older and more mundane than this, the propaganda was not wholly false.*

It was true that the Age of Reason had long since led to a radical questioning of the idées reçues *of strategy and tactics and had opened men's minds to the potentialities of military technology; that the staff of the French army had long been versed in the new theories of war.*

Yet two conditions had still been wanting before use could be made of this heritage: a field commander with the executive genius to make use of it, and the sort of army that could quickly and faithfully follow his directions.

Carnot had satisfied the second of these conditions by mobilizing the youth of France and forming of the Republican armies a unique and powerful weapon backed by an industry established on a war footing and capable of producing in a single year 7,000 pieces of artillery. One of these armies, the Army of Italy, though badly clothed and fed, was, after four years, of campaigning, a well-disciplined and seasoned force capable of great achievements.

It but awaited its ideal commander. And in Napoleon it found him. The small, young general took with him his volumes of Guibert and Bourcet; he sent to Paris for an account of Maillebois's 1748 campaign in Piedmont. But to emphasize the debt he owed to his predecessors is not to decry his own genius, as has been well observed.

As he said at St. Helena, "Everything is in the execution." The planning which preceded a battle was an intense and painful process. "I am like a woman in labour." At St. Helena he pointed out, "Few people realize the strength of mind required to conduct, with a full realization of its consequences, one of these great battles on which depends the fate of an army, a nation, the possession of a throne. Consequently one rarely finds Generals who are keen to give battle..." "I consider myself the boldest of Generals." The earlier Generals of the Revolution were unable to apply the new theories successfully; they tended to disperse their divisions too widely, and failed to concentrate them at the decisive point. Jomini, who was one of Napoleon's staff officers, describes in his *Précis de l'Art de Guerre* (1838) how Napoleon "decided in a moment the number of marches necessary for each of his columns to arrive at the desired point by a certain day."

It follows from the flexible nature of this new war of movement that Napoleonic strategy can, least of all, be reduced to a formula or a system. Jomini and Clausewitz tried to draw general conclusions from the Napoleonic experience, but they never succeeded in seizing the subtlety of Napoleonic warfare, and they often produced dangerously misleading conclusions. Clausewitz did, however, recognize that strategy cannot be reduced to a "system". "What genius does must be the best of all rules." Napoleon at St. Helena ridiculed maxims of war. "Of what use is a maxim which can never be put into practice and even if put into practice without understanding would cause the loss of the army?"

It is for this reason that, while Napoleon's Italian campaigns contain in essence all the subsequent campaigns no two Napoleonic battles are alike. The most that can be said is that Napoleon's favourite strategical maneuvers fell into two patterns – first, the classic flanking attack on the enemy's rear and communications, exemplified by the Marengo campaign, Ulm, Jena, Friedland, Smolensk (where it failed to come off), Montmirail; secondly, the attack on the centre of an enemy dispersed on a wide front, so as to defeat him successively in detail. This is the strategy of his first campaign in Piedmont, and also of his last campaign of Waterloo.[9]

On May 15, 1796, Napoleon entered Milan.

The pope, the king of Naples, the dukes of Parma and Modena were placating him with tribute in cash and art treasures. He fought, organized, negotiated as though he were the sovereign of Italy. The Directory could not rebuke the upstart of their own creation, for he was shedding glory on their pitiful regime and replenishing their yawning coffers.

Mantua, the last obstacle, was at last taken. Bonaparte was crossing the Alps toward Vienna when, in April, 1797, he decided to make peace. The best Austrian general, Archduke Charles, was at last to be his antagonist. The mountaineers of Tyrol were being called to arms. In addition Hoche and Moreau had started a lightning campaign north of the Alps, which might have compelled him to share his glory with them. The preliminaries, dictated by Bonaparte, were signed at Leoben on April 18; the final peace, which closely followed the same pattern, at Campo Formio on October 17. That peace was brilliant and realistic, that is to say, unscrupulous. Bonaparte, without a qualm, gave away the Republic of Venice to the Austrians: it took seventy years to repair that injustice. The complicated secret articles were at least as important as the published terms. It was not peace, but a deal: the kind of settlement for which neither side could feel any respect.

England remained. Bonaparte declined to take command of an expedition in Ireland. He agreed – the thought may have originated with Talleyrand – to lead a campaign into Egypt: the idea was as old as Leibniz, and even as St. Louis. Since there was no Suez Canal at the time, the possession of Egypt would be vital only as a steppingstone through the barren Near East to the fabulous empire of India. The enterprise was therefore gigantic and vague; the means, without command of the sea, wholly inadequate. Bonaparte himself had a romantic hankering for the "gorgeous East"; excellent historians believe that it was the key to his whole career.

Miraculously, the French fleet eluded the far superior British squadrons. On the way Bonaparte captured Malta from its Knights. He took Alexandria, marched on Cairo, and defeated at the Pyramids the colorful and antiquated cavalry of the Mamelukes. "Soldiers," said the general, "from these Pyramids forty centuries are looking upon you."

As he had done in Italy, Napoleon in Egypt showed himself a born ruler no less than a soldier. He had with him a scientific mission which did excellent work. He reorganized the country with due regard for the customs of the inhabitants. A thorough Voltairian, not quite sure that Jesus had ever existed, he found it easy to flirt solemnly with Islam. But Egypt was of little value except as a starting point, and the French were hemmed in. Their fleet was destroyed by Nelson in the bay of Abukir (Battle of the Nile). A campaign into Syria proved a failure: Bonaparte could not capture Acre, and his plague-stricken troops hastily returned to Egypt. Warned of the desperate plight of the Directory, Bonaparte escaped, abandoning his own army. His successor, Kléber, was assassinated; and Menou had to capitulate. It was, on a much smaller scale, as complete a disaster as the Russian expedition in 1812; yet it enhanced Napoleon's prestige, and to the present day it has preserved its romantic glamor.

In the meantime Russia, hitherto neutral, had struck an alliance with England. Austria, Naples, Portugal, the Ottoman Empire had joined them; the Second Coalition was more formidable than the first. The French were driven out of Italy by the Russian Suvorov and the Austrian Melas, and the British effected a landing in Holland. The situation, not so desperate as in 1793, was ominous; and people yearned for the wonder worker of Italy, Bonaparte.[10]

Soon the wonder-worker was First Consul. He discarded his military uniform and silenced his guns. A portrait of him at this time has been painted by his private secretary, Méneval, who greatly admired him:

Napoleon was of average height [about five feet six inches] and well built. His head was big and the skull largely developed. His neck was short and his shoulders broad. The size of his chest bespoke a robust constitution, less robust, however, than his mind. His legs were well shaped, his foot was small and well formed. His hand, and he was rather proud of it, was delicate, and plump, with tapering fingers. His forehead was high and broad, his eyes gray, penetrating and wonderfully mobile; his nose was straight and well shaped. His teeth were fairly good, the mouth perfectly modelled, the upper lip slightly drawn down toward the corner of the mouth, and the chin slightly prominent. His skin was smooth and his complexion pale, but of a pallor which denoted a good circulation of the blood. His very fine chestnut hair, which, until the time of the expedition to Egypt, he had worn long, cut square and covering his ears, was clipped short. The hair was thin on the upper part of the head, and left bare his forehead, the seat of such lofty thoughts. The shape of his face and the ensemble of his features were remarkably regular.

When excited by any violent passion his face assumed an even terrible expression. A sort of rotary movement visibly produced itself on his forehead and between his eyebrows; his eyes flashed fire; his nostrils dilated, swollen with the inner storm. But these transient movements, whatever their cause may have been, in no way brought disorder to his mind. He seemed to be able to control at will these explosions, which, by the way, as time went on, became less and less frequent. His head remained cool. The blood never went to it, flowing back to the heart.

In ordinary life his expression was calm, meditative and gently grave. When in a good humour, or when anxious to please, his expression was sweet and caressing, and his face was lighted up by a most beautiful smile. Amongst familiars his laugh was loud and mocking...

He lived in a very homely manner, especially when at La Malmaison. He used to spend the hours which were not taken up by work, exercise, or shooting, with Josephine. He used to lunch alone, and during this repast, which was a relaxation for him, he received the persons with whom he liked to converse on science, art, and literature. He dined with his family, and after dinner would look in at his cabinet, and then, unless kept there by some work, would return to the drawing-room and play chess. As a general rule he liked to talk in a familiar way. He was fond of discussions, but did not impose his opinions, and made no pretension of superiority, either of intelligence or of rank. When only ladies were present he liked to criticize their dresses, or tell them tragical or satirical stories – ghost stories for the most part. When bed-time came, Madame Bonaparte followed him to his room. Napoleon wasted very little time in preparing for the night, and used to say that he got back to bed with pleasure. He said that statues ought to be erected to the men who invented beds and carriages. However, this bed into which he threw himself with delight, being often crushed with fatigue, was quitted more than once during the course of the night. He used to get up, after an hour's sleep, as wide awake and as clear in his head as if he had slept quietly the whole night. As soon as he had lain down his wife would place herself on the foot of the bed, and begin reading aloud. As she read very well he took pleasure in listening to her...

I could not master my surprise at finding such simplicity of habits in a man like Napoleon, who from afar seemed so imposing. I had expected to find him brusque, and of uncertain temper, instead of which I found him patient, indulgent, easy to please, by no means exacting, merry with a merriness which was often noisy and mocking, and sometimes of a charming bonhomie. This familiarity on his part did not, however, awake any ideas of reciprocity. Napoleon played with men without mixing with them…

The Emperor used to have me waked in the night, when – owing either to some plan which he considered ripe for execution, and which had to be carried out, or to the necessity of maturing the preliminaries of some new project, or to having to send off some courier without loss of time – he was obliged to rise himself. It sometimes happened that I would hand him some document to sign in the evening. "I will not sign it now," he would say. "Be here to-night, at one o'clock, or at four in the morning; we will work together."…

When, by chance, he had got to the study before me, I used to find him walking up and down with his hands behind his back, or helping himself from his snuff-box, less from taste than from pre-occupation, for he only used to smell at his pinches, and his handkerchiefs were never soiled with the snuff. His ideas developed as he dictated, with an abundance and a clearness which showed that his attention was firmly riveted to the subject with which he was dealing. When the work was finished, and sometimes in the midst of it, he would send for sherbet and ices. He used to ask me which I preferred, and went so far in his solicitude as to advise me which would be better for my health. Thereupon he would return to bed, if only to sleep an hour, and could resume his slumber, as though it had not been interrupted...

Napoleon rarely wrote himself. Writing tired him; his hand could not follow the rapidity of his conceptions, he only took up the pen when by chance he happened to be alone and had to put the first rush of an idea on to paper; but after writing some lines he used to stop and throw away his pen. He would then go out to call his secretary.

His writing was a collection of letters unconnected with each other, and unreadable. Half the letters to each word were wanting, he could not read his own writing again, or would not take the trouble to do so. If he was asked for some explanation he would take his draft and tear it up, or throw it into the fire, and dictate it over again – the same ideas, it is true, but couched in different language and a different style.

Although he could detect faults in the spelling of others, his own orthography left much to be desired. It was negligence which had become a habit, he did not want to break or tangle the thread of his thoughts by paying attention to the details of spelling. Napoleon also used to make mistakes in figures, absolute and positive as arithmetic has to be. He could have worked out the most complicated mathematical problems, and yet he could rarely total up a sum correctly. It is fair to add that these errors were not always made without intention. For example, in calculating the number of men who were to make up his battalions, regiments, or divisions, he always used to increase the sum total. One can hardly believe that in doing so he wanted to deceive himself, but he often thought it useful to exaggerate the strength of his armies. It was no use pointing out any mistake of this kind; he refused to admit it, and obstinately maintained his voluntary arithmetical error.[11]

A more recent portrait has been painted by the distinguished English historian of modern France, Professor Alfred Cobban:

Short, but thin and muscular, he had good looks, though little notice should be taken of portraits in which he is already the Byronic hero of the coming romantic movement. He had tremendous energy and a powerful and disciplined memory. He could work continuously for long periods, with only snatches of sleep. In order not to disturb his habits, says his police official, Réal, he had taken care not to form any. He had a thirst for glory, fed partly on the writings of the pre-romantics but more on the history of the great conquerors of the ancient world, Caesar and Alexander, for this was also the period of the classical revival. Although he read Rousseau and was not uninfluenced by the ideals of the Enlightenment, his contribution to the legal code which bears his name showed a natural preference for the more conservative and less enlightened ideas of the *ancien régime*. Politically his bent was towards despotism untrammelled by divine right. His experience of the Revolution had left him with a deep contempt, not unmixed with fear, for the people. For politicians he had the dictator's natural aversion. He was not without humane instincts, and was capable of kindness in private life, to say nothing of the charm he could turn on at will; but such qualities vanished when they stood in the way of his success. Even early in his career, before overweening egoism had quite mastered him, when military considerations demanded it he was entirely ruthless. There is no evidence that bloodshed mattered a scrap to him, or that he ever thought, as a Marlborough or a Wellington did, of economizing in the lives of his soldiers. The mass attack on which he relied depended on not counting the cost in dead and wounded. A French Colonel describes him riding, as was his custom, over the field of Borodino after the battle, rubbing his hands and radiant with satisfaction as he counted five dead Russians to every one French corpse. I suppose, the Colonel adds sardonically, he took the bodies of his German allies for Russians. Such nobility as might have been given, even to the career of a military despot, by the service of some end, although a mistaken one, was lacking. Apart from his own personal glory, the only other ambition he had at heart was to found a dynasty. When, in his last campaign, he might have saved much for France by abandoning his dream of Empire, he was incapable of such moderation, or even realism. After all this, to say that he was an adventurer is an anti-climax; but it is not irrelevant or unimportant. Coming from islanders whose social institutions were the *banditti* and the *vendetta*, he carried the same standards into a country where the Revolution had already shown how uncertain were the conquests of the Enlightenment. For fifteen years France and Europe were to be at the mercy of a gambler to whom fate and his own genius gave for a time all the aces. He always cheated at cards and his carriage had diamonds concealed in its lining in case of hurried flight.[12]

In the early days of his triumph there had seemed no fear of flight.

To most French people Napoleon remained a consummate hero. The Consul became the Emperor, setting the crown on his head himself, in the presence of the Pope in Notre Dame. The Emperor created a new aristocracy and a new court – though bringing in as many survivors of the old regime as could be persuaded to enter it – and he took a new wife, Marie-Louise of Austria, to set the seal upon his triumph and to provide himself with an heir.

The peace signed with the Austrians at Lunéville (February 9, 1801) and with the English at Amiens (March 27, 1802) could not, however, be preserved.

England was no more satisfied with the truce than Napoleon was; while Austria was no more willing to resign herself to her loss of influence in Italy than Prussia was able to forget the glories of Frederick the Great.

Before Napoleon ascended the throne, there was already rising through the huge and-ill-compacted Germanic body a new consciousness of pride, and romantic visions of the medieval emperors in their might.

Napoleon's task was easier than Hitler's. French culture was still supreme among the ruling classes. The French were bringing with them genuine reforms, ideological and practical. They roughly and efficiently swept away the cobwebs of medievalism. But Napoleon, like Hitler, was incapable of treating his satellites with consideration. His "New Order" was geared to the interests of France not of Europe as a whole. The Continental Blockade (Berlin Decree, 1806), closing the Continent to all English goods, might have been a decisive weapon. Only Napoleon disregarded altogether the interests of the local populations. Holland, the Hanseatic Cities, association with France meant ruin; so every bight in the immense coast line became a nest of smugglers. The conquered learned that the first "natural right of man" for a German or an Italian was the right not to be a Frenchman. The economic hardships sharpened national consciousness.

The French not only plundered, with Napoleonic efficiency, the lands nominally associated with the Empire, but they also destroyed their sources of wealth. It was not Fichte in his *Addresses to the German Nation* who created German patriotism: Herder had laid deep foundations before. But there was fraternity in Herder's soul; Fichte, inspired by Napoleon's oppression, fostered the nationalism that is filled with hate, and which still poisons Europe today.[13]

So while there could be truces, there could be no real end to the war. Fighting had begun again in 1805; and Napoleon, once more, had been triumphant. Though Nelson had nearly destroyed the French fleet at Trafalgar (October 21, 1805), though Austria, Russia, and Sweden had joined forces against him, Napoleon, at Vim, at Austerlitz, at Auerstedt, at Jena, and at Friedland, had ensured that his Empire remained in existence. At Tilsit he made peace with the Czar, the last enemy left in the field.

Whatever men might say of his character and political wisdom, his military genius could not and cannot be questioned.

The comprehensive view of positions, the eye for the key point, the capacity to read the mind of his opponent, the ability to take quick decisions, a personality powerful enough to impose obedience, all these qualities Napoleon possessed in their highest form. If the fact has sometimes been denied, it has only been in a paradoxical fashion or from hatred of the man, and no historian of any importance has ever done so. Tolstoy's view of him in *War and Peace* is fundamentally unhistorical, even anti-historical; and he reduces the statesman, too, to nothing.[14]

In analyzing Napoleon's unquestionable genius as a soldier, Major General J. F. C. Fuller has reduced the elements to be considered in his characteristic style of warfare to three:

(1) Unity of Command; (2) Generalship and Soldiership; and (3) Napoleon's System of Planning.

Unity of command he held to be "the first necessity of war," and it should be borne in mind that in its full sense it is only possible when political and military direction are in the hands of a single man, as they were in Napoleon's after he became First Consul in January, 1800...

Unity of command was the foundation of Napoleon's many victorious campaigns and, strangely – as later we shall see – it became an element in his eventual downfall. Nevertheless, his maxims: "In war men are nothing, it is the one man who is all," and "One bad general (in command) ... is worth two good ones," remain as true today as when they were first uttered...

Napoleon's success as a planner of campaigns derived directly from his position as autocrat, which empowered him to combine in his own person the political and strategical conduct of war. This advantage, coupled with his single-mindedness and enormous industry, enabled him to transfuse his genius into his plans, at times so much so that they were quite beyond the comprehension of his generals. As the war lengthened and his problems grew more complex, the lack of comprehending subordinates became increasingly dangerous, and especially so during the Leipzig and Waterloo campaigns, when his brilliant maneuvers were botched by the stupidity of his marshals. This is why, when at St. Helena, he said: "If I had had a man like Turenne to second me in my campaigns, I should have been master of the world."

To him the planning of a campaign was an exacting work of art...

Napoleon entered upon each of his campaigns with a precisely premeditated plan which admitted of variations, each of which corresponded with an hypothesis he had made on his enemy's probable and possible movements. The plan was what he intended to do, and the variations covered the modifications he might have to make in it. Once the plan was activated, his problem became one of exploration. The current use of exploratory cavalry was to seek out the enemy's forces and report back on them. But, because Napoleon was more concerned with his own plan than his enemy's positions, and because normally they had changed by the time the cavalry reports were received, the object of his system of exploration – which included spies, agents, letters seized in post offices, etc. – was to confirm or eliminate his hypotheses. Therefore his cavalry, agents, etc., were directed in predetermined directions to elucidate doubtful points, knowledge of which was essential in order to confirm or eliminate an hypothesis. Thus, by reducing uncertainty to a minimum, by either eliminating or confirming his hypotheses, he not only simplified his own plan, but at the same time uncovered his enemy's. To discover what his enemy intended, more so than what his positions were, was the aim of Napoleonic exploration.

Although Napoleon frequently wrote or talked about principles of war, nowhere does he enumerate them. Once he said in the hearing of Saint-Cyr: "If one day I can find the time, I will write a book in which I will describe the principles of war in so precise a manner that they will be at the disposal of all soldiers, so that war can be learnt as easily as a science." Unfortunately he never did so; nevertheless, a study of his campaigns reveals: (1) His invariable reliance on the offensive; (2) his trust in speed to economize time, and (3) to effect strategic surprisals; (4) his insistence on concentrating superiority of force on the battlefield, particularly at the decisive point of attack; and (5) his carefully thought out protective system.[15]

The American military historian, Colonel Dodge, has drawn attention to some of Napoleon's supreme qualities as a general:

Some of Napoleon's qualities as a commander-in-chief were exceptionally developed. Such were his power of clear vision, his innate boldness, and his capacity for hard unceasing work. "War is an earnest game in which one can ruin one's repute and one's country; if one is sensible, he will test himself and know whether he is made for this craft or not," Napoleon wrote to Eugène from Burghausen, April 30, 1809. "I look upon myself as the boldest man in war who perhaps ever lived," he said at St. Helena. This self-praise is possibly overdone. The soldier cannot forget Hannibal's march from Spain across the Alps to the Po, or Alexander's advance from Macedon to the Indus. But Napoleon was bold and able enough to be dubbed by his enemies "The Hundred Thousand Man."

His power to gauge a situation, or estimate the numbers of a force which he could see, even in parts, was exceptional. "One look through his glass, and he had seized the picture of the whole army with incredible speed. He thus judged, from some height, whole corps of fifty or sixty thousand men, according to space and position," says Odeleben, in speaking of the campaign in Saxony. Comeyras wrote Napoleon from Milan, July 15, 1796: "I have recognized in you a habit of seeing very accurately, though very quickly." [16]

Colonel Dodge goes on to list Napoleon's imagination, his insistence that his officers should keep up the appearance of success, his self-reliance, his inventiveness, and his reputation for doing "sudden, unexpected and dangerous things [which] puzzled his antagonists."

These sudden, unexpected moves sometimes puzzled even his own staff:

Napoleon's separate headquarters stood under control of Grand Marshal of the Palace, Duroc, who, with Caulaincourt, Master of the Horse, always accompanied the emperor in his rides and drives, remaining near him and subject to his call. Two mounted *chasseurs*, under Caulaincourt, carried in leather portfolios the maps of the region involved, so as to put them at any moment before His Majesty. The imperial traveling coach was so arranged that Napoleon could lie down in it and drive all night if necessary. Either Berthier or Murat was apt to be with him, and Caulaincourt rode at the carriage step. The members of the personal staff, consisting of adjutants and staff officers to bear dispatches and orders, followed hard upon the emperor's coach, each one to be ready at call, knowing full well that Napoleon wanted a thing done as soon as spoken. On long journeys they followed in carriages. In 1807 there were twenty-one of these officers. Four pages were in attendance on His Majesty, and his body servant, the Mameluke Rustan, saw to his intimate wants. The escort was a detail of the *Chasseurs de la Garde*, and whenever Napoleon alighted, four of these men dismounted and with fixed bayonets formed an open square around him, which quietly moved in any direction Napoleon took, keeping the view open for him and preventing intrusion. At times they remained mounted. The imperial cortège was closed by couriers and orderlies, under the Master of the Horse, and grooms, with generally eight or nine horses for the emperor, and mounts for other service, servants and numerous camp-followers. The train finally grew so large that it became noticeable and dangerous in the presence of the enemy, and in 1813, after Duroc was killed, an order was issued that there should remain near Napoleon's person only Berthier, Caulaincourt, the Marshal of the Day, the commanding officer of the escort, two adjutants, two aides, two officers familiar with the language of the country, one page and one groom, and Rustan, thirteen in all.

For emergencies requiring long rides or drives, there were sent ahead relays of nine saddle-horses, two for Napoleon and seven for his necessary followers, or relays of carriage-horses, if he was to drive. These were so arranged that he had a fresh mount or relay every six or eight miles. The emperor was not an expert horseman, and his saddle-beasts were selected and trained for him with the utmost care.

The general staff proper stood under Berthier, who had in 1806 thirteen adjutants; and under three chiefs, with five adjutants each, were thirty-one general staff officers and thirty engineers and topographical officers. Songis, Chief of Artillery, had a staff of eighteen members. Chasseloup, Chief of Engineers, had one of nineteen. Daru, General Intendant, had forty-three officials. These were not all present at headquarters, being generally detailed on duty in every direction. To these various subordinate departments Napoleon was in the habit of constantly sending for information wanted at the moment, to precede formal reports, later rendered.

On arrival at any given place, the first thing done was to prepare the emperor's office. It was generally ready by the time he came up and dismounted. In the middle of this office, be it tent or room, stood a table, upon which were spread the best maps of the theatre of war, under direction of the Chief of the Topographical Bureau, Baeler d'Albe; and on these were indicated by colored pins the location of the troops from latest reports. In the four corners were tables for the four private secretaries, who took down the emperor's orders. These, dictated with incredible speed while Napoleon paced up and down the floor, formed the basis on which Berthier issued orders to the army; or they might be addressed to the ministers at home. Next was prepared the emperor's sleeping-room, in front of the door of which Rustan invariably slept; then a bedroom and office for Berthier near Napoleon's; and last the rooms for the officers on duty. The rest found quarters as best they might. In bivouac there were usually five tents: Napoleon's office, his sleeping-tent, Berthier's, and two for the rest.

During peace Napoleon was wont to retire towards eleven, rarely after midnight, and he rose between seven and eight. In the field he cut down this allowance markedly. After his dinner, to which he devoted a bare twenty minutes, eating little but hastily, he lay down at six or seven p.m., and rose at one, to issue orders for the day. This was a tax on himself and the whole staff; but it had the marked advantage that he did not, in the early evening, issue orders for the morrow before all reports had run in; neither did he sleep beyond the hour when, these being on hand, he could prepare and send out well-considered instructions for early morning marches, with full knowledge where every corps stood, and the latest news about the enemy. It was a thoroughly practical system.[17]

A picture of Napoleon in the field has been given by a German officer attached to his staff, General Baron Odeleben:

All that was happening at headquarters came without a moment's warning, and yet everyone had to be ready at once to perform his task. Unexpected moments of rest, unforeseen departures, changes of appointed times, and often of roads and stopping places as well, followed each other unceasingly. Even when the Master of Horse had some hint of them, the execution was left to the last moment, and all the others had to cudgel their brains to guess what would come next.

Very often the march would be held up for several hours, or even half a day, and to the last word Napoleon dictated in his closet was appended a curt order:

"The carriage! to horse!"

With that, all who had to attend him would be in motion, as though struck by an electric shock.

Not till then was it announced which way we were going.

The Master of Horse or, if he were on detached service, an equerry rode on the right hand of the coach. General Guyot or the officer next him in rank was on the left. The aides-de-camp on duty, the equerries, the orderly officers, the pages, a few lead horses for Napoleon and Berthier, Roustam, the keeper of the portfolio, and another outrider at Caulaincourt's disposal, were directly behind Bonaparte's carriage.

This whole throng was followed by an escort of twenty-four mounted chasseurs with an officer in command.

This grouping, settled once and for all, was obligatory, and was uniformly maintained with the greatest exactness. Not all the officers who were required or permitted to follow in his train dared to overtake the escort. Only those of high rank had leave to ride either behind or alongside the carriage.

Thus the cohort swept on like a thunderstorm, at a fast trot, by day or by night, for several leagues at a stretch, and those who had to follow this whirlwind through the night were rather hard put to it. Where the road was narrow all would be charging each other, so to speak, with brutal zeal. Those who were best off were the two orderly officers in front of the carriage, and two chasseurs who were still further ahead. All the rest were in peril of breaking their necks or their legs. The servants leading Napoleon's horses thought they were leading the convoy. The keeper of the portfolio, the orderly officers and the pages had the same pretension. And indeed each became an important man when Bonaparte called for him. Thus the whole troop went crowding, scurrying, jostling each other in the heat of the day, in dust and fog, and in the darkness of night.

When Napoleon stopped, the saddle-horses had to do likewise, and four chasseurs from the head of the escort dismounted, fixed their bayonets to the end of their carbines, presented arms, and posted themselves round him in a square. It was the same when a call of nature forced him to alight from his horse or carriage, or when he stopped for a walk round, to observe the enemy. Then the square was larger and kept pace with his movements; but loosely, so that he had a clear space and could observe in all directions. If the objects were distant, the page on duty would come forward with the spy-glass, which Bonaparte propped on his shoulder or on that of Caulaincourt.

When Napoleon was obliged by circumstances, either in the early morning or the evening, to spend some time in the open, the chasseurs made him a good fire. This fire was always fed with an extraordinary amount of wood; great chunks of wood and, whenever possible, whole beams were set ablaze, by way of a signal marking the spot where Bonaparte might be found.

Berthier was his companion there, as at table. He rarely had any other. Everyone kept at a certain distance, forming a semi-circle, or they would show the same eagerness to draw near the marshals' fire so as to be admitted to their table.

Napoleon would walk about musing by himself or chatting with Berthier, as he awaited the sound of gunfire or other signals from his generals. When he was growing bored he took snuff, or amused himself by flicking pebbles here and there with his feet, or pushing wood up to the fire. He was incapable of doing nothing.

Though a bad rider, he would often commit himself unreservedly to the skill of his horses which were usually small and mean-looking. Very often he ventured into the narrowest, the swampiest of bridle-paths, and on deplorable and dangerous roads, through flood-water.

The Master of Horse, who, by virtue of his office, was his immediate forerunner, spent most of the time looking for the most practicable places. [Napoleon] himself once remarked very ingenuously that he had learnt a great deal, but had never been able to familiarize himself with the horse. Nor was his physique adapted to this exercise. At the gallop he would let himself slump in the saddle, usually managing the reins with his right hand, while all the upper part of his body, with the motion of the horse, was jerked sideways or forward, and the left arm hung carelessly down. If the horse chanced to put a foot wrong, he immediately lost his balance.

It was Napoleon's habit to study the field of battle in detail after the engagement, whenever the weather made it possible. He seemed to be scanning the position that had been occupied by the enemy as a means of learning about his forces and probing his designs.

When Napoleon went over the battlefield, the French dead had usually been buried and the wounded of that nation removed. It was known for a fact that he found the sight of his losses very disagreeable.

By an unbridled impetuosity, he often gave even his generals cause to make him pretty rough answers. One day he began upbraiding General Sebastiani, affirming that his cavalry had done less than that of General Latour-Maubourg, which had captured so many flags and guns, and had made so many prisoners, and concluding with these terrible words:

"F—! do as much yourself! Your men are riff-raff, not soldiers."

"Sire, my men are not riff-raff," retorted Sebastiani in a dry and firm voice; and he pointed out that considering the state they were in and all the privations they were suffering, his troops could not have done more.

The Duke of Taranto (MacDonald) backed this up, and between them they were able to silence him, while Caulaincourt, to avoid a scandal, had desired all those present to fall back.

At Muglitz near Pirna, Napoleon, giving way to a fit of spleen, struck one of his generals in the face.

This tendency to inordinate rage was well known, and yet I have heard some high-ranking officers say of him:

"Believe me, he's not ill-natured."

When he had been dispensing some favour, his guards commonly looked for some very hot affair. The most certain preludes were harangues to the men and the delivery of the eagle to the battalions. If his hopes had been deceived or if, despite these preambles, no bloody scene had taken place, which happened with several battles he had meant to fight, owing to the skilfully calculated retreat of the allies, then Napoleon's fury burst out. He was annoyed that these theatrical forces had missed their aim.

On more than one occasion Napoleon's words affected the troops like witchcraft.

At the end of the campaign misery and privation lost him the hearts of the rank and file, who preferred facing death on the battlefield to enduring hunger. Yet a part of the Young Guard went on raising their customary shouts, and even when fortune had forsaken him, at the time when he was beaten and forced to leave Saxony, these shouts were reiterated with incredible vehemence, as though to comfort him in adversity. At the time of the forced marches, which went on and on without victuals, in the neighborhood of Dresden, Bautzen and Pima, the huzzas of this same corps had only a feeble ring, and a number of men could be heard saying:

"Nobody will shout!"

His travelling-coach was so arranged that he could sleep in it and stretch out on cushions. Between the seat he occupied and that of Berthier there was some difference, so that his travelling companion could not lie down.

Dressed in uniform, his head done up in a parti-coloured handkerchief, he could sleep on the road as though he had been in bed. Inside his carriage were a quantity of locked drawers, containing the news from Paris, reports as yet unopened, and books. Opposite Napoleon was a list of the relay stations, and a big lantern hung up at the back of the carriage lit the inside, while four more lanterns shed their light on the road.

The cushions which Roustam arranged were deftly packed up in the carriage, and under the magazine a number of spare candles were stowed away. Roustam sat on the box by himself, and there were six heavy Limousin horses, driven by two coachmen, to draw the coach, which was plain, green, seating two and well sprung.[18]

Napoleon's powers of inspiration, mentioned by Baron Odeleben, was one of the most cultivated and calculated of his effects:

The charm which Napoleon could turn on at will was used unscrupulously to fortify his mastery over men's minds. He told Caulaincourt, "When I need someone I am not squeamish, I would kiss his arse." His surest touch, was, of course, with his soldiers. A record of victory and professional skill is the first requisite for a commander in gaining the confidence of his soldiers; but to this Napoleon added an uncanny insight into the psychology of the soldier. As he said, "The military are a freemasonry: and I am its Grand Master." His constant reviews, and his presence on the battlefield, enabled him to establish an extraordinary degree of personal contact, particularly with the Guard. One letter will illustrate his attention to details of morale. In May 1807 he wrote from Poland to the Chancellor of the Legion of Honour thus: "Write to Corporal Bernaudet of the 13th of the Line and tell him not to drink so much and to behave better. He has been given the Cross because he is a brave man. One must not take it away from him because he is a bit fond of wine. Make him understand, however, that he is wrong to get into a state which brings shame on the decoration he wears." Marmont writes that "it was by familiarities of this kind that the Emperor made the soldiers adore him, but it was a means only available to a commander whom frequent victories had made illustrious; any other general would have injured his reputation by it."

Napoleon played on the emotions of glory, adventure and comradeship with the skill of a sorcerer. The Comte de Narbonne, who was a survivor of the *ancien régime* and went through the Russian campaign at the age of sixty, described the spirit in Napoleon's army as "a democratic chivalry." Wellington reckoned that the moral effect of Napoleon's presence with his army was worth 40,000 men. Even Private Wheeler, of Wellington's army, records in his diary his admiration for "Boney". Not even slaughter, defeat and disaster could break the bond. At the costly battle of Essling in 1809 the Guard refused to fight unless the Emperor retired to a less exposed position. In the appalling conditions of the retreat from Moscow, there were no signs of mutiny, even of grumbling; less so than in Wellington's army which was at the same time retreating from Burgos. The most extraordinary example of Napoleon's moral ascendancy was on the return from Elba in 1815. When Napoleon faced alone the battalion which had been sent to stop him and cried: "Kill your Emperor if you wish," they ignored the commands of their officers to fire, broke ranks, and crowded round him.[19]

The veneration in which Napoleon was held by his men is emphasized by Thiard in this description of the Emperor on the day before Austerlitz:

I have rarely seen Napoleon as cheerful, as contented, as he was all that day. More than once I caught him rubbing his hands joyfully, as though saying to himself: "I've got them," or "They shan't escape me." This confidence was shared by the whole army, and anyone suspecting the possibility of a reverse would have been thought out of his mind. The day before a battle is a great day, when one has faith in the general. There is only one finer – the day of action.

Supper showed the influence of this happy frame of mind. The conversation was never brisker or more lively. At first it turned on the theatres of the capital, to which it had been led by a feuilleton we had received in the morning. From there it moved on to the respective rank which should be assigned to our three great tragic dramatists. Junot, who had as much education as mother wit, took a large part in it. There was no argument except on Voltaire, whom in my judgment Napoleon ran down too much. He brought out very forcibly all the faults and the want of local colour in *Zaïre*, *Alzire* and *Tancrède*. Of the tragedies of Racine, those he put first were *Bajazet*, *Mithridate* and *Britannicus*. But above all, he gave the palm to Corneille. And there we had no quarrel with him.

As soon as the meal was over, Napoleon said:

"Let's go and see the Guards."

We all turned out. But by the end of the round, which was exhausting, if I remember rightly there was no one with him but M. de Caulaincourt, Junot, Rapp and myself.

Scarcely had we reached the line when Napoleon was recognized, and the men stood up at sight of him.

We had hardly gone fifty paces when a bit of wood across our path made him stumble. But luckily we caught hold of him in time, and he did not lose his balance. Then the grenadiers, of their own accord, took the straw on which they were lying, twisted it up to provide something like torches, which they set alight, and then walked in front of us to light the general, making the air ring with their shouts. This impulse was electric. All down the line torches were made, and each troop, as it were, took over escort duty from the one before. Then, as always happens at these moments of enthusiasm, what remained of the beds was soon ablaze. This demonstration was not without its risk, because of the cartridges. And so we kept on shouting to the men: "Mind your pouches!" And luckily no mishap occurred.[20]

Even when wounded and in defeat the Emperor's soldiers could still find it in their hearts to cheer him, as Earl Stanhope learned after Waterloo:

In the evening we went to a little party at Deal Castle. In conversation with Captain Bridges, R. E. – a very accomplished and agreeable man – he told me that he had been at the hospital at Brussels after the battle of Waterloo, and had seen limbs amputated from several of the French wounded prisoners, but such was their enthusiastic devotion to Napoleon, that even during the operation, and amidst their sufferings, they called out "Vive l'Empereur!"[21]

The devotion that his men bore to him as a fighting general was counted by the English historian J. Holland Rose as perhaps the most important of the secrets of Napoleon's success:

The fighting instinct throbbed in his blood during his tender years, witness that curious piece of self-revelation imparted to Antommarchi at St. Helena. When teased by his companions for his fondness of a little girl, he would pick up sticks or stones, and pelt or rush at his tormentors without thinking of their size or number. What is bred in the bone, comes out through life; and this extraordinary hardiness and pugnacity, inherited seemingly from the Pietra-Santa family, distinguished him from first to last, from the first charge at Montenotte to the onset of the Imperial Guard at Waterloo. In this combative instinct lies the secret of his power over the soldiery. Men will do anything and go anywhere for a fighting general, provided that he cares for their interests and touches their imagination.

Here again he was an ideal leader. To his generals he, for the most part, turned the colder side of his nature, exacting instant and unquestioning obedience, giving them abundant opportunities to enrich themselves at the expense of the liberated people, and finally dowering them with immense domains. Sometimes, however, he fired them with burning words, as in the parting injunctions to General Lauriston, to whom he entrusted the command of the troops on Villeneuve's fleet designed for a landing in England: "If you experience reverses, always remember these three things – union of your forces, activity, and a firm resolve to die with glory. These are the three great principles of the military art, which have made Fortune favour me in all my operations. Death is nothing; but to live vanquished and without glory is to die every day."

His proclamations to the soldiers pulsate with national pride. Never has a man of different race so profoundly stirred great armies. From the time of his first appeal in the spring of 1796, to march onward and conquer Italy, to the last proclamation, five days before Waterloo, urging every Frenchman to conquer or die, he showed a supreme art in kindling the passion for glory in the rank and file; and when that flame burns brightly in Celts they will do anything. As Napoleon said, love of glory is with Frenchmen a sixth sense. He set himself to develop it, often treating his men with the old republican *camaraderie*. In times of exceptional strain, as on the night before Jena, he encouraged the engineers and artillery men by appearing at their side, watching their toil, and speaking the words that change men into Titans. Or again, he would go over the battlefield, feeling the pulse or the heart of the recumbent forms, and showing genuine satisfaction when he discovered signs of life that had not been before observed. Especially he loved to talk with his Old Guard, asking them how long and where they had served, the number of their wounds and so forth. He it was who nicknamed them *les grognards*, the very best means, surely, of keeping grumbling within bounds.

What wonder that Wellington calculated the presence of Napoleon on a battlefield to be worth 40,000 troops, not only because his moves were skilful, his blows telling, but because his very presence nerved the men to do their utmost, and gave them supreme confidence in the result.[22]

Even the great losses which, unlike Wellington, he could afford and did not appear to regret had little effect on the veneration in which the survivors held him.

Inspiring boundless enthusiasm in his men, he expected them to perform prodigies of endurance; and when they fell, another host arose at the stamp of his foot to repeat the miracle, until generous France was bled white by her adopted son. Wellington, austere and uninspiring, got far less out of his troops before and after battles. On the field they fought with native hardihood; but on no occasion did the Duke win a campaign by continuous forced marches like those of the French before Ulm; and never did he spur on his army to the extraordinary feats which in a fortnight after Jena laid Prussia at the invaders' feet.

Napoleon personified the fire, the dash, the brilliance of the south. Wellington, an Irishman only in the place of his birth, certainly not in character, embodied the hardness, caution, sound sense and stubbornness characteristic of the Anglo-Saxon. By temperament and of necessity he waged a defensive warfare. The puny land forces of England having to be husbanded at every turn, his first thought was to save his army from destruction. That was the last thought of Napoleon, who in his later years recked little of losing 100,000 men if he could inflict a loss of 120,000 on his enemy.[23]

Perhaps, though, this emphasis on Napoleon's callous disregard of his casualties has been exaggerated:

Much has been said of Napoleon's callousness about human life, and on the battlefield. This is less shocking to the professional soldier; even the amateur soldiers and civilian combatants of twentieth-century wars have experienced the strange, unfortunate capacity of the human race to suspend the normal revulsion to death, wounds, and mutilation in the heat and smoke of battle. Both Napoleon and his soldiers knew well that, in the conditions of the time, a decisive battle was far less costly in human life and misery than the attrition of a protracted campaign. Disease and privation were more to be feared than the risks of death in battle. A Napoleonic veteran would greet the day of decisive battle, under the eye of the Emperor, as a *jour de fête.* The supply, movement, medical services and even the training of the Napoleonic armies continued the tradition of the revolutionary armies in being, in the words of Professor G. Lefebvre, "a continual improvisation." The army was expected to live off the country; and everything was sacrificed to mobility and the quick knock-out blow. As the conscript armies grew in size and rawness, and as the campaigns moved out of the fertile areas of Italy and Germany into Poland, Spain and Russia, the inadequacy of this system became steadily more serious, and wastage, pillaging, indiscipline mounted.

It is easy to exaggerate the manpower losses of the Napoleonic wars. Taine, writing immediately after the disastrous fall of the Second Empire, estimated that 1,700,000 French soldiers were killed between 1804 and 1815. This figure would imply a casualty rate approaching one hundred per cent, as the total number of men actually enrolled in the army from the eighty-six Departments of France proper in this period was little more than two million. Between 1800 and 1812, 1,400,000 men were enrolled out of 4,350,000 of military age. In 1813, after the losses in Russia, 800,000 men were called up, and in 1814, for the first time, an entire class was summoned without exemptions, though, in fact, barely 100,000 new conscripts actually served. It is known that 15,000 officers were killed or wounded between 1800 and 1815; and the proportionate casualties in the ranks would not exceed 400,000. In the four years of the 1914–18 war, 1,360,000 French soldiers were killed.[24]

Also, a large proportion of Napoleon's losses were of foreign troops.

To picture a French army, using French resources, as conquering Europe, would, however, not be correct. From the beginning of the Revolutionary War the French armies had lived off the country, and as their wars were always, until 1813, fought on foreign soil, the main burden did not fall on France. The numbers of men raised from France, though large by *ancien régime* standards, were not excessive. Up to 1812 the annual average works out at some 85,000, and this from a France which was steadily expanding its frontiers. As well as Piedmontese, Belgians, Dutch, and inhabitants of some German states, which were subjected to the laws of conscription when they were annexed, levies were raised from the satellite states. The army that invaded Russia in 1812 had contingents from every nation of Europe: of its 700,000 men only a third were French.[25]

It says much indeed, for Napoleon's powers of inspiration that during the retreat from Moscow in 1812, few of his men, whether French conscripts or foreign levies, raised their voices to lay their sufferings at his door. General Caulaincourt said that "not one word against the Emperor was heard in the whole course of this disastrous retreat."

Napoleon's relationships with his senior officers were not always so happy.

The Marshals, Generals, and staff officers frequently behaved like spoilt prima donnas; and Napoleon liked to manage them by keeping them in a constant state of jealous rivalry for his favours, by alternate slaps and caresses. When enraged with Napoleon, Marshal Lannes used to exclaim that "he should be pitied for having conceived an unfortunate passion for this harlot". When

Lannes was killed at the battle of Essling, Napoleon wrote to his widow, "I lose the most distinguished General, my companion in arms for sixteen years, the man whom I considered my best friend". On the evening after Essling, Napoleon sat with tears running down into his soup. No less genuine was his sorrow at the death of Bessières at the battle of Lützen and of Duroc at the battle of Bautzen in 1813. Junot, the companion of his youth, and Gourgaud, his aide who accompanied him to St Helena, tried Napoleon's patience by their tantrums of jealous devotion. Napoleon complained that Junot was "*sentimental comme une jeune fille allemande*": that Gourgaud was "jealous, in love with me. Hell ... I was not his wife, and I could not sleep with him."

Napoleon was a shrewd judge of the qualities and limitations of his Generals. He thought that Desaix would have been the first soldier of France, if he had not been killed at Marengo; Lannes might have become so. Ney and Murat were incomparably brave leaders of men on the battlefield, but no more. Berthier was a superb chief of staff, but a muddler if left to himself. Only Masséna, Davout, and possibly Soult were capable of independent command of large armies, Napoleon told Eugène in 1809 that "Masséna has military talents before which one must bow"; but he also told Joseph that "Masséna is no good at civil government; he is a good soldier, but he is completely dominated by the love of money".

Napoleon frequently criticized his Generals' mistakes, but he never made any systematic attempt to teach them his methods, or to form a Staff College. He relied entirely on himself. But why did he put Junot in command of the Army of Portugal, knowing his inadequacy for command? Why did he make Marmont a Marshal, and leave him to face Wellington? Why did he continue to employ Bernadotte, whose defects he summed up in 1809, "Bernadotte is an intriguer whom I cannot trust. He nearly lost me the battle of Jena, he was mediocre at Wagram, he never turned up at Eylau, when he could have, and he did not do what he might have done at Austerlitz"? The answer seems to be that Junot and Marmont were the companions of his youth; that Bernadotte had married Désirée, his ex-fiancée, and was Joseph's brother-in-law. Napoleon was, in fact, influenced by old associations and family ties a great deal more than he would have liked to admit; it may be a persisting trait of his Corsican origin.[26]

He had other, more serious, weaknesses. His determination to be implicitly obeyed at all costs could have dangerous consequences, as Constant records at Boulogne when England was threatened with invasion:

One morning, as he mounted his horse, Napoleon announced that he was going to review the naval forces, and gave orders for the ships lying at anchor to quit their moorings, saying that he meant to inspect them in the open sea. He set off with Roustam for his usual ride, expressing the wish to find everything ready on his return, at an hour he mentioned.

Everyone knew that Napoleon's wish was his will. During his absence this one was conveyed to Admiral Bruix, who replied with imperturbable coolness that he was very sorry, but the review would not take place that day. In consequence, not a vessel moved.

On his return Napoleon asked whether all was ready. He was told what the admiral had said. This reply, so unfamiliar in tone, had to be twice repeated to him, and, with a violent stamp of his foot, he sent for the admiral, who waited on him directly.

Napoleon, as the admiral was not quick enough for his liking, went to meet him half way from the hut. His Majesty was attended by his staff, who gathered round him in silence. His eyes were flashing fire.

"Admiral," he said in a choked voice, "why have you not carried out my orders?"

"Sire," replied Admiral Bruix with respectful firmness, "there is a frightful storm getting up. Your Majesty can see that as well as I. Your Majesty does not wish to expose so many brave fellows to needless danger?"

And in fact the heaviness of the air and the low rumbling that could be heard in the distance bore out the admiral's fears only too well.

"Sir," returned Napoleon with increasing irritation, "I gave an order. Once more, why did you not carry it out? I am the sole judge of consequences. Obey!"

"Sire, I shall not obey!"

"You are insolent, sir!"

And Napoleon, who was still carrying his riding-whip, advanced on the admiral with a threatening gesture. Admiral Bruix fell back a step, laying his hand on his sword-hilt.

"Sire," he said, turning pale, "be careful!"

All who stood by were frozen with terror. For some time Napoleon remained motionless, his hand raised, and his eyes fixed on the admiral, who, on his side, retained his terrible posture.

At last Napoleon threw down his whip. Bruix let go his sword-hilt, and awaited bareheaded and in silence the outcome of this horrible scene.

"Rear-Admiral Magon," said Napoleon, "you will instantly carry out the movement I ordered. As for you, sir," he went on, looking once more at Admiral Bruix, "you will leave Boulogne within twenty-four hours and retire to Holland. Go."

Napoleon immediately walked off. As they went, some officers, but only a very few, clasped the admiral's outstretched hand.

Meanwhile Rear-Admiral Magon was putting the fleet through the fatal movement Napoleon had insisted on.

Hardly had the first arrangements been made when the sea became dreadful to behold. The sky, dense with black clouds, was streaked with lightning, thunder rolled continually, and the gale broke all the lines. In short, what the admiral had foreseen took place, and the most appalling storm scattered the vessels till it seemed there could be no hope for them.

Napoleon, with head bent and folded arms, was anxiously pacing the beach, when suddenly dreadful cries were heard. More than twenty gunboats full of soldiers and sailors had been flung on the rocks, and the unhappy men on board, struggling with the raging waves, were crying for help no one dared to give. Napoleon saw his generals and officers shuddering with horror around him.[27]

Potentially more damaging than this neurotic self-will were Napoleon's fits of abstraction. General Thiébault remembered one such fit and its sequel.

I felt obliged, before the Emperor should leave Compiègne, where he had betaken himself immediately after the marriage ceremonies, to make some show of zeal by going to pay my court to Their Majesties. I spent three days there.

The second of them ended like this. I was in the card-room, the furthest of the apartments used as reception-rooms. The Empress was at cards. And while so many kings, archdukes, princes, foreigners of the highest rank, and so many illustrious Frenchmen followed the Emperor with their eyes and hung on his slightest movements, he himself was exchanging a few words with one, honouring another with a nod, going from one card-table to the next and greeting the ladies with remarks more pungent than gallant.

At the end of his circuit, finding himself by the door between this card-room and the adjoining salon, he passed through it. And at once an immense train hurried in his wake.

Rolling to and fro, he came to the middle of the room, stood still, crossed his arms over his chest, bent his gaze on the floor six feet ahead of him and became fixed.

The kings, Archduke Ferdinand, the Empress's uncle, and the other exalted persons who were following, also stopped. Some of them fell back. Others drew aside. All crowded together. And a pretty wide circle was formed, with the Emperor at its centre in a fixity copied by one and all, and a silence which nothing broke.

To start with, all had avoided even looking at each other. Gradually, eyes were raised, and each looked about him. A few moments more, and these glances became so interrogative in character that all seemed to be asking each other what this stage business was leading up to. A tacit inquiry, which, in the presence of so many and such foreigners, made every Frenchman uncomfortable.

And indeed, an abstraction so sudden, but equally bizarre and ill-timed, might for three or four minutes be set down to the Emperor's wish to concentrate on some important idea which had unexpectedly occurred to him.

But after five, six, seven, eight minutes there was no one who could make head or tail of it. However, it stood to reason that at a moment when a haughty and vainglorious master was pleased to make such a peculiar exhibition of himself, the thing to do was to do nothing.

Unhappily Marshal Massena, who was in the front row, and behind whom I was standing, thought differently. Indeed I felt convinced that this man, who had such felicitous promptings and such an unerring glance on the field of battle, but who retained none of his advantages at court, thought he would be doing Napoleon a service by enabling him to put a natural end to this absurd scene – in its way the most ludicrous I have ever seen in my life.

He did not realise that if he provided a leader "offended at his glory" with a chance of mortifying him, he would get him out of the scrape just as well, but by substituting cruelty for claptrap.

As a result, when not a soul budged or thought of budging, he left his place, entered the circle which an evil genius seemed to have drawn on purpose to lure him in quest of an affront, and then walked slowly up to the Emperor…

Amazement and curiosity were depicted on every face. Mine could express nothing but dread. In any case, the suspense was brief. For no sooner had the marshal uttered a few words too low to be heard than, without raising or turning his eyes, without moving a muscle, the Emperor pronounced in a voice of thunder:

"Mind your own business!"

And the old marshal, who, in spite of his glory and his dignities, had just been humiliated before all Europe, instead of taking leave on the spot and hiding his shame in his own house, dumbly returned to his place and, to complete my discomfiture, returned to it backwards.

Never have I felt more mortified. Never was Napoleon the despot revealed to me in a more arrogant and impudent light. For this was an equally gratuitous and cruel insult to France in the person of one of her oldest and most illustrious defenders.

As for Napoleon, after awarding this prize for such great services, he continued his statue scene a few moments longer.

Then, as though emerging from a dream, he raised his head, uncrossed his arms, threw a scrutinizing glance on all about him, turned without speaking to anyone, and went back into the card-room.

At a sign, the Empress threw down her cards and rose. All the games stopped and all got to their feet.

Passing Marie-Louise, he said to her in rather a sharp tone:

"Come, Madam..."

And he walked on, while she followed three steps behind. As soon as he approached the door of the inner apartments, this door opened, and the moment the Empress had passed through, it closed on them. The time was not half-past nine.[28]

Napoleon's treatment of one of the most distinguished of his marshals is characteristic of his attitude toward mankind in general. He despised mankind, General de Ricard thought:

Where did Napoleon get that contempt for mankind which, they say, never ceased to grow on him? To be sure he had about his person, in his entourage (and in his family – perhaps one may say: especially in his family), beings who really deserved contempt. But yet there were, in his time, steadfast characters and virtues, men he could neither tame by his caresses nor cow by his threats. Even among those who were devoted to his fortunes from admiration of his genius, there were men of honour and spirit. If he had ministers to whom he could take his fists, he had others who gave him "an inkling that they would forget his station, if he forgot theirs" (the Duke of Gaeta).

Napoleon could not, *in petto*, despise such men. I believe rather that contempt for humanity was with Napoleon a matter of pose and policy. He wished to debase and corrupt men. Therefore it suited his ambition to think them base and corruptible.

Napoleon's genius remains incomparable. But alas, his heart … And it was by his heart that he judged mankind. What right had *he* to despise mankind who, to attain power, had taken Josephine almost from Barras's lap, and who went on to discard his Josephine for a Marie-Louise?[29]

And it was ultimately this inability to comprehend mankind, to understand its faults and sympathize with its aspirations that was to lead to his downfall. For no empire, however militarily strong, can permanently withstand the forces of human revolt. First in Spain at Baylen, then in Austria at Wagram, Napoleon was made to feel conscious of a new spirit awakening.

Ostensibly the Wagram campaign had produced for Napoleon even more brilliant results than that of Austerlitz. But when, on his return to Paris, one of his Ministers spoke contemptuously of the Austrians, Napoleon replied sharply, "It is evident that you were not at

Wagram." He had been impressed by the stoutness and enthusiasm of the Austrian resistance. The costliness of the Wagram battle, the greatest artillery battle yet known, which had caused some of his second line troops to panic, had shaken his confidence in battles as the trump card. In August 1809 he had written in an unaccustomed vein, "Battle should only be offered when there is no other turn of fortune to be hoped for, as from its nature the fate of a battle is always dubious."

It was not only in the military but also in the moral sphere that his confidence had been shaken. Shortly before he left Schönbrunn a young German student, Frederick Staps, had tried to assassinate him when presenting a petition at a military review. In the course of a long interview with this young man, Napoleon tried to persuade himself that the assassin was mentally deranged, but he refused to recant and went to his execution crying, "Long live Germany. Death to the tyrant." General Rapp wrote to the Burgomaster of Schönbrunn: "You have no doubt heard of this man who wished to assassinate His Majesty last Thursday: it is I who was lucky enough to stop him. He has confessed everything to His Majesty. He is to be executed tomorrow. It is incredible that he is the son of a Lutheran minister from Saxony." Hitherto Napoleon had only had to face assassination from Bourbon agents: that an educated young man of the middle class should wish to murder Napoleon, the champion of enlightenment, he found puzzling and shocking. He was forced to recognize that there was a new spirit stirring in Europe.[30]

After Wagram the tide turned. Another treaty was signed with Austria; but the relations between the Czar and the Emperor, so friendly at Tilsit, were showing how transient all treaties were.

On June 25, 1812, a French army of nearly half a million men crossed the Niemen; six months later, when Ney led the rear guard out of the Russian wastes, scarcely more than 50,000 of them had survived. The disasters of this gigantic, ill-conceived expedition were cataclysmic: by the time Napoleon arrived back in Paris a new and powerful coalition was being formed to bring about his ruin.

For a year he held out. His alert genius, which seemed to have deserted him at Borodino, was not yet exhausted; he showed that he could still win victories in the old, grand manner. But then, on October 16, 1813, the end came at Leipzig.

Again he abandoned his troops to reorganize resistance from Paris. Luckier than their comrades in Egypt and Russia, his soldiers made good their escape. As late as November 8 the allies were still offering Napoleon their willingness to respect the "natural frontiers." They knew his unyielding temper, and they wanted to expose him as the sole obstacle to peace. Perhaps, remembering 1793, they had misgivings about attacking those frontiers which had become dear to the French, and which might be defended with savage energy. Napoleon gave an evasive answer. No further compromise was possible.

By the end of 1813 the allies had crossed the Rhine and entered old France. Schwartzenberg and his Austrians, Blücher and his Prussians were converging on Paris. For three months Napoleon played a magnificent game worthy of his greatest achievements in Italy. With raw recruits, some of them eighteen years old, he rushed from one invading army to the other and sent them reeling back at Champaubert, Montmirail, Château-Thierry, Vauchamp, Nangis, Montereau. Once more victory went to his head: he dreamed of reconquering all that he had lost and refused a last offer, with the boundaries of 1792.

The French were of clearer sight than their leader: they shrugged their shoulders wearily when a fresh victory was announced. Every passing advantage won by Napoleon brought about a drop in the Paris stock exchange: the same realistic barometer that had indicated his rise served to register his fall. All the prodigies of tactics and endurance proved unavailing; the imperial troops were beaten at Laon, Arcis-sur-Aube, La Fère-Champenoise. The allies captured the heights of Montmartre, and Paris capitulated. The British were at Bordeaux.

Napoleon at bay still refused to understand: he heaped abuses on Marmont for surrendering Paris and urged his marshals to make a supreme effort. They shook their heads. He may have attempted suicide: reports on this point are at the same time definite and irreconcilable. Then, at Fontainbleau, he abdicated, at first in favor of his son, then, under allied pressure, unconditionally (April 11). He took a well-staged, heart-rending farewell of his Old Guard. Already his Senate had turned against him and declared that he and his race had forfeited the throne.

The allies, many of whom had professed to be his friends, one of whom was his father-in-law, treated him with singular consideration. He kept his imperial title; he was given, instead of a jail, a toy kingdom, the island of Elba, with an army of four hundred men. France deeply felt her defeat but not the fall of the autocrat. As he himself had prophesied, his exit was hailed with a sigh of relief. If he had few friends left, he still had bitter enemies: he was insulted on his way to exile and had to disguise himself to escape lynching. On May 4 he arrived at Elba. The strangest chapters of his career were still to be written.[31]

2

1814: Peace and Congress

"What is it you want of me?" Napoleon had asked Metternieh at Dresden in the summer of 1813. "That I should dishonour myself? Never! I shall know how to die, but never to yield an inch of territory. Your sovereigns, who were born on the throne, may get beaten twenty times and yet return to their capitals. I can't do that. I am a self-made soldier."

It was this intractable spirit, rather than the military disasters which were soon to follow, which compelled Napoleon's abdication. Even after the crushing victory at Leipzig, where the last great Napoleonic army, raised by incredible exertions, was fatally broken, the allies offered to retreat (November 1813), on the basis that France should retain her natural frontiers, the Rhine, the Alps, and the Pyrenees. That offer was rejected. Later when France had been invaded and one signal defeat had been inflicted on the defending army, the terms were harder, but even then (February 4, 1814), with the sacrifice of Savoy and Belgium, and the acceptance of the old frontiers of the French monarchy as they existed before the revolutionary conquests, Napoleon might have retained his throne. After this last chance had been rejected, there was no other thought in the mind of the allies but that he, like so many of his royal victims, must cease to reign…

It was Talleyrand, a renegade priest and a married bishop, who persuaded Alexander I that the Bourbon House must be recalled to rule in France. Improbable as it might seem that France would willingly accept the government of a fat old gentleman, who for twenty-five years had lived in exile estranged from all the stirring events and glories of that time, there was, in truth, no alternative. Louis XVIII at least represented a principle, a tradition, a fragment of the political faith of France. He at least might be thought to promise repose and the goodwill of Europe to a much tried and deeply apprehensive people. After the escapade of the Revolution and the Empire the old monarchy seemed to be the least unsafe of expedients; but not even the pen of Chateaubriand, most eloquent of French writers, could make it glorious; nor the English-looking constitution imposed by the allies convert it into an instrument of wise and generous liberty. The white flag, by which the famous tricolor was replaced, was a fitting emblem of the family which returned to its home, having learnt nothing and forgotten nothing in an epoch of tumultuous change.

The terms accorded to the conquered country (Treaty of Paris, May 30, 1814) were marked by a politic moderation.

The detailed settlement of Europe was left to a Congress summoned for November to Vienna. Here the aristocracy of the old *régime*, light-hearted in the moment of their great release, surrendered themselves to an orgy of brilliant dissipation. As Paris danced after Thermidor, and London after the 1918 Armistice, so through that autumn and winter Vienna danced while the Corsican was safe in Elba and the officials were working out the structure of a new Europe. In this circle of emperors and kings, princes, nobles, and diplomats Marie Louise, the faithless wife of Napoleon, was studious to display her tiny feet.

The new map was shaped by statesmen for whom revolution emanating from France was the greatest of all dangers to the well-being of mankind.

The eastern frontier of France was therefore lined by a series of buffer states or provinces destined to protect the tender body of central Europe from revolution: in the north a kingdom of the Netherlands, which lasted till 1830, when the uneasy union between Calvinist Holland and Catholic Belgium was dissolved; in the south a Sardinian kingdom, strengthened by the incorporation of Genoa and Savoy, while the intermediate region of the Rhineland was entrusted, mainly at the instigation of the British Government, to the wardship of Prussia. Nobody then foresaw the union of Germany under the Prussian crown, or that change in the balance of European power which still makes Germany formidable to her neighbours.[32] Far otherwise was the outlook in 1914. Then France was regarded as the general enemy, and Prussia as the power best qualified to keep a watch upon the Rhine.

With the same idea of recalling Europe to conservatism and sobriety, the Austrians were accorded that dominant position in northern and central Italy which soon provoked the conspiracies and wars of Italian nationalism...

These arrangements were reached without great expense or controversy as part of a general design for repelling the influence of France from those countries in which it had been spread by the conquests of Napoleon. The principal difficulty arose in that region of the middle east of Europe where the problem is still most thorny. What was to be done with the Grand Duchy of Warsaw, which Napoleon had carved out of the Polish Provinces of Prussia and handed over to be governed by the Saxon King?

What was to be done with Saxony itself? Russia wanted Poland, Prussia wanted Saxony, and had these two states been left to their own devices, Poland and Saxony would have been wiped off the map. Such a prospect, however, was most unpalatable to Austria and France, the one refusing to see her Prussian rival so aggrandized, the other cherishing strong views upon a liberated Polish state. It was a question which brought the Congress to the brink of war. Eventually a compromise was reached under which Prussia received some two-thirds of Saxony and the Rhine provinces, while Poland was erected into a constitutional kingdom under the Tzar.

Talleyrand's formula of legitimacy summed up the spirit of the settlement.[33]

It was a spirit with which Metternich was entirely in sympathy.

Among the remarks (and they were numerous) which Metternich made about himself there is one which appears sincere enough, and which is difficult to reconcile with the charge of invariable opportunism. "I am bad at skirmishes," he said, "but I am good at campaigns." Flattered as he was by all the talk of a "Metternich system," he affirmed none the less that he had no system, but only certain fixed principles. It is in fact arguable that, although in the day to day conduct of affairs he displayed an opportunism which bounded upon levity, the main principles which guided his political course were unvarying and rigid. What were those principles?

In his attitude both to internal and to external affairs the whole of Metternich's political theory can be summarised in the one word "equilibrium." He interpreted that word in an almost mechanical sense, having a tendency to approach politics as he approached the astronomical clocks, the astrolabes and the other scientific instruments with which it was his hobby, in spare moments, to amuse himself. In internal affairs the pendulum had swung too far to the left and in the direction of chaos; repression was necessary to restore the balanced functioning of the machine. The only antidote to the disarrangements of revolution was the sacred word "stability." Similarly in international affairs the Balance of Power was an almost cosmic principle. Without internal and external equilibrium there could be no repose; and repose was essential to the normal happiness of man.[34]

So the formula of legitimacy became the rule by which the Congress acted:

It was legitimacy which restored the Bourbons to France, saved Saxony for the Wettins, and confirmed the power of the royal house of Sardinia. No respect was paid to nationality or to the wishes of the population concerned. In all essentials, therefore, the statesmen who drew up the settlement at Vienna were sharply opposed in aims and principles to the artificers of the Europe in which we now live. The Peace Treaties of 1920 constituted a democratic settlement made possible only by the downfall of those very monarchies to which the Congress of Vienna had entrusted the policing of Europe. The settlement of 1920 created new Republics, redistributed frontiers, accepted the dissolution of the old Austrian Empire, and built up a Europe on that principle of self-determination which had been preached by the French revolutionaries, but was afterwards long lost to view. To the Congress of Vienna the principles of President Wilson would have been anathema. Guided by Metternich, Talleyrand, and Castlereagh, it held that the well-being of Europe was to be secured not by compliance with the assumed wishes of the peoples concerned, but only by punctual obedience to legitimate authority.

By a stroke of fortune for the conservative cause the allied sovereigns and ministers were still gathered in Vienna when it was learnt (March 7, 1815) that Napoleon was once more on the soil of France.[35]

3

The Flight of the Eagle

When Napoleon landed on the island of Elba he sincerely declared that "he wanted nothing but to rest". Still smarting from the catastrophe which had befallen him, he believed that he could get used to living like a minor Italian prince. He seemed to be relaxed, without regrets and almost happy; but soon he felt the need for action again. He busied himself with the organization of his tiny state. He created a fleet, built roads, worked the iron mines, extracted salt from the marshes, and kept his minute army in trim with drills, reviews and digging operations. This "army" was composed of eight hundred veterans of the Old Guard who had followed him and three hundred men from the island's former garrison. He promised himself that in his leisure time he would write a history of his reign. He freely discussed the major events of the period with his officers, particularly those which led to his downfall. In the course of discussion he referred several times to the German campaign and his refusal to accept peace at Prague.

"I was wrong," he said, "but you must put yourselves in my place. I had won so many victories, Lutzen and Bautzen being the most recent, when I recovered my power in two days. I had full confidence in my soldiers and in myself, and I wanted to throw the dice one last time. I lost. But those who blame me have never drunk from the intoxicating cup of success."

The respectful silence of his listeners left him alone with his thoughts and his regrets. After this period of heart-searching he plunged into reading. He had a country house built and enlarged his residence at Portoferraio. He beautified his little capital, had the streets paved, installed a fountain, repaired and dredged the port. From early morning he was on horseback with the Grand Marshal Bertrand and the good and faithful Drouot, riding across the island to supervise the progress of his various projects. Sometimes he boarded a long boat and toured the coasts. In the evenings he held social gatherings as he had done during his reign, and arranged for concerts and theatrical performances to be given for the local residents and soldiers. Madame Mère and Pauline Borghèse came to join him and preside at his modest court, while he awaited the arrival of Marie-Louise and her son, which he believed must be imminent.

As the weeks passed, this hope gradually faded. His letters to her were by turn affectionate and peremptory; soon she stopped replying to them. She had been taking the waters at Aix and instead of returning via Italy as he begged her, she went straight back to Vienna, accompanied by General Neipperg, who soon became her lover. Napoleon had not believed that she could be unfaithful to him so quickly; he imagined that his wife, being young and innocent, was being closely watched by her family. He shuddered at the thought of his son being brought up as a German prince.

Soon, despite his economies, he began to run into financial difficulties. He had brought with him 3,400,000 francs, the remains of the immense sums he had amassed during his triumphal years and which he had spent recklessly in his attempts to stem the invasion. But his public works, the maintenance of his army, his ships and his house, had considerably reduced this hoard. The two million-franc Civil List pension which had been guaranteed him by the Treaty of Fontainebleau, was still to be paid by the Bourbons; he assumed, however, that they would never fulfil their obligations. Once his personal funds were gone, he would be unable to pay or feed his small army. If he were forced to disband it he would be left undefended, which would doubtless be welcomed in certain quarters. There was a real danger of assassination. At home hot-headed Royalists spoke openly of doing away with him or of deporting him far across the ocean, to St. Helena or St. Lucia.

This idea was unbearable to him:

"I am a soldier," he said to Bertrand, "if someone comes to assassinate me, I will bare my breast, but I do not want to be deported."

In fact, deportation would mean the death-blow to his confused but still lively hopes. From newspapers and friends still in France he knew what was going on in Paris and Vienna. It did not seem possible to him that the Revolution, of which more than ever he claimed to be the heir, could be stifled by the Holy Alliance, or that Europe could quietly settle down into the old framework of 1789.

All the elementary mistakes which the restored monarchy should have avoided were, astonishingly, committed one after the other. The Army was angered by the actions brought against the former generals of the Empire, the *bourgeoisie* by the insolent attitude of the

Court, the constitutional liberals by the prorogation of the Chambers, and industry by the excessive customs concessions granted to English goods. The peasants feared that the sale of national property would be revoked, a measure threatened by the émigrés. Taxes, already so burdensome, continued to be levied, although the Government had promised to abolish them. A mood of suppressed anger began to mount throughout the country; already the Emperor was missed.[36]

Erckmann-Chatrian well convey the unrest in France – the anger caused by the returning émigrés, *the trouble spread by the discharged soldiers:*

Then Father Goulden said to me with an ominous air, "Things are going badly, Joseph. Do you know what all these people will do in Paris? They will demand back their fishponds, their forests and parks, their chateaux, their pensions, to say nothing of high offices and honours and distinctions of all kinds. You think their dress and their wigs very antiquated. Those people are more dangerous to us than the Russians and Austrians – for the Russians and Austrians will go away, and these will remain. They will come and destroy what has taken us five-and-twenty years to effect. You see how proud they are! Many of them have been living in great poverty beyond the Rhine, but they consider themselves of a different race to us – superior beings; they think the people are always ready to be fleeced, as they were before 1789. They say that Louis XVIII has good sense; so much the better for him. If he is so foolish as to listen to these people, if they even think he can be got to listen to their counsels, everything is lost. It will be a war against the nation. The people have been thinking for twenty-five years; they know their rights, and know that one man is as good as another, and that all talk about noble races is nonsense; every one wants to keep his field, each one wants equality of rights, and all will defend themselves to the death."...

Thus the whole winter passed away. The indignation became greater from day to day. The town was full of half-pay officers who dared no longer stay in Paris – lieutenants, captains, commanders, colonels of all the infantry, and cavalry; people who lived on a small glass of cognac and a crust of bread, and who were the more unhappy inasmuch as they had to keep up appearances. Imagine men of this kind, with hollow cheeks, close-cut hair, their eyes flashing, with their great moustaches, and their old regulation greatcoats, the buttons of which they had been obliged to change. Fancy them walking about three or six, or ten in a group, on the great square, with great sword-sticks hanging from their button-holes, and their great cocked hats set square across their shoulders, always well brushed, but so worn and shabby that you felt sure they could not have a quarter enough to eat. Still you could not help saying to yourself, "These are the victors of Jemmapes, Fleurus, Zurick, Hohenlinden, Marengo, Austerlitz, Friedland, and Wagram; if we are proud of being Frenchmen, it is not the Count of Artois or the Dukes of Berry or of Angoulême who can boast of being the cause of our pride, but these men themselves. And now they are left to die, and even bread is refused them while emigrants are put in their places. It's really an abomination." It was not necessary to have much good sense, or kindness, or justice to see that this was against nature.

For my part, I could not bear to see these wretched people; it made my heart ache. When a man has served, if it be only for six months, the feeling of respect for his old chiefs, for those whom he has seen in the front under fire, always remains with him. I was ashamed of my country for allowing such scandalous things to be done.[37]

Napoleon, aware of all this, soon decided to return.

Early in 1815 he had virtually made up his mind to attempt returning to France. His companions were bored and his soldiers asked him in a familiar way, "Sire, when are we leaving?"

The announcement that the Congress of Vienna would soon be over was also encouraging, since once the allied sovereigns had dispersed, it would be harder for them to act in consort against him. Thanks to Pauline, he had made his peace with Murat, who, cold-shouldered by his new masters, had come to ask the Emperor's pardon. Madame Walewska spent two days on Elba with her son, and then proceeded to Naples to warn Murat to be ready for action.[38]

Napoleon had already made his preliminary preparations when a messenger arrived on Elba sent by one of his former ministers, Hugues-Bernard Maret, Duke of Bassano. This messenger, Fleury de Chaboulon, recorded his impression of the interview – how Napoleon strode up and down, violently agitated as he listened to accounts of the state of public opinion in France, and at length said:

"I could be in France in two days, if the nation were to recall me... Do you think I ought to go back?"

As he spoke these words, Napoleon averted his eyes, and I could easily see that he attached more importance to the question than he wished to reveal, and that he was awaiting my answer with anxiety.

"Sire, I dare not decide such a question of myself, but..."

(*Abruptly*) "That's not what I'm asking you. Answer yes or no!"

"Yes."

(*With emotion*) "You think so?"

"Yes, sire, I am convinced, like the Duke of Bassano, that the people and the army would welcome you as a liberator and embrace your cause with enthusiasm."

(*In an anxious, disturbed manner*) "So Maret advises me to come back?"

"We foresaw that Your Majesty would question me on that point, and here are his exact words:

"'You will tell the Emperor that I dare not take it on myself to decide such an important question, but that he may regard it as a positive and incontestable fact that the present government has ruined itself in the eyes of the people and the army, that disaffection is at the highest pitch, and that the regime is not expected to hold out for long against the general censure. You will add that the Emperor has become the object of the regrets and wishes of the army and the nation. After that the Emperor will decide, in his wisdom, what he has to do.'"

Napoleon became pensive, was silent, and after a long pondering said to me:

"I will think it over. You are to stay here. Come at eleven o'clock tomorrow."[39]

He discussed his problem constantly with his family and his companions.

"I cannot die here," he confided to Madame Mère, "France is in turmoil, the Bourbons have stirred up against themselves all the beliefs and hopes associated with the Revolution. The Army wants me back; everything leads me to believe that they will welcome me with open arms. There is certainly the chance of coming across some unexpected obstacle, of meeting some officer, loyal to the Bourbons, who would destroy the enthusiasm of my troops and defeat me in a few hours. But such an end would be better than staying indefinitely on this island, and the future in store for me here. So I want to leave and tempt providence once more. What is your opinion, Mother?"

This remarkable woman, a tower of strength, both in good times and bad, thought for a moment and then replied simply.

"Go, my son, and follow your destiny."

Napoleon then consulted Bertrand and Drouot. The former agreed with his plan, the latter was less sure. Might the Emperor's return not tear the country apart? Napoleon set his mind at rest. Everything, he said, had changed including himself. He no longer wanted to be a conqueror, but a liberal monarch who would give the French unity and peace.

Taking advantage of the absence of the English commissioner, Sir Neil Campbell, who was on holiday in Leghorn, Napoleon placed an embargo on all ships bound for Elba. On February 26 he embarked with eleven hundred men and four pieces of artillery on a flotilla consisting of the brig *Inconstant*, the schooner *Caroline* and five other light craft. He informed Murat of his departure, but ordered him not to act until he knew how things were going in Paris.

It was a fine moonlit night when Napoleon went aboard the *Inconstant*, but the wind, which had been favourable, suddenly dropped, and the next morning found the little fleet still struggling between Elba and Caprera in waters which were guarded by two cruisers, one English, one French. Napoleon's captains, Chautard and Taillade, were uneasy and recommended returning to Portoferraio; but Napoleon refused. A little later the breeze freshened and the flotilla bore northwards. Near Leghorn, the *Inconstant* came up with an armed brig, *Zéphyre*, commanded by Lieutenant Andrieux. They could have captured the ship, but this seemed too risky. The Emperor ordered his grenadiers to take off their fur caps and to lie down on the deck. Taillade took a megaphone and hailed Andrieux while Napoleon listened anxiously to their conversation.

"Where are you bound for?" – "Leghorn, and you?"

"Genoa." "How is the great man?"

"Wonderfully well." "Glad to hear it!"

The *Zéphyre* stood off and the *Inconstant* continued on her course towards France. Napoleon spent the best part of the two days' journey on deck, glasses in hand. He spoke to his soldiers, reminded them of their battles and revealed to them that he was going to free France from the foreign yoke.

Despite all that had occurred to disillusion him, their joy moved him deeply. To those who could write he dictated the proclamations he had drawn up before leaving, for distribution among the army and the civilians. He was confident that the country would respond to his final appeal:

"Soldiers, we have not been defeated. In my exile I have heard your voice. Your general has returned; come and join him again. Put on the tricolour cockade which you used to wear in the days of our greatness. Victory will come marching at the double, the eagle with the national colours will fly from steeple to steeple to the very towers of Notre Dame. Then you will be able to boast of what you have done, you will be the liberators of your country."

To all grenadiers who had not yet received it, he awarded the cross of the Legion of Honour. They remained awake throughout the night of the 28th, silent, happy, full of hope, resolved as one man to die for their Emperor.[40]

Napoleon's small army landed near Cannes on March 1.

Towards midnight, after the men had cleaned their arms, eaten their soup and received a fortnight's pay, they were formed into column and marched into Cannes under a glorious moon. In Cannes, people had thought at first that Algerian pirates had landed and the inhabitants had actually barricaded their houses. The arrival of the vanguard removed one source of fear only to create another. The crowd gathered round the grenadiers and questioned them with more anxiety than sympathy. Only the children showed real joy. As the detachment had marched past them, the shadow of the bearskins had fallen on the ill-cleaned school windows and, heedless of cane or threatened imposition, they had poured out of their classrooms.

Cambronne without loss of time proceeded, purse in hand, to requisition provisions, mules and horses. He was in the middle of an argument with the mayor, a stout royalist who would rather have seen the Dey of Algiers himself than a Bonapartist general, when an emblazoned travelling carriage emerged from the Aix road. It carried the duc de Valentinois who was on his way to his principality of Monaco. Cambronne forced him to descend and confined him in the Hotel de la Poste until further orders. The main body, which did not arrive till after one o'clock, halted within half a gunshot of the outskirts, not far from where the road from Grasse joins the main road. This wonderful night was bitterly cold and the Emperor ordered a vine-wood fire to be made whilst awaiting the distribution of rations. In spite of the advanced hour the whole population rushed out to see Napoleon and crowded round him. Their attentions were so pressing that he was forced to summon a few grenadiers, telling them to show no roughness. "Don't worry the people," he said, and went on warming himself, stirring the fire with the toe of his boot.

"The people of Cannes received the Emperor with an enthusiasm which was the first presage of the success of the expedition." Thus the *Moniteur*. From other sources we learn that the attitude of the crowd was one of anxious curiosity rather than of enthusiasm. It is even said that a butcher of the name of Bertrand took deliberate aim at the Emperor from behind his window, and would have fired had not a neighbour, in terror of the reprisals which such a crime might provoke, snatched his weapon from his hands. Some encouragement Napoleon got from the courier of the duc de Valentinois who declared that, once out of Provence, he would find everybody on his side, but that was probably all. The prince was conducted to the bivouac. "Are you coming with us, Monaco?" said the Emperor laughing. "Sire, I am going home." "And so am I" was the answer. After a halt of some two hours the column resumed its march towards Grasse without entering Cannes.

At Grasse, about twelve miles distant, the rumour of a Corsair landing had spread, as at Cannes, but it was not long before the mayor, the marquis de Gourdon, had learned the real facts. In the absence of the sous-préfet, he summoned the municipal council during the night and sent for General Gazan, who had lately retired on half-pay and was living in his native town. The councillors talked of arming the population and opposing any attempt of the usurper to march through Grasse, but Gazan, whose loyalty was above suspicion, for by ten o'clock he had already sent an urgent message to Marshal Soult, began by enquiring into the defensive resources of the town. On the mayor informing him that he had altogether thirty muskets, of which only five were serviceable, and not a round of ammunition, he advised this ardent warrior to take no action.

There was, besides, some doubt as to whether Napoleon intended to march by way of Grasse or by Aix. A man who was sent out to bring in information met the advanced guard halfway. Cambronne, suspecting him to be a spy, called out to him: "You look very tired, my friend. You needn't go any further. I will tell you everything you want to know." The General hurried on, leaving his detachment behind him and entered Grasse alone. Heads appeared at all the windows, and soon fifteen hundred persons ("many old heads and white ribbons," as he picturesquely described them) were assembled in the public square and the place du Clavecin. The mayor asked Cambronne in the name of which sovereign he was requisitioning, and, on receiving the answer that it was in the name of Napoleon, replied, "We have our sovereign and we love him." "Monsieur le Maire," replied Cambronne, "I am not here to talk politics with you but to ask for rations, as my column will be here shortly." The mayor bowed to the inevitable and obeyed. "Yet nothing would have been easier," as Cambronne said later before the court martial, "than to kill me, alone there among the people of the town. It was easy to say 'I love the King'. He ought to have shown it."

Napoleon, who was anxious as to the course of events in this town of twelve thousand inhabitants, was advancing very slowly. Near the village of Mouan he halted on hearing the sound of bells and only resumed his march after learning from a carrier, whom he cross-questioned, that the bells were tolling for a funeral. On arriving in sight of Grasse, and being told of the excited condition of the town, he made a circuit, instead of marching through it, and halted for the night about a mile and a half further on, on the plateau of Roccavignon. There were others beside royalists in Grasse and many people climbed the heights bringing wine for the soldiers and flowers for the Emperor. By a happy chance the violets were just in flower. A blind old officer came to see the Emperor, his wife leading him, and asked permission to kiss his hand. Napoleon embraced him. It was when bivouacking at Grasse that he heard again for the first time the cry of "*Vive l'Empereur!*" from French throats...

Napoleon's march, almost furtive at first, successful only by its rapidity, was soon to become the flight of the eagle. In Eastern Provence the populace had been indifferent or covertly hostile. As he drew nearer to Dauphine there was a marked change. The peasantry flocked to meet him, and after looking first at their five-franc pieces to be sure he was really the man, they would break into cheers and wish him victory. At Sisteron the crowd had greeted him with the cry of "*Vive l'Empereur!*" At Gap the préfet and the general had found it impossible to organise a defence and, unable to stem the general tide of feeling, had withdrawn to Embrun with the garrison. At Saint-Bonnet the inhabitants, in their anxiety at the smallness of his force, offered to join him, and proposed to sound the tocsin and rally the whole population of the neighbouring villages to march with him. "No," said the Emperor. "Your feelings are to me a sure guarantee of what the army will feel. Every soldier that is brought against me will come over to my side. The greater number of them, the greater the certainty of my success. So stay quietly at home."[41]

By March 6 Napoleon was at Corps, about fifty miles south of Grenoble, which was the headquarters of the 7th Division under General Marchand.

Marchand still hoped to march against "Bonaparte's brigands", as Fournier called them, but, at a second meeting on March 6th, the commanding officers were no longer so keen to fight. They reported that their men could not be counted on, especially those of the 3rd Engineers and the 4th Artillery, in which Bonaparte had served before the Revolution, that there was no eagerness to take the oath a second time, and, in fact, that it would be rash to take the field with such unreliable troops. When Marchand's order containing the statement that Bonaparte had only a thousand men was read out, some of the men had called out, "What about us? Don't we count?" Others had struck out the General's signature and written an unmentionable word in its place. The following conversation between two gunners had been heard on the ramparts: "He's always been our friend, he has – and they want us to do him harm – no bloody fear!" "Blasted idiot! If it comes to firing, we might be firing in the other direction."[42]

On March 7 Napoleon moved on toward Grenoble through La Mure.

He rode through La Mure, acknowledging graciously the greetings of the inhabitants, and dismounted a hundred yards outside the village, on a hillock near the high road. He was followed by a cheering crowd of more than fifteen hundred. A picket of light infantry formed a ring round him. He chatted at length with the mayor and municipal councillors, questioning them as to the state of opinion in the countryside, its products and its needs, and discussing their personal situation. There was a blazing sun. A corporal brought wine in a bucket for the men of the picket, and when they had all drunk, Napoleon took the glass which his *grognards* had used, and drank from it as well. It was by acts of this kind that he endeared himself to his men.

At eleven, the column moved on, headed by the Poles and followed by the light infantry of the Old Guard, some on foot and others riding in carts provided by the inhabitants, the Emperor bringing up the rear in his carriage, his led charger alongside. The main body was still some way behind. Three and a half miles before reaching Laffray the high road enters a long defile bordered on one side by hills rising to a height of nearly 400 feet, and on the other by a chain of lakes. The light infantry were suddenly surprised at the sight of the Poles galloping back helter-skelter. They jumped out of their carts and, hastily taking up a formation, began loading. The Emperor left his carriage, mounted and galloped forward with the lancers. After a short while he drew rein. A force of infantry was drawn across the end of the defile between him and the village. It was a battalion of the 5th Regiment and the company of engineers. Delassart, their commander, had, during his night retreat, been assailed by doubts as to whether, in view of the fact that circumstances had made it impossible for him to carry out his original instructions of delaying Napoleon by blowing up the Ponthaut bridge, he ought not to report to General Marchand and await further orders before returning to Grenoble. His men showed no signs of disaffection, not one of them had deserted, Laffray offered a splendid defensive position which it would be difficult to turn. He therefore decided to occupy the outlet of the pass, hoping to hold the rebel forces in check long enough to be able to receive an answer to the two messages he had sent to Marchand during the night and in the morning. Between 12 and 1 o'clock, an a.d.c. [aide-de-camp] of the General, Captain Randon, arrived, but this officer brought no instructions, having left Grenoble before the arrival of Delassart's dispatches. He had been sent to find out what was happening. This young man of nineteen, a nephew of Marchand, and destined later to be a marshal of France and Minister of War under the second Empire, was particularly hostile to Bonaparte. He insisted that they must fire on him. He stayed on with Delassart who deployed his battalion in front of the village with his company of *voltigeurs* in the first line.

Delassart recognized Napoleon by his grey coat. He watched him dismount. The Emperor, who appeared agitated, was striding up and down the road, stopping occasionally to observe the battalion through his glass.

Many peasants had accompanied him and some of them approached the *voltigeurs* and offered them the proclamations, but not a man moved from his place in the ranks. Delassart drove the peasants away with threats. Later an officer of the guard, an old comrade-in-arms of the commandant, came across to parley with him. Delassart turned a deaf ear to his promises and exhortations and cut in with "I am determined to do my duty. If you do not leave at once I will have you arrested." "Just one thing – are you going to fire?" "I shall do my duty," the commandant repeated, and, seeing the officer making as if he wished to address the troops, he carried his hand to his sword. At that moment Captain Raoul, one of the Emperor's a.d.c.'s, rode up to the front of the battalion and cried: "The Emperor is on the point of advancing towards you. If you fire, he will be the first to fall. You will answer for it before France."

Not a man stirred, not a man spoke. They seemed insensible as a row of statues. And then the little troop of Polish Lancers began to advance, while, one hundred yards behind them could be seen the long blue coats and the bearskins of the Old Guard. The 5th Regiment seemed to waver. The commandant watched the faces of his men. He saw terror. "Battalion! right about turn, march!" He gave the order hurriedly, hoping even if resistance was impossible, as it now seemed, to prevent desertions. He turned to Marchand's a.d.c.: "How can I take men into action who are trembling in every limb and pale as death?" The Poles drew nearer. He made his men quicken their step, but the *voltigeurs* could now almost feel the breath of the horses on their backs. Delassart felt that in a moment his battalion would be broken into from behind. "Halt! Right about face," came the order. With bayonets at the charge he made his men, still mechanically obedient, advance once more. The Lancers, knowing that on no account must they charge, wheeled and retreated to the right of the Old Guard.

And then the Emperor told Colonel Mallet to make his men put their muskets under their left arms. The Colonel protested that it would be dangerous to advance practically unarmed against a force whose intentions were to say the least uncertain, and whose first volley would spread havoc, but the Emperor replied: "Mallet, obey your orders."

And, alone, leading his veterans with arms reversed, he marched towards the opposing line.

"There he is! Fire!" rang out the frenzied shout from Captain Randon.

The wretched men were livid, their knees shaking, their quivering hands clutching at their weapons.

Napoleon halted within pistol shot. "Soldiers of the fifth," said he, and his voice was steady and clear, "I am your Emperor. Know me." He drew nearer and threw open his coat: "If there is one among you who would kill his Emperor, here I am."

The men could stand no more. "*Vive l'Empereur!*" The mighty shout burst forth, a pent up torrent suddenly released. In a moment ranks are broken, white cockades lie scattered in the dust, shakos are waving on bayonet points. The men are thronging round their Emperor, cheering, kneeling at his feet, touching his boots, his sword, the skirts of his coat – worshipping. Under cover of the confusion Captain Randon, whose order to fire would have gained him but short shrift from the men, sets spurs to his horse and is gone. Delassart, humiliated and desperate, yet deeply moved, and overcome with tears, hands his sword to the Emperor who folds him in his arms in a gesture of consolation.[43]

The road was now open to Grenoble, which Napoleon entered in triumph. "Before Grenoble," he was to say later, "I was an adventurer. At Grenoble I was a reigning prince."

At Lyons, Napoleon resumed his full status of Emperor. He addressed the people, he reviewed the troops, he received the municipal council, the court, the clergy, the faculties, the deputations sent by the workshops. He appointed and dismissed officials. He decorated a National Guard for being the only man who had escorted the comte d'Artois to the town gate. He filled the vacancies in the commands of the 7th and 19th military divisions. He issued decrees suppressing the use of the royal standard and the white cockade, abolishing the old noblesse and feudal titles, suppressing the orders of Saint-Louis and of the Holy Ghost. He disbanded the Swiss regiments and the *Maison du roi*, annulled all appointments and promotions made during the preceding twelve months in the army or in the Legion of Honour, as well as all changes in the Courts of Appeal or First Instance. He re-established the tricolour flag and made the wearing of the national cockade compulsory. He restored the electoral rights and the salaries of the legionaries, he abrogated all laws of deprivation enacted against communes and charitable establishments, he sequestrated the estates forming the apanage of princes of the House of Bourbon, he banished from French territory all émigrés who had returned since the invasion. On March 13th he issued eleven decrees of which the last abolished the Chamber of Peers and summoned an extra-ordinary session of the electoral colleges to meet in Paris as a kind of assembly of the nation.

The people never left him. They stood outside his house cheering, they followed him wherever he went, and when he left Lyons on March 13th they accompanied him beyond the limits of the faubourg of Vaise. At Villefranche trees of liberty were set up in all the public places, the houses were decorated with the national colours and with eagles of gilt paper. Sixty thousand peasants from all the country-side had gathered in haste in this little town of barely four thousand inhabitants to see the Emperor. The villages were deserted for more than twenty miles around. The royalist writer, Fabry, tells the story of two peasants who bought from the inn-keeper the bones of the chicken which the Emperor had eaten at luncheon, to preserve as relics. From Villefranche, Napoleon went on to Macon where he slept. Germain, the préfet, and the mayor had left the town the day before amid the jeers of the populace. The préfet's substitute received him and paid him this rather naïve compliment: "Your Majesty always works miracles. When we heard of your landing we thought you were crazy." He was prevented from continuing by the cheers of the populace.

On arriving next day (March 14th) at Tournus and at Chalon, where tricolour flags had been displayed since the 12th, the first words of the Emperor were of congratulation to the inhabitants on their gallant behaviour during the invasion. "I have not forgotten," said he, "that you resisted the enemy for forty days, and how bravely you defended the passage of the Saône." On asking for the names of those who had particularly distinguished themselves, the crowd shouted out that of the mayor of Saint-Jean-de-Losne. "I hereby decorate him," said the

Emperor, "it is for gallant fellows like him and like you that I created the Legion of Honour, not for émigrés drawing pensions from your enemies."

The Emperor had heard at Lyons of the arrival of Ney in Franche-Comte. According to Rovigo, Ney was, of all the Marshals, the one whom Napoleon feared most. Fleury de Chaboulon on the contrary declares that he learnt with satisfaction that the command of the first troops that were to be brought against him had been entrusted to Ney. Evidently the two views cannot be reconciled. It is, of course, possible that Napoleon, who knew Ney's violence of character, was afraid of some rash act on his part, on the other hand he probably had more to hope from Ney's impressionable and impulsive nature than from the dourness of a Macdonald or a Suchet. So on leaving Lyons he sent several emissaries to Marshal Ney and to some of his generals. The spell which he had so successfully cast over the troops at Laffray, the conduct of the garrison in Grenoble, and the enthusiasm of the garrison in Lyons left him in no doubt as to the feelings of the Army in general. It seemed as if nothing could now arrest his triumphant progress. Yet some desperate move on the part of Ney might stain it with blood.

-

Ney had arrived on March 10th under the spell of his own words to the King, that he would bring back Bonaparte in an iron cage. He was so pleased with this expression that he repeated it to the sous-préfet of Poligny, who retorted that it would be better to bring him back dead in a cart. "No, no," said the Marshal, "You don't know Paris. They want something they can see," and he added: "It's lucky the man from Elba has launched this madcap enterprise. It means the last act of his tragedy. It's the dénouement of the Napoleonad." Every word he spoke breathed an inspired hatred. "Yes," he repeated, "leave Bonaparte to me. We'll attack this wild beast."

But the difficulty was to find a pack of hounds. Besides, he had no definite instructions. First he was to act under the duc de Berry. The duc de Berry had stayed in Paris. Now he was told to take his orders from the comte d'Artois. Ney wrote to him that his [Ney's] presence in Besançon seemed to serve no useful purpose and asked to be summoned to Lyons "to be employed in the front line" of the comte's army. The comte d'Artois being no longer in Lyons, and no longer having an army, his letter remained unanswered.

Ney's first thought was to join Monsieur at Roanne, but he finally decided on the more soldierlike course of concentrating his troops at Lons-le-Saunier. He would be there in the centre of operations and would be able to debouch through Bourg either on Napoleon's flank or on his rear according to circumstances. On arriving at Lons-le-Saunier in the night of 11th-12th he sent for the préfet, the marquis de Vaulchier, and held council with him. Next morning he saw the commanders of the various units, sent out riders to hasten the concentration of the troops and wrote a second letter to Soult to the effect that, as soon as his artillery had arrived, he would march on Bourg and manoeuvre towards Maçon.

Ney knew that the comte d'Artois had left Lyons, but he did not yet know whether Napoleon had entered the town. That evening (the 12th) he learnt the news from a merchant called Boulouze who had fled from Lyons on the morning of the 11th to escape from the tumult.

Boulouze described to him the frantic enthusiasm of the soldiers and of the populace on seeing the grey coat. He added, "when Bonaparte reviewed the troops in the place Bellecour he said to them: 'My friends, we shall go to Paris with our hands in our pockets. Everything is prepared for my journey thither!'" Boulouze also showed the Marshal the proclamation to the Army dated from the golfe Jouan. The Marshal read it unconcernedly and put it in his pocket. On Boulouze remarking that Bonaparte claimed to have the support of Austria, Ney burst out angrily, "What next! It's only his usual boastfulness." Boulouze was carried away by Ney's confidence and exclaimed: "Ah, monsieur le maréchal, you have already been the saviour of France by forcing Napoleon to abdicate; you will now be doubly her saviour." Ney liked the expression and repeated it in another form before Major de la Génetière: "If I can secure the triumph of the King, I shall be the liberator of my country."

Left alone, Ney read the proclamation once more. This time he was so struck by it that he could not refrain from showing it to the préfet of the Jura and to the marquis de Saurans, aide-de-camp of the comte d'Artois, who happened to come in at that moment. "People don't write like that now," he said, "The King ought to write like that. That's the way to write to soldiers – that gets them." And striding up and down his room he repeated: "*La victoire marchera au pas de charge. L'aigle avec les couleurs nationales volera de clocher en clocher jusqu'aux tours de Notre Dame.*" And then getting excited, as was his way, he began to attack the conduct of the comte d'Artois at Lyons – the comte d'Artois "who has never even condescended to take a Marshal of France in his carriage," the comte who leaves him, Ney, without troops and without orders. He blamed the King for having refused to retain the Old Guard with him the year before, he accused the party of the émigrés, he recalled the humiliations which the princesse de la Moskowa[44] had suffered at court. He was equally severe on Napoleon. "That madman will never forgive me his abdication. He would probably have my head cut off in six months." In spite of his grievances against the Bourbons he remained ardent and resolute. "The first soldier who moves," he cried, "will get my sword through his body, the hilt can be his poultice … but soldiers always march to the sound of guns. Vavasseur, my aide-de-camp, knows how to manage them."

Next day, March 13th, the Marshal had a hundred thousand cartridges brought from Besançon. He hastened the arrival of his artillery, he sent an officer to prison who had called out "*Vive l'Empereur!*" and dispatched some disguised gendarmes and well-disposed royalists to bring in information from Mâcon. He wrote to Suchet: "I hope we shall see the end of this crazy enterprise." He studied the comparative strength of the forces – his great inferiority in numbers merely drew from him the remark to Bourmont: "We shall be the smaller force, but we shall give them a drubbing." To Bourmont's remark that the troops were unreliable, he answered: "I will take a musket and fire the first shot and everyone will follow."

Meanwhile the news grew blacker and blacker. Not only Lyons, but all the towns of the Rhône, the Ain and of Saône-et-Loire were in open insurrection. In the evening Capelle, préfet of Bourg, arrived half dead with fright. He had been hunted from the town by the inhabitants, and the 76th Line Regiment which formed the advanced force of Ney's corps had gone over to Napoleon. Capelle was in terror of mob violence. "We're back in the Revolution," he said. He did not think the Marshal could take the risk of attacking Bonaparte; he advised him either to join Masséna and fall on Napoleon's rear, or to make for Chambery whence he could obtain help from the Swiss who were quite ready to come to the King's help. But at these words Ney's true French heart revolted. "If foreigners put their foot in France, every Frenchman will declare for Bonaparte," he cried.

The Marshal's loyalty was unshaken as yet, but he was uneasy in his mind. He remarked to Capelle that the only thing for the King to do was to put himself on a stretcher and have himself carried at the head of his troops, in order to revive their courage. It was after the visit of the préfet of the Ain Department that emissaries from Lyons contrived to enter the Hôtel de la Pomme d'Or where Ney had his quarters. They gave him a letter from Bertrand written certainly under Napoleon's inspiration if not actually to his dictation. The letter stated that the Emperor was embarked on no crazy enterprise, success was certain whatever action might be taken against him, everything had been arranged and everywhere the population and the army would declare against the Bourbons. If civil war occurred and blood was shed uselessly, he, Ney, would stand responsible before France. In this letter were enclosed an order to march and an autograph note from the Emperor, as follows: "My cousin, my major-general sends you the order to march. I feel sure that, directly you heard of my arrival in Lyons, you restored the tricolour flag in your command. You are to carry out Bertrand's orders and join me at Chalon. I will receive you as I did on the morrow of the battle of Moskowa." According to Ney the messengers also brought a proclamation to the troops of the 6th military division, which had been dictated by the Emperor and already bore the signature of the Marshal himself. Ney questioned the emissaries. They were officers of the guard whom he knew personally. They had entered Lons-le-Saunier in mufti. Later, at his trial, Marshal Ney generously refused to reveal their names. They told him with a mass of detail everything they had seen and heard: France was wild with enthusiasm, the tricolour was floating over every town, there would be no resistance anywhere, the King had already left Paris, Europe was favourable to the re-establishment of the Empire, Marie Louise and the Prince Imperial were to return from Vienna, the English squadron had had orders not to interfere with Napoleon's crossing. These letters and conversation seriously unsettled the Marshal. Everything that they had said was but a confirmation, at any rate as far as France was concerned, of the reports which Ney had received from the staunchest loyalists, such as the duc de Maille, the préfets of the Ain and the Jura, Colonel de Saint Amour and Major de la Génetière. In the reckless night which followed, it may be that he fought out this great problem of his conscience in an agony of irresolution – but it is far more probable that, carried away by the impetuosity of his nature, he took the plunge unhesitatingly, much as in the past he had flung himself at the cannon's mouth. The call of fate had come and he answered it unresistingly, however great the mental pain. At the thought that an act of his might deluge France with the blood of civil war his oaths melted into thin air. "I was caught in the whirlwind and I lost my head," were the words in which he defended himself at his trial.

But even if Ney had wished to keep his promise to the King and fight Bonaparte (and such was his firm intention until the night of March 13th) he could not have done so.

Delassart at the pass of Laffray, Marchand at Grenoble, Macdonald at the Guillotière bridge, one after the other these men had found resistance impossible. All that had happened several days ago, and, now that the little band from Elba had swollen to the dimensions of an army, now that the task before Ney was no longer that of awaiting an opponent in carefully chosen positions, but of following him by forced marches and attacking him in the open, was it likely that he would be able to carry his men with him? Even on the impossible assumption that, after facing the break-up of his forces through mutiny and desertion, he could have saved a quarter or perhaps a third of his army, already two marches ahead, even if he had been able to come up with them and by seizing a musket and firing the first shot had induced his men to attack their comrades, what then? A deplorable, useless struggle, ending in the defeat of Ney's little force by an enemy five or six times their number and the probable massacre of the scattered remnant by the indignant Burgundian peasantry. And who shall say whether posterity which has readily forgiven Ney his breach of faith, which remembers him only as the hero of many a victory, as the gallant general of the retreat from Russia, who shall say whether posterity would ever have forgotten that he ordered Frenchmen to fire on Frenchmen?

It has been suggested that Napoleon's words "I shall receive you as I did on the morrow of the battle of the Moskowa" had allayed Ney's anxiety as to Napoleon's attitude towards him, and that ambition and resentment for the humiliations inflicted on him at the Tuileries were at the root of his betrayal. That was not the case. The truth is that Ney, the bravest of the brave, was for once afraid of a battle; the truth is that events were too strong for him, that, chained to his army, he was not a free agent; the truth – do we not hear it in his own strangely moving words "could I hold back the sea with my hands?"

On the morning of March 14th, Ney sent for Lecourbe and Bourmont. He declared, and he believed his own words, that he had done so to seek their advice, but he really wished, though unconsciously, to convince them of the inevitability of his decision, and to justify himself in his own eyes by their expected adhesion to his course of action. He repeated to them what Napoleon's envoys had told him of the irresistible force of the Bonapartist tide and of the connivance of Austria and England, and then, whether it was that he had confused in his mind the words of Napoleon's emissaries and the revelations which had doubtless been already made to him in Paris of a plot among the patriots and the generals, or whether the emissaries themselves had informed him of the existence of this conspiracy, he added: "The whole matter is settled. We have been in agreement for the last three months. You would know it if you had been in Paris. As the King has not kept his promises, it has been decided to de-throne him. They thought at one time of the Duke of Orleans, but the Bonapartists carried the day. A commissioner was sent to Elba to lay the conditions before the Emperor. The Minister of War is himself in the plot. The King must, by this time, have already left Paris. If not, he will have to be removed, but no harm will be done to him. Everything will go off quite quietly." Lecourbe, who hated the Emperor, and Bourmont, who was a royalist by feeling and tradition, protested. Bourmont, respectfully, but firmly, reminded Ney that, as a Marshal of France and Prince of the Moskowa, he had accepted from the King the mission to fight Bonaparte. Lecourbe was more violent: "How do you expect me to serve that b—? He has done me nothing but harm and the King has done me nothing but good. Besides, I am in the King's service and – well – *monsieur le maréchal, I* have a sense of honour."

Stung by these words, Ney flew into a passion, and, instead of setting forth the real reasons for his decision, that is to say the impossibility of moving the troops and his own scruples about letting loose a civil war, he began passionately to declaim against the Bourbons: "And so have I a sense of honour. That's why I don't intend to go on being humiliated. I am tired of seeing my wife come home crying at the snubs she has received. The King doesn't want us, that's clear. It's only from a soldier like Bonaparte that the army will receive proper consideration," and, taking from the table the service order issued by the Emperor and bearing Ney's name, he handed it to the two Generals with the words, "Here is what I am going to read to the troops." After further discussion, Lecourbe and Bourmont, who shared Ney's conviction as to the impossibility of commanding the obedience of the troops, reluctantly made up their mind to throw in their lot with him. On Ney's instructions, Bourmont ordered the troops to parade at 1 o'clock, and shortly before that hour, he and Lecourbe went to meet the Marshal at the Hôtel de la Pomme d'Or, and conducted him to the ground. Both knew the purpose of the parade and by appearing at the side of the Prince of the Moskowa, they sanctioned his desertion to the Emperor and shared his responsibility.

The troops formed a hollow square. The Marshal and Generals Bourmont and Lecourbe, surrounded by their staffs, took up their positions in the centre on foot. The drums beat. "At that moment," says an eye-witness, "I looked at the soldiers. All looked gloomy and pale. I feared the return of one of those days of the Revolution, when the officers fell victims to their men." Ney drew his sword and in his clear and resonant voice he read: "Officers, non-commissioned officers and men, the cause of the Bourbons is for ever lost..." He was interrupted by a great shout of, "*Vive l'Empereur!*" arising from every side of the square. It was a cry of joy and a cry of relief. The Marshal continued: "The legitimate dynasty which the French nation has chosen, will ascend the throne once more. Only the Emperor Napoleon is entitled to rule over our beautiful country... Soldiers, I have often led you to victory, now I am leading you to join the immortal phalanx that follows the Emperor to Paris..." His voice was drowned in cheers. The men were falling on each other's necks. Ney, carried away by the general enthusiasm, embraced his officers who crowded round him, and then mingling with his men, he gave the *accolade* to the soldiers. "He went through the ranks like one possessed, embracing even the drummers and fifers."

Only a few superior officers remained aloof in indignant consternation. Colonel Dubalen, commanding the 60th Regiment of the line, approached Ney in the midst of all this embracing. "*Monsieur le maréchal*," said he, "my oath to the King does not permit me to change my allegiance. I ask you to accept my resignation." "I do not accept it," answered Ney. "But you are free to withdraw. Go quickly and take care that the men do not handle you roughly."

That evening, whilst soldiers and people fraternized, singing and drinking, breaking shop-signs that bore the *fleur de lys*, sacking a café because it was called the Café Bourbon, the Prince of the Moskowa was entertaining at dinner his staff and the generals and higher officers. It was a gay, noisy, animated feast. Only one man there was gloomy and silent – the Marshal himself. His excitement was gone now, and his conscience began to prick him. "From the moment of that unfortunate proclamation," he said later, "I only longed for death. Many a time I have thought of blowing my brains out."

From that time forth, the hero's spirit was troubled within him, and never again was he to know serenity of mind until the day when he faced the firing squad.[45]

In Paris the atmosphere was rising toward panic. Newspapers either made no announcements or printed false news; but it was known that:

...the Government had sent the crown jewels and fourteen millions in scrip to London. The discontented elements – not the leaders, who, feeling themselves watched, dared not move, but the obscure masses, who feared nothing because all the prisons in the state would not have held them – spoke openly of the unheard-of success of the Emperor and of his expected entry into the capital. The bourgeoisie were dumfounded; panic reigned on the Bourse. Government stock which had stood at 78.75 had fallen to 71.25 on the news of Napoleon's landing, and was now fluctuating between 66 and 68 francs. All confidence had gone. On the boulevards and in the Palais Royal white cockades were falling like leaves in autumn. From morning till night, small groups of young men still wandered round the precincts of the Tuileries shouting "*Vive le roi!*" but these cries no longer found an echo. Money was being sent to England, crowds were besieging the passport offices and the booking offices of the stage-coaches. The supervisor of the College Henri

IV was endeavouring to cure the pupils of the habit of crying "*Vive le roi!*" and, with admirable prudence, was having the bust of Napoleon removed from the latrines to a more honourable position.

Even the general officers, so confident and resolute at first, were getting anxious. On March 13th, Oudinot wrote to Clarke: "I don't know what to think of the spirit of the troops. The grenadiers are to march tomorrow. I hope they will behave." Next day his doubts were changed to certainty. He hastened to telegraph: "Not only will the troops refuse to fight; but they will go over to the enemy on the first opportunity." On the 15th General Ornano said to the Countess Dupont: "As for me, I shall keep my oath to the King, but there is not a soldier who would not throw down his musket in the presence of Napoleon."

From all sides the same reports were coming in to the War Office, for everywhere the openly expressed feeling of the Army was the same. On entering Le Mans all ranks of the 61st, including the colonel, were wearing bouquets of violets. The 11th Light Infantry were declaring gaily that they were being sent to Paris on behalf of the King, but that they were going there on behalf of the Emperor. The colonel of the 41st told the préfet of Limoges frankly that he had the eagle of the regiment in his portmanteau. In the cantonments of Villejuif the men declared their determination, "to do no harm to the King, but never to fire on the *petit caporal*" On the barracks in Paris the men were heard shouting, "*Vive le Père la Violette*" At the gates of La Flêche the comte de Luce had a conversation with a foot-soldier. "So you're going to Paris?" "Yes, but the little general will be there first." "You've been deceived. He's very likely dead by now." "You know no more about it than our colonel. He said the same thing. Do you suppose that any French soldier would ever fight against the Emperor for your Louis XVIII?"[46]

It seemed, indeed, that no French soldier would.

After Ney's desertion a paper was found on the railings of the Vendôme Column: "From Napoleon to Louis XVIII: My good brother, there is no need to send me any more troops. I have enough."

And so the monarchy crumbled like a house of cards. The King, with few defenders either in the army or amongst the people, fled from the Tuileries at midnight on March 19th. The following evening Napoleon once more entered Paris.

His astonishing tour de force, *which had begun less than three weeks before at Cannes, had ended in triumph. Royalist writers have tried to represent the restoration of the Empire as the outcome of a purely military movement. But it was not:*

It was hatred of the *ancien régime* that stirred the peasants, it was love of their Emperor that moved the soldiers. The twin feelings united them in a common action – their impulse was one – their confidence was mutual and together they marched as comrades to meet him. Hence the ease and rapidity of his success, hence the overwhelming triumph of his march from the golfe Jouan to Paris.

Looked at in this way, Napoleon's epic enterprise, which has been called "one of the most astonishing exploits known to history or mythology," loses something of its magic. The spell of the grey coat did not work everything. Given the state of public opinion, given the mentality of the Army, one might almost say that this enterprise, rash and presumptuous as it appeared, could not fail. Once in France, the Emperor had nothing to fear but a few brigades of gendarmerie, the fanatical bands of Provence, and the troops of the Royal Household. His eleven hundred grenadiers were ample protection against the gendarmes, and by taking the Alpine route he could and did avoid the Provençaux. As for the household troops, twelve stages of more than ten leagues each lay between them and Lyons. The battalion from Elba would have grown into a little army before they could make contact with it.

It has been said a hundred times that a single shot fired from the ranks would have arrested Napoleon's march. That may be so, but it is by no means certain. Assuredly the Old Guard would never have answered a single shot, so that the battle which his enemies were anxious to engage would have been avoided. In any case the difficulty was to get anyone to fire this fateful shot. Captain Randon in the Laffray pass certainly gave orders to fire, but he did not seize a soldier's musket and put his own fingers to the trigger. Again at Grenoble there were many royalist officers standing beside the shrapnel-loaded guns, but not one of them dared fire a piece. They knew that such an action meant being "hacked to pieces by their gunners." At Lyons, Macdonald sought in vain among the national guards, among the royalist volunteers, even with promises of gold among the rabble, a single man prepared to fire that first shot, and although he had even resolved to do so himself, he shrank from that extreme step, as others had done before him, when, surrounded by his mutinous troops, he found himself face to face with the vanguard of the Emperor, and heard behind him the great cry of a city in revolt: "*Vive l'Empereur!*"[47]

Paris, however, on the eve of the Emperor's reentry was far from being a city in revolt. The early excitement had subsided and the Comte de Lavallette, a Bonapartist, remembered that:

Paris was quiet. Those who lived at a distance from the Tuileries kept their distance. Each kept to his own house. The King's going, the Emperor's coming were an enormous event, and one so strange that the fourteen centuries of the monarchy had offered nothing so extraordinary. And yet indifference seemed to rule every mind.

Was the event above the compass of vulgar souls? Or was it the common sense of the people, which declared it was not well for them that these two monarchs should come to grips, and that they could expect nothing from it but pain and sacrifice?[48]

The Duc de Broglie confirmed this impression:

The day that followed the going of the man they were letting go, and saw the coming of the man they were letting come, turned out even drearier than the day before. Paris was lugubrious, public squares deserted, cafés and places of assembly half closed. The passers-by avoided each other. In the streets one met hardly anyone but belated soldiery, officers on the spree and men in their cups, shouting, singing the Marseillaise, the rowdy's everlasting refrain, and offering all comers, in jeering tones and almost at the point of the sword, tricolour cockades.[49]

In the Tuileries excitement mounted as the hour of Napoleon's arrival drew nearer.

Five or six officers on half-pay were strolling in the vast courtyard, embracing each other, rejoicing that Napoleon was coming back.

In the apartments the Emperor's two sisters-in-law, the Queen of Spain and the Queen of Holland, were awaiting him with deep emotion. They were soon joined by their ladies and those of the Empress. Everywhere fleurs-de-lis had expelled the bees. However, on inspecting the immense carpet covering the throne-room in which they were, one of them observed that one of the lilies seemed to be loose. She tore it off, and presently the bee could be seen. The ladies all set to work, and in less than half an hour, to peals of laughter from the whole bevy, the carpet again became imperial...[50]

At nine o'clock the cabriolet in which Napoleon had driven through the city stopped before the entrance by the gateway on the Quai du Louvre. Lavallette described the scene:

Scarcely had he alighted when a shout of "Long live the Emperor!", but a roof-splitting, a tremendous shout, made itself heard.

It was that of the half-pay officers, packed, jammed together in the entrance-hall and crowding the staircase to the top.

The Emperor was in his famous grey overcoat. I advanced towards him, and the Duke of Vicenza called out to me:

"For heaven's sake, get in front of him, so that he can move!"

He began to climb the staircase.

I went before him, backwards, one step ahead, gazing on him with deep excitement, my eyes suffused with tears, and repeating in my delirium:

"What! It's you! It's you! It's you at last!"

As for him, he went slowly up, his eyes closed, his hands stretched out in front of him, like a blind man, expressing his happiness only by a smile.[51]

4

The Hundred Days

The France to which Napoleon had returned was a very different place from the country he had left; and he soon learned that Colonel La Bedoyère, one of his former aides-de-camp, was right when he told him, "You can no longer reign in France except on liberal principles."

To reassure the Jacobins and to combat the royalists Napoleon recalled Fouché as Minister of Police; Carnot, who had refused to take part in the aggressive wars of the Empire, was appointed Minister of the Interior; Marshal Davout, who had also never been fully identified with the autocratic Empire, became Minister of War; and Benjamin Constant, leader of the liberal opposition in the Tribunate in 1802, was asked to draft an "Additional Act to the Constitution of the Empire," which was intended, in Napoleon's words, to inaugurate a constitutional monarchy.

The Emperor's whole system, so he protested to the outspoken General Rapp, was changed.

My system is changed. No more war, no more conquests. I mean to reign in peace and make my subjects happy.

Rapp: So you say. But already your anterooms are filled with the time-servers who always humoured your bent for arms.

Napoleon: Fiddlesticks! Experience... Did you often go to the Tuileries?

Rapp: Now and then, sire.

Napoleon: How did those people treat you?

Rapp: I have nothing to complain of.

Napoleon: It seems you were well received by the King on your return from Russia?

Rapp: Extremely well, sire.

Napoleon: I dare say. Wheedled to start with, then shown the door. That's what was coming to all of you. For, after all, you were not their men. It was impossible you should suit them. It takes other claims, other rights to please them.

Rapp: The King has relieved France of the allies.

Napoleon: All right, but at what a cost! And his promises – have they been kept? It was that, it was the insolence of the nobles and the priests that made me leave Elba. I might have returned with three million peasants who were flocking to complain and offer their services. But I was sure I should meet with no resistance before Paris. It's very lucky for the Bourbons that I came back. But for me they'd have wound up with an appalling revolution.

Have you seen Chateaubriand's pamphlet, which doesn't even allow me courage on the battlefield? I think you've seen me in action sometimes? Am I a coward?

Rapp: I shared the indignation felt by all honest men, at a charge as unjust as it is ignoble.

Napoleon: Have you seen anything of the Duc d'Orléans?

Rapp: I only met him once.

Napoleon: That's the one with a sense of conduct and tact! The others have bad friends, bad advisers. They don't like me. They're going to be more furious than ever. And well they may be. I got here without striking a blow. Now they'll be denouncing my ambition with a vengeance. That's the everlasting reproach. It's all they can find to say.

Rapp: They're not the only ones to accuse you of ambition.

Napoleon: What – me ambitious! Would a man with ambition be as fat as this?

(He was slapping his belly with both hands.)

Rapp: Your Majesty is joking.[52]

Napoleon lost few opportunities of protesting this change of heart:

Napoleon on several occasions announced that, whereas in the previous fifteen years he had, admittedly, begun to found "the Grand Empire" in Europe, he was now resolved to concentrate exclusively on "the happiness and consolidation of France alone." Nothing reveals the new thinking into which the Emperor had been persuaded by his entourage more clearly than this seemingly self-evident pledge. It meant nothing less than Napoleon's adhesion to the principle of nationality, which the Grand Empire had violated with brutal persistence. Although it is well-known that, during the Empire, relations between the Emperor and his brothers, whom he had made Kings of Spain, Holland and Westphalia, were tense and full of conflicts, it is less often understood that these relations deteriorated because these sovereigns stood up as boldly as they dared for the interests and national concerns of the various peoples whom they ruled. The Emperor wanted satellites; but they, stauncher sons of the Revolution, insisted on "the happiness and consolidation" of their new dominions...

Although the author of the *Additional Act to the Constitution of the Empire* was Benjamin Constant, and although without any doubt Mme de Staël's former protégé and friend had been able to embody a number of his – and her – most cherished liberal ideas into this document, the part played by Joseph Bonaparte as the great persuader and protagonist of true Bonapartism was infinitely more decisive and effectual than the contributions, important though they were, from that brilliant but wayward intellectual, the Benjamin among Bonapartists. For had not Joseph even persuaded Mme de Staël, then at her château of Coppet on Lake Geneva, that Napoleon had returned from Elba a chastened and changed man? Joseph very nearly succeeded in turning the Emperor himself into a Bonapartist…

[But many Frenchmen], perhaps even the majority, could not bring themselves to believe that the liberal Empire, a constitutional Monarchy under the Bonaparte dynasty, would be permitted by Monarchical Europe to establish itself in France. The commercial and professional classes especially feared that Napoleon's return must mean war… They welcomed the liberal reforms that the Government promulgated in a series of emphatic announcements; when, after the elections in May, the two Chambers assembled on June 3rd, they saw with satisfaction that both Houses were swarming with their political friends. Now that the reactionary Royalists had been silenced and the outmoded alliance of throne and altar no longer impeded progress, it seemed entirely possible that the constitutional Charter of 1814, which the *Acte additionnel*, drawn up in April 1815, so closely resembled, would at last come into its own. Many intelligent people would have agreed with Michael Bruce, another English sympathiser with the new turn of events, that Napoleon had forged "too many chains for himself" to make a return to his former unfettered despotism feasible. Even so, however, few believed that Napoleon would remain chained, Prometheus-like, to the constitutional rock for long. They knew that the Congress of Vienna had placed him "beyond the pale of civil and social relations", that they had "delivered him to public vengeance". The tricolour cockades, like the Bourbon lilies on the carpets of the Tuileries, were therefore highly movable emblems, but the work of giving Continental Europe a lead in representative government nevertheless went ahead.[53]

In May elections were held for a new Chamber of Representatives and Napoleon professed impeccable democratic sentiments in public: "Emperor, Consul and soldier, I owe all I hold to the people." But at the same time

intense preparations to bring the army up to full strength went ahead under Davout's highly efficient direction. Wellington and Blücher were known to confer together in Belgium – the country Napoleon had always maintained had become French since its conquests by the armies of the Revolution. So, from May onwards, we find him more often pouring over maps and scrutinising lists, statistics and reports submitted by the Ministry of War than discussing constitutional niceties with Benjamin Constant and Carnot. "I need a *coup d'éclat*," he told the latter, possibly with the events of Brumaire 1799 in mind. He had also, at a meeting of the now responsible Council of State, protested that the new constitutionalism weakened him and put him in chains. "France seeks me," he had suddenly exclaimed, "and cannot find me." And then, all this talk of goodness, abstract justice and natural law! "It is not in my nature," he added very reasonably, "to be an angel.

The first law is necessity." And he ended on this menacing note: "I repeat, *Messieurs* – the old arm of the Emperor must be found again and must be seen." And what had always been the function of that arm? "France," he told them, "needs my arm to subdue Europe." Now that the Allies had supplied the necessity, the Emperor seemed to be flexing his muscles. Fouché remained unimpressed. "Let him win a battle or two," he remarked not long after this outburst. "He will lose the third, and then our part begins." As he explained, "us" meant "we, the advanced men of the Revolution."

From then onwards, Napoleon's second reign moved along on the parallel tracks of preparing for war and inaugurating the parliamentary regime. It all seemed a little contradictory.[54]

Nothing seemed more contradictory than the elaborate ceremony of the Champ de Mai *held on June 1 when the* Acte additionnel *was formally promulgated. General Thiébault, in fact, was conscious of an air even of absurdity:*

For how deliver an almost revolutionary speech in the costume in which Napoleon had resolved to appear? The contrast would have been as strange as, in their incongruity with the circumstances, his speech, his articles and that same costume were shocking.

Never has an orator shown more adroitness in substituting thrilling phrases for positive concessions, and referring everything to a future in which he still expected to be once more lord of all. Never was an actor at more pains to depict imperial majesty in all its splendour, but never did Napoleon choose a worse time to exchange his war costume, his grey overcoat, his old sword, his little hat and his boots, for white silk stockings, embroidered shoes with rosettes, a stage sword, a coat, a sash, a cloak dazzling with embroidery, and the crown of a Roman emperor.[55]

The Duc de Broglie confessed that the ceremony left him both indignant and contemptuous:

I saw the imperial squad go by, in full gala dress – waving plumes, cocked hats, short Spanish cloaks, white satin panteloons, shoes with rosettes and so on. This masquerade, in the shadow of such a crisis, with France on the brink of being invaded and carved up, owing to and for love of these fine gentlemen – this masquerade, I say, filled me with as much indignation as contempt.

I saw the Guard and several line regiments go by, with martial air, proud step and anxious brows, like men ready for a game at double or quits. As they marched past the Emperor, their eyes were glittering with an ardent and sombre fire. One seemed to see *Morituri te salutant* hovering on their lips, and the frantic cheers which were being drawn from them by order marred the effect without dispelling it.

In the Emperor's speech there was loftiness, to be sure, brilliance, majesty. But even so, it smacked far too much of the theatrical hero, the upstart of glory. Why should he have perched himself up on stilts to take a high tone, and opened a big mouth to recall big things? And was this the moment in any case – when France, reduced by one invasion to her old boundaries, was struggling under the threat of a second, from which it seemed only a miracle could save her? [56]

A few days after the ceremony of the Champ de Mai

...the session of the Chambers opened. Napoleon was at last reconciled with his brother Lucien; he, like Madame Mère, Joseph and Jérôme, was now back in France, and it was he whom Napoleon proposed should be elected president of the representatives. The man who had been president of the Five Hundred on the 18 Brumaire could have been especially valuable to Napoleon in this vital post. But there were objections and the chamber put forward the former Senator Lanjuinais, a lifelong opponent of Napoleon, one of the first in 1814 to propose his abdication.

The Emperor, incensed, refused at first to approve this election.

"They have deliberately slighted me by choosing an enemy!" he said. "In return for all the concessions I have made, they wish only to insult and weaken me. Very well, in that case, I intend to resist; I shall dissolve this Assembly!"

Fouché evidently considered it his duty to give the widest possible publicity to these remarks. The Chamber was indignant. On the advice of Carnot and Regnault de Saint-Jean d'Angély Napoleon agreed to modify his attitude. He received Lanjuinais at the Elysée Palace (where he had been residing since mid-April, in order to avoid undue ostentation) and had a frank discussion with him.

"The past is nothing. I only take into consideration a man's character and present attitudes. Are you my friend or my enemy?"

Lanjuinais was moved and offered to support the Emperor, if he acted as a constitutional monarch.

"We are agreed," said Napoleon, "I ask nothing more of you."

And he confirmed Lanjuinais' presidency.

The Chamber of Peers, appointed by the Emperor, resembled the former Senate. Princes, marshals, generals, ministers and prelates sat in it, together with members of the old aristocracy. But Napoleon could no more rely on this assembly than he could on the Representatives. The first debates which took place left him no illusions.

He called the two Chambers to an Imperial session on June 7. His speech was serious and forceful.

"Our enemies are banking on our internal feuds... The army and I will do our duty. You, Peers and the Senate of that great people of ancient times, you must be resolved to die rather than survive the dishonour and degradation of France."

Though he was applauded, he knew full well that these men would only remain loyal to him if he were the victor. In his imagination he already saw the muddy plains of Flanders where the enemy was massed against him. It was there that the final, decisive game would be played.

"If I am victorious," he said to his closest friends, "we will force everyone to attend to their own affairs and we shall have time to get used to this new régime. If I am beaten, God knows that will happen to you and to me. In twenty or thirty days everything will be decided."[57]

It seemed to some of those who watched Napoleon in these days that he no longer had the drive and energy to force this decision in his favor. General Thiébault recalled:

...the longer I looked, the less I could find him as he had been in his strength and greatness.

Never has the impression I felt at the sight of him, at the moment when fate was about to decide between the world and him – never has that impression left my mind.

His glance, so formidable of old in its searching quality, had lost its power and even its steadiness. His face, which I had so often seen as though beaming with grace or moulded in bronze, had lost all expression and all appearance of strength. His contracted mouth retained none of its old magic. Even his head had no longer the carriage that marked the overlord of the world, and his gait was as awkward as his bearing and gestures were uncertain.

Everything about him seemed distorted, blighted. The usual pallor of his skin had given place to a very decided greenish hue, which startled me.[58]

Despite his appearance, however, he turned his attention to the organization of the country for war with his accustomed energy and drive. As well as men and horses, hundreds of tons of materials had to be found quickly – uniforms, weapons, ammunition, wagons, harness. And they were found in an astonishingly short time. But one harassing problem remained: a lack of reliable generals.

Many generals had uncompromisingly identified themselves with the royalists or had withdrawn into retirement, pleading illness or fatigue. Napoleon had hoped that Berthier, his former chief of staff, would join him. But Berthier, tired and disillusioned, went away to Bamberg, and there threw himself from a window. The news of his death for a time unnerved Napoleon, one of whose companions had never seen him so melancholy:

He did not stir from a little room leading to the one in which we were received, and he spent, alone with Count Boulay de la Meurthe, a full hour, throughout which his face was drawn, his attitude sombre, his speech more laconic than usual. His haughty head drooped in spite of him, there was something fateful in his glance, and his gestures were all the more eloquent of grief because his slightest movements had something convulsive about them.[59]

Soult, who had had no experience of such an important post, and although he had been Louis XVIII's Minister of War, was appointed chief of staff in Berthier's place. It was an unfortunate choice. But there seemed so few alternatives. Napoleon felt that Davout could not be spared from his duties as Minister of War in Paris; Murat, who had rashly moved north with an untrustworthy Neapolitan army in April, had been routed at Tolentino and was now in disgrace; Junot's mind had given way as a result of the Russian campaign; Suchet, it was felt, should not leave his command in the Alps. There was Ney and there was Grouchy; but although both of these men were brave officers neither was to be fully trusted in independent command.

Yet, with or without trustworthy generals, the war would have to be fought. The allied sovereigns had still been in Vienna when it was learned that Napoleon had returned from Elba, and it had only taken a fortnight to draw up the terms of a military alliance against the man who was condemned as an outlaw. A plan had been formed for six armies to cross the French frontier simultaneously – an Anglo-Dutch-Belgian army of 93,000 under Wellington, a Prussian army of 117,000 under Blücher, a 200,000-strong army of Austrians and Bavarians, 150,000 Russians, and two Austrian-Piedmontese armies, which would cross the Alps and march on Lyons and Provence; more than half a million men in all.

This threat had to be met, and would be met in Belgium. A campaign there offered the best chance of rallying the people of France behind him.

For centuries, seeing that it brought with it the great estuary of the Rhine, Belgium had possessed a symbolic, almost mysterious, value in the eyes of the French people. Over and over again the soil of this little country had been watered with French blood, nor had the ambition to acquire it ever failed to haunt the imagination of French statesmen. As the conquest of Belgium had been the first and principal glory of the young French Republic and its loss the most damaging commentary on the Empire, so its recovery now would be a prize than which none would be more welcome to the heart of France.[60]

There were economic reasons, too. Even Louis XVIII, who had stood for peace, had stressed that union between what became Belgium after 1830 and France was an important French interest.

Cheaper coal and more manufactured goods were now seen as war aims no less urgent than political and national self-determination.

In the second week in June Napoleon signed the decree by which, during his absence on the forthcoming campaign,

the ministers and his brothers would form the Government under Joseph's presidency.

He smiled bitterly as he remarked:

"Yes indeed, it is very important to you that I should win this battle."

During the night of the 12th, after dining with his family in the Elysée, he whispered in the ear of Mme. Bertrand, half-joking:

"Let us hope that we shall not soon wish ourselves back on Elba!"[61]

5

Wellington and the British Army

Arthur Wellesley, third of the four surviving sons of the first Earl of Mornington, was born in Ireland on April 29, 1769. Like Napoleon, born in the same year, he did not consider that his childhood had been a happy one.

Childhood and early youth were stages in the duke's existence of which he seldom spoke; and never except abruptly, and as it were by accident. But enough escaped him from time to time to show that he did not look back upon them with much pleasure. There is reason to believe that, from some cause or another, he was not a favourite with his mother till his great deeds in after life constrained her to be proud of him. She seems to have taken it into her head that he was the dunce of the family, and to have treated him, if not harshly, with marked neglect; and being herself a woman of great ability and strength of character, she gave the law in this as in other respects to her own household. While the utmost pains were taken with the education of his brothers, Arthur was sent, being very young, to a preparatory school in Chelsea, where he learned little, and to which the only references he was ever known to make were the reverse of flattering...

From the Chelsea school, young Wellesley was transferred to Eton, where he remained only long enough to make his way into the remove. He was indifferently instructed when he arrived, and he never by such diligence as the case required succeeded in taking a good place among his class-fellows. His habits, on the contrary, in school and out of school, are stated to have been those of a dreamy, idle, and shy lad. The consequence was, that besides achieving no success as a scholar, he contracted few special intimacies among his contemporaries, and laid the foundation of no lasting friendships. His was indeed a solitary life; a life of solitude in a crowd; for he walked generally alone, often bathed alone, and seldom took part either in the cricket matches or the boat-races which were then, as they are now, in great vogue among Etonians.[62]

Wellesley entered the army in 1787 as an ensign in the 41st Regiment of Foot. And thereafter, helped by political influence as well as by his talent, his promotion was rapid. He was in command of a battalion at the age of twenty-three, and before he was thirty he was in command of an army in India where his brother was viceroy.

Fortunately for Great Britain, it does not always follow that, because a man has been pushed rapidly to the front by political influence, he is therefore incompetent or unworthy of the place given him. Every one who came into personal contact with Arthur Wellesley soon recognized that Castlereagh and the other ministers had not erred when they sent the "Sepoy General" to Portugal in 1808, and when they, despite of all the clamour following the Convention of Cintra, despatched him a second time to Lisbon in 1809, this time with full control of the Peninsular Army. From the first opening of his Vimiero campaign the troops that he led had the firmest confidence in him – they saw the skill with which he handled them, and criticism very soon died away. It was left for Whig politicians at home, carpers with not the slightest knowledge of war, to go on asserting for a couple of years more that he was an overrated officer, that he was rash and reckless, and that his leadership would end, on some not very distant day, with the expulsion of the British Army from the Peninsula. At the front there were very few such doubters – though contemporary letters have proved to me that one or two were to be found.

To say that Wellington from the first was trusted alike by his officers and his men, is by no means to say that he was loved by them. He did everything that could win confidence, but little that could attract affection. They recognized that he was marvellously capable, but that he was without the supreme gift of sympathy for others. "The sight of his long nose among us," wrote one of his veterans, "was worth ten thousand men any day of the week. I will venture to say that there was not a heart in the army which did not beat more lightly when we heard the joyful news of his arrival." But this does not mean that he was regarded with an enthusiasm of the emotional and affectionate sort. Another Light Division officer sums up the position in the coldest words that I have ever seen applied to the relations of a great general with his victorious army. "I know that it has been said that Wellington was unpopular with the army. Now I can assert with respect to the Light Division that the troops *rather liked him than otherwise*... Although Wellington was not what may be called popular, still the troops possessed great confidence in him, nor did I ever hear a single individual express an opinion to the contrary."[63]

Yet, as Sir Arthur Bryant has commented, though he was no John Moore and planted few seeds of love in men's hearts, still he was adept in the difficult art of shaping human materials for the purposes for which he needed them. Not expecting much of men, he seldom tried them too high and, knowing where they were likely to fail, was always ready with the necessary corrective at the right place and moment. No one was ever a greater master of cold, scathing rebuke that, without exaggeration or provocative heat, left the victim without answer or escape. "It is not very agreeable to anybody," he told a refractory Portuguese magnate, "to have strangers quartered in his house, nor is it very agreeable to us strangers who have good houses in our own country to be obliged to seek for quarters here. We are not here for our pleasure."

During the quiet winter months of recuperation that followed the collapse of his hopes after Talavera, the British Commander-in-Chief – using the respite offered by Napoleon and Joseph – was transforming his still half amateur army into a professional fighting force. Under his easy, high-bred manner he reshaped it with a hand of steel. In this he was helped by the fact that he was a man of the world and of the highest fashion. Though of frugal and even Spartan tastes, he was accustomed to the best society, kept a mistress – in her due place – and understood the lure of pleasure. He was well able to deal both with senior officers who claimed a gentleman's right to go home for the winter to hunt and manage their estates, and with subalterns who neglected their regimental duties for the charms of the Lisbon opera house. "My lord," one of his brigadiers began, "I have of late been suffering much from rheumatism…" "And you wish to go to England to get cured of it," snapped the Commander-in-Chief, turning his back: "By all means. Go there immediately."

The rule of such a chief was as unpalatable to gentlemen who thought themselves above discipline as to marauders who deserted for drink or left the line to plunder. Just as the malingerers and column-dodgers of the base hospital at Belem – the notorious *Belem Rangers*, "noted," according to Rifleman Costello, "for every species of skunk" – were driven back to their regiments that winter by an icy wind, so gay sparks who tried to find in Lisbon a second Drury Lane were recalled in chilling terms to their duties. "The officers of the army," they were reminded, "can have nothing to do behind the scenes… Indeed, officers who are absent from their duty on account of sickness might as well not go to the playhouse, or at all events upon the stage and behind the scenes."

Nor would this unsympathetic Commander permit his officers the liberty of politics. He stigmatised the croaking which prevailed in the army as a disgrace to the nation. "As soon as an accident happens," he complained to one of his divisional generals, "every man who can write, and who has a friend who can read, sits down to write his account of what he does not know and his comments on what he does not understand." Such letters, diligently circulated by the idle and malicious, not only found their way into English newspapers, encouraging the anti-war Opposition and conveying valuable information to the French, but aroused partisan feelings in the field. These Wellesley would have none of; his wish, he stated, was to be the head of an army not a party, and to employ indiscriminately those who could best serve the public, be they who they might.

Yet his discipline was never negative. He made it his business to teach his officers the same meticulous care and attention to duty in which he had schooled himself. Success, he told them, could only be attained by attention to minute detail and by tracing every part of an operation from its origin to its conclusion, point by point. An indefatigable worker, he expected every one about him to be so too. He made it a rule, he said, always to do the work of the day in the day. Regular habits, a superb constitution and a well-regulated mind had been the foundations of all his triumphs. "When I throw off my clothes," he once remarked, "I throw off my cares, and, when I turn in my bed, it is time to turn out." He taught his army to do the same.

At the root of this punctilious, fastidious, clear-sighted man's nature was a deep and abiding sense of duty. It was not an inspired and burning passion like Moore's or Nelson's; Arthur Wellesley made no pretence of being at home in such altitudes. But, though his feet were firmly planted on his mother earth – one on the battlefield and the other in Bond Street – he was inherently a man of his salt. He spoke the truth, honoured his bond and kept faith. He regarded a lie as an act of cowardice and a breach of promise as a vulgar betrayal. He had learnt to eradicate these easy frailties from his own character, just as he had taught himself to be frugal and reticent, in his youth when he had had to master his Irish ebullience and artist's sensitivity in order to survive in a *milieu* of trustful elder brothers and inadequate family resources. Adherence to bond and duty was not so much a natural bent of his rather mysterious nature – in which ran suppressed rivers of deep emotion – as a close-fitting mask which he had early donned in self-protection and to which in due course his own features had come to conform. Yet it was one which, like his talent for economy, perfectly served his country's need. He spared himself no care or labour which could further her ends and made every man and every penny go as far as man or penny could go…

He was so industrious, clear-headed, sensible and efficient. For everything he did he had a reason and, when he chose to explain it in his clear, lucid way, it always proved unanswerable. As he himself wrote of Marlborough, he was remarkable for his cool, steady understanding. If any of his senior officers quarrelled – as in those days of hot tempers, hard drinking and prickly honour they were very apt to do – he was always ready with his moderation, balance and good sense to compose the difference. "A part of my business and perhaps not the most easy part," he told the fiery Craufurd, who had conceived a grievance against a brother officer, "is to prevent discussions and disputes between the officers who may happen to serve under my command… I hope that this letter may reach you in time to induce you to refrain from sending me the paper which you inform me you have written."

For here was a Commander-in-Chief who did not stand upon ceremony or take personal offence. It was hard to quarrel with him: he saw your point of view while clarifying and enforcing his own. "You and I necessarily take a different view of these questions," he told Craufurd, "I must view them in all their relations; your view of them is naturally confined to their relation with your own immediate command." Much of his time was spent in trying to adapt impossible War Office and Treasury regulations to the exigencies of a Continental campaign for which they had never been designed. Yet he refused to inveigh against them needlessly or to allow his subordinates to do so; all that could be done, he told the latter, was that they should assist each other as much and clash as little as possible. Adhering steadfastly to his chosen path, he was always ready to compromise on inessentials: to go down metaphorically on his knees, as he had done before Cuesta at Talavera. "Half the business of the world," he wrote, "particularly that of our country, is done by accommodation and by the parties understanding each other."

This genius for being reasonable, coupled with his clarity and common sense, enabled Wellington – unlike most men habituated to discipline and command – to deal with politicians. Being free from Moore's troublesome sense of moral indignation, he never made them uncomfortable with tedious reiterations of principle. So long as they ultimately came along with him, he always allowed them a way to wriggle round their difficulties. And though he left them in no doubt as to what he wanted and meant to do – there is nothing in life, he once remarked, like a clear definition – he never expected or asked them to do the impossible. "In my situation," he told a colleague, "I am bound to consider not only what is expedient but what is practicable." He remembered that Ministers had to do so too. He realised that they were harried and abused in Parliament and the country, that there was a shortage of money and troops. He made no more claims on them than were absolutely essential, told them the exact truth and explained, in language which the busiest fool could understand, the common-sense reasons for his requests. He only pressed them when he had to: "Would it be fair or indeed honest in me," he wrote to the British Ambassador at Lisbon, "to ask of a man more than I thought absolutely necessary."[64]

"Wellington's nerves," as Philip Guedalla says, "were always steady."

That was his secret; Lowry Cole had pierced it, when he termed his commander "a fine fellow with the best nerves of any one I ever met with." For the sharp gaze never wavered, and the upper lip drew tightly down over the slightly prominent teeth without a quiver. His nerves were admirable; exercise, long days in the saddle, and plain fare helped to keep them so. Did not Alava learn to dread his standing answer to the question at what o'clock the Staff would move and what there was to be for dinner? "At daylight," he invariably replied; and to the second interrogation, "Cold meat." "*J'en ai pris en horreur*," the anguished Spaniard moaned, "*les deux mots* daylight *et* cold meat." But Wellington throve on them. His night's rest varied between three hours and six; and for his first four years in the Peninsula, although he was Commander-in-Chief, he had reverted to the practice of his Indian campaigns and slept in his clothes. His days were regular; rising at six, he wrote steadily until breakfast at nine o'clock. Those quiet mornings served to dispose of his enormous correspondence with incredible punctuality; for "my rule always was to do the business of the day in the day." Then he breakfasted and transacted military business with the Staff. This lasted all the morning, except on hunting days when a gleeful Quartermaster-General records that he "could get almost anything done, for Lord Wellington stands whip in hand ready to start, and soon despatches all business." Those were the days that startled Portuguese on lonely hillsides beheld an unprecedented cavalcade, heard view-halloos and the sharp note of hounds, and marvelled at the strange proceedings of their incomprehensible allies. "Here," as Captain O'Malley loved to recall, "the shell-jacket of a heavy dragoon was seen storming the fence of a vineyard.

There the dark green of a rifleman was going the pace over the plain. The unsportsmanlike figure of a staff officer might be observed emerging from a drain, while some neck-or-nothing Irishman, with light infantry wings, was flying at every fence before him" – and the Peer himself followed his hounds in the sky-blue and black of the Salisbury hunt. Such was the impressive apparatus with which Lord Wellington toned his nerves in winter-quarters.

His nerves, indeed, were admirable; and a becoming sense of who he was and what he had achieved contributed to steady them – "I am the mainspring of all the other operations, but it is because I am Lord Wellington; for I have neither influence nor support, nor the means of acquiring influence, given to me by the government." Small wonder that his correspondents never ventured upon a more familiar address than "My dear Lord". Even behind his back he was "the Peer" to Generals and "our great lord" to ardent subalterns; although an intoxicated private once alluded (in the presence of a scandalised staff officer) to "that long-nosed b—r that beats the French," and the army had been known to call him "Atty". But such diminutives were rare; for he kept his distance.

Not that he kept it by conventional distinctions of uniform and entourage. Headquarters, as one observer noted, were "strikingly quiet and unostentatious. Had it not been known for a fact no one would have suspected that he was quartered in the town. There was no throng of scented staff officers with plumed hats, orders and stars, no main guard, no crowd of contractors, actors, cooks, valets, mistresses, equipages, horses, dogs, forage and baggage waggons, as there is at French or Russian headquarters! Just a few aides-de-camps, who went about the streets alone and in their overcoats, a few guides, and a small staff guard; that was all!"[65]

His appearance is described by a contemporary, the Reverend G. R. Gleig:

Nature had endowed him with a robust frame and an iron constitution. In height he measured about five feet nine inches – I speak, of course, of what he was in the vigour of his days, for latterly old age had shrunk and bowed his frame, and given him the habit of stooping. His shoulders were broad, his chest well developed, his arms long, and his hands and feet in excellent proportion. His eyes were of a dark violet blue, or grey, and his sight was so penetrating, that even to the last he could distinguish objects at an immense distance. The general expression of his countenance when silent or preoccupied, was grave; but his smile had a charm about it which, when once seen, could never be forgotten. A forehead not very high, but broad and square, eyebrows straight and prominent, a long face, a Roman nose, a broad under-jaw, with a chin strongly marked, gave him a striking resemblance to more than one of the heroes of antiquity, especially to Julius Caesar. His hair, which was originally a clear brown, had become white as silver before he died, but to the last there was no baldness, even at the temples. If you met him in a crowd or upon the street, and were entirely ignorant that he was a great man, you would be impelled by some secret impulse to fix your eye upon him, and to turn round and look after him when he had passed. I saw him for the first time as he crossed the line of march during a military operation in Spain. Only three mounted officers attended him, and he was simply dressed in a grey frock, a cocked hat covered with oil-skin, and grey trousers; but instinctively he was recognised as the commander of the forces, and the impression then made upon the mind of a boy, never in after life passed away.

The military costume of the duke on active service was singularly plain, though becoming, and very peculiar. On state occasions he wore the full dress of his rank, with all his orders and decorations; but in the field his garb was either a blue or a grey frock – blue when fighting was not expected; grey, if a battle were in preparation or in progress. Over this, that he might be more easily recognised from afar, he often threw a short white cloak, which is still in existence, and may be seen in a glass case at Apsley House. His cocked hat was very low, rising but little above the crown of the head, and he rarely surmounted it with a plume. The boots known as "Wellingtons" were of his own invention, and outside the trousers he used often to wear mud-guards of strong leather, which overlapped and were fastened with straps and buckles.[66]

The army, which he had joined at the age of seventeen, was not a good one. As its historian, Sir John Fortescue, has said:

For the British soldier, the ten years that intervened between the end of the American rebellion and the beginning of the war of the French Revolution were among the very worst in his history. In the first place, the army had returned from America defeated and discredited. The war had been enormously costly, and the first and most natural economy was to reduce the military forces to the lowest possible strength. This would have signified less if any pains had been taken to maintain their efficiency, whatever their numerical weakness; but, on the contrary, they were allowed to fall absolutely to pieces. The pay of the private soldier was literally insufficient to keep him from starvation, and the result was that recruits could hardly be obtained, or, if beguiled into accepting the shilling, deserted immediately. In Ireland, particularly, the average number of deserters amounted to one-sixth of the whole establishment. Thus, weak though the regiments would have been even if their ranks had been filled, they were weaker still from want of recruits. In other words, the officers had no men to command. It must be remembered, too, that regiments were rarely kept together in those days. In England there were, except in a few fortresses – such as the Tower – no barracks; and the men were billeted in small bodies, often no more than troops or companies, in the ale-houses of provincial towns. In Ireland there were barracks, but these were mostly small and widely distributed, so as to enable the troops to do the work of police. In either country it might take a colonel a day's journey to visit the whole of his regiment. Thus there was every facility for slackness on the part of the officers, and every difficulty in the way of a commander who disapproved of such slackness.

Moreover, there were plenty of colonels who gave themselves no trouble about their regiments; and, despite of periodic inspections by generals, it was almost impossible to stir such commanding officers into activity. A colonel was the proprietor of his regiment, having paid hard cash for it, and, within certain limits, did very much what was right in his own eyes. Even in the matter of drill no uniformity was enforced until March 1792. A colonel might be an able and enthusiastic soldier who gave his men training that was far in advance of his time, or he might be a hard-drinking old dullard who was quite content if his battalion could blunder through the prescribed movements somehow. At the best, all that was expected of a battalion or a regiment of cavalry was extreme precision of drill with, in the case of the infantry, very exact performance of the manual and firing exercise...

That better material should be obtained under existing conditions was not to be expected. In barracks the men were infamously housed, being huddled together by fours in wooden cribs to sleep, and having only their sleeping-rooms in which to do everything but their drill. They drank hard, as did every class at that time, and they could buy fiery spirits in the barrack-yard; it being judged impossible to prevent them from smuggling liquor into their quarters, and therefore a less evil to permit them to purchase it. There was no encouragement to good behaviour; and one principal punishment, merciless flogging, was inflicted for misconduct. There were, on the other hand, always officers who sought, and with great success, to rule their men with kindness and consideration; but their great difficulty was that they could not afford to rid themselves of bad characters. A soldier was enlisted for life, and, if he were discharged, he must be replaced, which was a matter of expense to the officers, for the country did not grant bounty enough to attract recruits. In 1790, for instance, an alarm of war with Spain led to sudden augmentation of the army. The Treasury offered a bounty of five guineas; but the actual price of recruits rose to fifteen guineas. Hence officers were obliged by sheer penury to keep not only undesirable men, but decrepit old veterans who could hardly stand on their legs and were utterly useless except on parade. It was not that they wilfully defrauded their country, but that the Treasury, by its extreme niggardliness, forced such fraud upon them...

Apart from the prohibitive expense of recruits, the pay of subalterns of cavalry was, owing to the high price of forage, scarcely equal to the maintenance of their servants and their horses; and the result was that vacant cornetcies could not be filled. The pay of an officer gave him only an absurdly trifling sum over and above the interest on the price of his commission; and it was too much to expect that gentlemen should invest money in a dead loss. The Adjutant-General in vain pressed the hard case both of these subalterns and of the private soldier upon the Chancellor of the Exchequer. But William Pitt, who was busy with the task of putting the finances of the country on a sound basis – in itself a transcendent service – turned a deaf ear. In 1792 he did improve the position of the private soldier so far as not only to deliver him from starvation, but actually to allow him the munificent sum of a trifle under one penny one farthing a day; but this he did at the cost of leaving the subalterns unrelieved. The general result of Pitt's parsimony and of civilian control of the army was that discipline among the officers was extremely bad. Colonels could not be hard upon their officers for not keeping the ranks of their companies full, when they literally could not afford to pay the cost of recruits; and a subaltern took little account of his military superiors when, if he were refused leave of absence by them, he could obtain it, through political influence, directly from the Secretary at War.[67]

One of the worst problems in the army was drunkenness. In Spain this had affected the French army as much as the British.

Englishmen drank hard in those days, and the wine-vaults of Spain were a terrible temptation. Harry Smith has drawn for us a ludicrous picture of the Light Division essaying to make a night-march, when every soul, except himself, was drunk; the commanding general in particular being so much exhilarated by wine that no entreaties could prevail with him to cancel his orders. On one day during the retreat from Burgos twelve thousand British soldiers were hopelessly drunk at the same moment; but the French were fortunately unable to take advantage of the opportunity, for the number of their drunkards exceeded even that of the red-coats. And this was no solitary instance of such weakness on the part of the French. There is evidence that a principal cause of Masséna's failure to turn Wellington's right at Fuentes de Onoro was that most of his cavalry were drunk. They galloped in every direction with great intrepidity, but accomplished nothing, and were easily driven back by a handful of fortunately sober British squadrons. It must be added that at the sack of Oporto and elsewhere the French army was guilty of excesses which, if possible, left the British behind in the race of misconduct. But what Wellington deplored was that his soldiers should sink to the level of their enemies. The French had to look after themselves, and there was some excuse for them if they helped themselves; but the British were regularly fed; and any misbehaviour on their part was in his eyes unpardonable. If they were not better than the French in their conduct, they could not beat them in the field; and better they should be, morally superior in every respect, or he would know the reason why.[68]

Discipline was maintained largely by means of the lash.

Floggings were inflicted by the drummers of the regiment, under the superintendence of the drum-major and the adjutant. The culprit was bound by his extended arms to two of three sergeant's halberds, planted in the ground in a triangle, and lashed together at the top. The strokes were inflicted at the tap of a drum beaten in slow time. Each of the wielders of the cat retired after having given twenty-five lashes. The surgeon was always present to certify that the man's life was not in danger by the further continuance of the punishment, and the prisoner was taken down the moment that the medical man declared that he could stand no more. Often this interference saved a culprit from the end of his punishment, as if the tale was fairly complete he might never be called upon to undergo the balance. But in grave cases the prisoner was merely sent into hospital till he was sufficiently convalescent to endure the payment of the remainder of his account. Inhuman commanding officers sometimes refused to allow of any abatement, even when the crime had not been a very serious one, and insisted that the whole sentence should be executed, even if the culprit had to go twice into hospital before it was completed.[69]

But it was not the certainty of punishment alone that improved the discipline of the army:

The "new spirit" which [Wellington] joyfully marked (for it was of his own creation) in his officers was far more potent towards the same end. In the Peninsula, as in India, he raised the standard alike of professional knowledge and of moral conduct; and it was when he invaded France that the military harvest of his sowing was gathered. The French peasants sold their produce to him and refused to sell it to Soult. Draught-cattle were always forthcoming for the English commissaries, while the French went away empty; and Soult's poor soldiers staggered away half-starving over the wretched roads under pouring rain, while the British followed them, knee-deep in mud and drenched to the skin, it is true, but with stomachs full, waggons loaded, and teams complete – food, waggons, and bullocks all honestly sold and peaceably delivered in return for good money by the French inhabitants. Well had Wellington verified his prediction that, when once the seat of war were transferred to French soil, hostilities would speedily end.

His great triumph came when the regiments sailed away either for service in America or for return to England. One division traversed the greater part of France to its port of embarkation not only without a single crime, but without a single complaint of any inhabitant against a single British soldier.[70]

As well as the discipline of the troops, the quality of the officers had greatly improved since the Napoleonic Wars had begun, though promotion was still most haphazard.

Promotion in the British Army at this period was working in the most irregular and spasmodic fashion,- there being two separate influences operating in diametrically opposite ways. The one was the purchase system, the other the frequent, but not by any means sufficiently frequent, promotion for merit and good service in the field. The practice at the Horse Guards was that casualties by deaths in action were filled up inside the regiment, without money passing, but that for all other vacancies the purchase system worked. When a lieutenant-colonelcy, majority, or captaincy was vacant, the senior in the next lower rank had a moral right to be offered the vacancy at the regulation price. But there were many cases in which more than the regulation could be got. The officer retiring handed over the affair to a "commission broker," and bidding was invited. A poor officer at the head of those of his own rank could not afford to pay the often very heavy price, and might see three or four of his juniors buy their way over his head, while he waited vainly for a vacancy by death, by which he would obtain his step without having to pay cash. The system of exchanges, which prevailed on the largest scale, also pressed very hardly on the impecunious; officers from other corps, where there was a block in promotion, managed for themselves a transference into battalions where there seemed to be a likelihood of a more rapid change of rank, by paying large differences for an exchange to those who stood at the head of the list. But there was also a good deal of exchanging for other reasons – officers whose regiments were ordered to unhealthy or unpopular stations, such as the West Indies or New South Wales, offered considerable sums to others who were ready to accept the ineligible destination in return for hard cash. By careful management of this sort, a wealthy officer could procure himself very rapid promotion – e.g., a lieutenant might buy a captaincy in a West India regiment for a comparatively modest sum, and then, as a captain in such a corps, exchange on a second payment with a broken or needy captain in some other regiment on a European station, to whom money was all-important, and so get well established in his new rank, without ever really having quitted home, or served in the corps into and out of which he had rapidly come and gone on paper only. It is said that one young officer, who had the advantages of being wealthy, a peer, and possessed of great family influence in Parliament, was worked up from a lieutenancy to a lieutenant-colonelcy in a single year. This, of course, was a very exceptional case, and happened long ere the Peninsular War began; but it may be remembered that Wellington himself, was, through similar advantages on a smaller scale, enabled to move up from ensign on March 7, 1787, to lieutenant-colonel in September 1793 – five steps in seven years, during which he had been moved through as many regiments – two of horse and five of foot. He was only nineteen months a captain and six months a major, and he had seen no war service whatever when he sailed for Flanders in command of the 33rd at the age of twenty-three! The Duke of York later insisted on a certain minimum of service in each rank before promotion could be obtained.

Contrast with such promotion that of the poor and friendless officer who, after twenty-five years of service, six Peninsular campaigns, and two wounds, found himself still a captain at the age of forty-three!...

Professional training for officers had perforce been nonexistent in the early years of the French war. There was no institution which supplied it, and all military knowledge had to be acquired by rule of thumb at regimental headquarters. An improvement of the greatest importance was made by the establishment in December 1801 of the "Royal Military College" at High Wycombe for the use of young officers, followed by the creation of its "Junior Department" in May 1802, "for the instruction of those who from early life are intended for the military profession." The latter, the origin of the college at Sandhurst, to which the department was removed in 1811, accepted boys as early as thirteen. Its first inspector-general was the French *émigré* Jarry, to whom we owe the "Instructions for Light Infantry in the Field" of

1804, while Colonel John Gaspard Le Marchant was "Lieutenant-governor and Superintendent General." This was the accomplished cavalry officer who fell in 1812, at the head of his brigade, in the crisis of the battle of Salamanca, when he had just delivered a decisive charge. The military college men were already numerous when the Peninsular War began.

The French General, Foy, a witness whose authority can hardly be called in question, for he is making grudging admissions, says that he considered the general mass of the British officers excellent.[71]

Whether or not they were superior to the French officers, Wellington was certain that he could count on two points of superiority in the army as a whole. The first of these was

the superiority of the English formation for infantry in the two-deep line to the heavier order of the enemy's battalions. For this formation Wellington was, of course, not responsible himself: he took it over as an accepted thing, and thought that he knew how to turn it to the best account...

Sir David Dundas's drill-book of 1788[72] with its Prussian three ranks, which had been the official guide of the British infantry of late, was not formally cancelled at first, but it was practically disregarded, and the army went back to the two-rank array, which it had habitually used in the American War, and had abandoned with regret. Apparently the Duke of York[73] did not altogether approve this change; he at least once issued a General Order, to remind colonels that the formation in three ranks was still officially recognized and ought not to be forgotten. But the permission given by an order in 1801, that inspecting officers might allow regiments to appear "even at reviews" in the two ranks, probably marked the practical end of the Prussian system. It had certainly been disused by many officers long before that campaign date, and it is certain that in Abercrombie's Egyptian campaign the double instead of the triple rank was in general use. British military opinion had decided that fire was everything, and that the correct answer to the French columnar attack was to put more men into the firing line.

A conclusive proof of the efficacy of the double when opposed to the triple rank was very clearly given at the half-forgotten Calabrian battle of Maida, three years after the commencement of the second half of the great French War. At this fight the French General Reynier had deployed the whole, or the greater part, of his battalions, who were not as usual fighting either in *ordre mixte* or in battalion column. The result was very decisive – 5,000 British infantry in the thinner formation received the attack of 6,000 French in the heavier, and inflicted on them, purely by superior fire-efficiency, one of the most crushing defeats on a small scale that was ever seen, disabling or taking 2,000 men, with a total loss to themselves of only 320.

It is worthwhile remembering that some of the officers who were afterwards to be Wellington's trusted lieutenants were present at Maida, including Cole, Kempt, Oswald, and Colborne. This was about the only instance that I know where English and French came into action both deployed, and on a more or less parallel front. Usually it was a case of "column against line."

Sir Arthur Wellesley had been nine years absent in India before he returned to England in 1805, so that he had to learn the difference between the Republican and the Imperial armies by new experience. The problem had long been interesting him. Before he left Calcutta he is said to have remarked to his confidants that the French were sweeping everything before them in Europe by the use of column formations, but that he was convinced that the column could, and would, be beaten by the line. What he heard after his return to England evidently confirmed him in this opinion. A conversation which he had with Croker, just before he set sail on the expedition which was to end at Vimeiro, chances to have been preserved in the latter's papers, under the date, June 14, 1808. Sitting silent, lost in reverie for a long time, he was asked by Croker the subject of his thoughts. "To say the truth," he replied, "I am thinking of the French I am going to fight. I have not seen them since the campaigns in Flanders [1793–94] when they were capital soldiers, and a dozen years of victory under Bonaparte must have made them better still. 'Tis enough to make one thoughtful. But though they may overwhelm me, I don't think that they will outmanoeuvre me. First, because I am not afraid of them, as everyone else seems to be, and secondly, because (if all I hear about their system is true) I think it is a false one against steady troops. I suspect all the continental armies are half-beaten before the battle begins. I at least will not be frightened beforehand."

Wellesley went out to Portugal, there to try what could be done with steady troops against the "French system." But it would be to convey a false impression of his meaning if we were to state that he simply went out to beat column with line – though the essential fact is sufficiently true. He went out to try his own conception of the proper way to use the line formation, which had its peculiarities and its limitations. The chief of these were that—

1. The line must not be exposed before the moment of actual conflict: *i.e.*, it must be kept under cover as much as possible.
2. That till the critical moment it must be screened by a line of skirmishers impenetrable to the enemy's *tirailleurs*.
3. That it must be properly covered on its flanks either by the nature of the ground, or by cavalry and artillery.[74]

A second point of superiority in the British army was their skill in musketry, which was unrivaled.

In respect of musketry the British were far ahead of any army in Europe. During the War of American Independence they had been called upon to meet an elusive enemy, who had carried marksmanship in civil life to a high degree of perfection; and they had been obliged to adapt themselves to that enemy's tactics. The result had been not only great improvement in shooting, but a definite and far-reaching change in tactical formation. Hitherto the British infantry, even as all the infantry of Europe, had been drawn up three ranks deep for action, the front rank kneeling and the two rear ranks firing over their heads. In America the British soon learned to fight in two ranks only, frequently also loosening their formation to encounter scattered sharpshooters in woodland fighting. This formation in double rank, though not laid down by regulation, became the rule after the end of the war, and it signified the very important fact that, given an equal number of men, the British front of fire was longer than that of any other nation.[75]

Also, the British musket, antiquated as it now seems, was superior to the French.

The musket with which three-quarters of the English army were armed seems at first sight to belong to an almost mythical past, and the tactics to which it gave rise quite absurdly heroic; yet the tactics of the early nineteenth century were anything but unscientific, and represented the best use to which the arms of the period could be put.

The English musket, the Brown Bess, was in essence a smoothbored, muzzle-loading, late seventeenth-century flintlock, to which the passage of a century and a half had brought only a few minor improvements. In the hands of well-trained troops it might be fired as often as twice a minute, but such a rate could not be kept up for long. The cartridges were made by hand, usually by women, the cases consisting of strong paper, hence the modern stationer's term, cartridge paper, and were well waxed to preserve them against damp. Using them was a complicated operation. The cartridge had to be cut with a knife or torn open with the teeth, and a small amount of powder sprinkled in the firing pan; the rest of the explosive was poured down the muzzle, with the ball and a small wad, and rammed tight with a ramrod. The charge was fired by a spark from the flint igniting the powder in the priming pan which in turn detonated the explosive in the barrel.

Gunpowder, a mixture of charcoal, sulphur and saltpetre, had first appeared on the battlefield in the early fourteenth century, but for the next 500 years no substantial advance was made on this rather unsatisfactory propellant. When a musket was fired, half the powder remained as a deposit fouling the barrel or left the muzzle in a cloud of dense white smoke. Until smokeless powder was introduced in the 1880's, battles were fought in very poor visibility, and it was common for troops to fire on their own side, and for generals to mistake what was happening in the enemy lines, as a number did at Waterloo. The flint which ignited the powder in the priming pan had to be changed after every thirty shots, and when the pan became foul from the priming, which it frequently did, the flint missed fire. Ramming became more difficult after the first few shots because of the deposits accumulating on the side of the barrel, and if it was dispensed with, the escape of gases was so great that the ball lost most of its force. "When hard pressed," wrote Sergeant-Major Cotton of the 7th Hussars, "the infantry would resort to the French skirmishers' method of loading in order to save time. After priming, they would shake the rest of the powder into the barrel, dropping the ball after it, and then giving the butt a rap or two on the ground, which was quite soft after so much rain. The ball, in consequence, not being rammed down to confine the powder, came out at times quite harmless." Yet however cumbersome and inefficient a weapon the English musket may seem, the French pattern was inferior. Its greatest shortcoming was that it was used with coarser powder, so that although English shot was a quarter as heavy again, and therefore required a heavier charge, the French barrel needed washing out twice as often, after every fifty shots instead of every hundred. Rifles made their appearance some time before Waterloo, but without a breech-loading mechanism to accompany the rifling, they were not really suitable for military purposes. The Rifle Brigade, who took part in the Waterloo Campaign, were equipped with Baker's rifle, which was much more accurate than the musket, and had a longer range, but could only be fired a third as often, so great was the difficulty of ramming a charge down a rifle barrel.

A musket ball could inflict mortal injury at a distance of as much as 500 yards, but the weapon was so inaccurate that at this range a hit was completely accidental; at 250 yards the French musket was subject to an error of 9 feet. Troops usually held their fire until the enemy were within 100 yards of them, and the returns of a practice company of ordinary German soldiers of the period explain why this was so. The Germans ranked above the French and below the English in accuracy of fire, and their performance, although without the distraction of battlefield conditions, may be taken as giving a reasonable picture of the value of musket fire. Firing at a target 100 feet long and 6 feet high, that is to say at the kind of target a company of infantry would offer in action, 60% of their shot hit the screen at 75 yards. At double this distance only 40% of their rounds were successful, and at 225 yards only one ball in four found the target.

With the help of such facts the tactics of the Napoleonic Wars begin to make sense. The infantryman was compelled to fire from the shoulder in an awkward and vulnerable standing position because he could only load standing up. He waited to fire until he was almost upon the enemy because his musket was inaccurate, and because an appreciable time would have to elapse before he could fire again. The troops were drawn up almost shoulder to shoulder, and often in more than one rank in order to achieve a reasonable concentration of fire-power. Because the enemy was no better armed, the massed infantry formations of Wellington's army were not as dangerous as they seemed. The deployment and evolutions of the early nineteenth-century army may still be studied on the modern parade-ground, where they have survived virtually unchanged. In those days parades had more than a ceremonial and vaguely disciplinary value; they provided a daily opportunity to rehearse the movements the soldiers would perform under fire. The pompous occasions which are now retained out of feeling for tradition were then largely practical affairs. Colours were trooped because the regiment fought closely grouped around its standard, which provided a convenient rallying point for stragglers gone astray in the smoke clouds surrounding their position, as well as being a focus of morale for troops compelled to stand their ground for long periods while the issue of the struggle was slowly, but nonetheless, bloodily, decided.

At Waterloo the English possessed a considerable advantage in fire-power over their opponents. Their superiority was of long standing, and possibly dated from the Middle Ages, when the English archers were renowned for their accuracy. This, like their reputation for steadiness in defence, probably owed as much to national character as did the French gift for swift manoeuvre and dash in the attack. Until a few years before Waterloo the English army, like the French, had arranged infantry in three ranks, the theory being that by the time the third rank had fired its volley, the first would have reloaded. It was noticed that the presence of the third rank tended to hinder the firing and reloading of the other two, and that given the well-trained soldiers of the English army, reducing the number of ranks to two did not diminish the rate of fire; moreover dispensing with the third rank increased the line, and therefore the regiment's fire-power, by 50%. Among the pioneers of the two-rank system was Sir John Moore, who fell at Corunna, and Wellington, his successor in the Peninsula, reaped the fruits of his innovations in Belgium as well as Spain. The English development of scientific infantry tactics was fostered by the possession of a small standing army, in contrast to the vast conscript force recruited by France to maintain the conquests of the Revolution and Empire. Nevertheless, it is surprising that after a brief experiment with two ranks the French should have returned to three, still not realising that fire-power was the decisive factor in infantry engagements.[76]

So far as artillery was concerned, the two armies were fairly well matched.

There was little difference between the performance of French and English guns. The rate of fire was about that of the musket, that is to say, with skill and exertion, the guns could be fired twice a minute. No means had been found to overcome recoil action, and the pieces had to be laid afresh after every round. The extreme range of a twelve-pounder, the largest gun commonly used in battle, was about 3,600 yards, but the extreme effective range was 1,200 yards to 1,700 yards. It was only at little more than half this distance, however, that firing usually began. A variety of shot was used, ball, canister and grape. The last two spread their contents over a wide area; at short range they were extremely effective against infantry and cavalry in close formations. Canister represented a crude form of machine-gun fire in that it contained ordinary musket balls, while grape composed of small iron scrap might be thought of as an equally remote forerunner of shrapnel. To achieve any kind of range, it was necessary to fall back on single balls, which inflicted serious casualties on columns of infantry, where they would knock several men down at once, remaining dangerous as long as they continued to travel.[77]

After the wars were over Wellington made a private comment which, for all its denigration of "the scum of the earth," cannot conceal his ultimate respect for his men. He was asked if the French soldier was flogged, and he replied:

"Oh, they bang them about very much with ramrods and that sort of thing, and then they shoot them. Besides a French army is composed very differently from ours. The conscription calls out a share of every class – no matter whether your son or my son – all must march; but our friends – I may say it in this room – are the very scum of the earth. People talk of their enlisting from their fine military feeling – all stuff – no such thing. Some of our men enlist from having got bastard children – some for minor offences – many more for drink; but you can hardly conceive such a set brought together, and it really is wonderful that we should have made them the fine fellows they are."[78]

6

Blücher and the Prussian Army

Gebhardt Leberecht von Blücher is a descendant of a very ancient and noble family whose barony is situated in the Dutchy of Mecklenburg-Schwerin. He was born at Rostock, in that Dutchy, on the 16th of December, 1742, being the youngest of six brothers. His father was a Captain of Dragoons in the service of the Elector of Hessen-Cassel.[79]

The father was

scantily endowed with wealth but had sufficient influence to obtain for his six sons positions in almost as many different armies. Gebhardt Leberecht von Blücher began his military career in the Swedish service at the age of sixteen, Sweden being at the moment one of Frederick the Great's many enemies in the Seven Years' War. Blücher's connection with the Swedish army, however, terminated very suddenly; for he was captured in a skirmish, brought before the Prussian Colonel Belling, made a very favourable impression on that fiery officer, and, apparently without the least struggle of conscience, allowed himself to be given a post in Belling's own regiment. Blücher always, in later life, spoke of the episode with amusement and declared that the thought of it refreshed him whenever he was sad. Belling proved a good friend to Blücher and exerted a strong influence over him. He helped the boy to procure the equipment necessary to a young hussar officer of that day – the fur-lined cloak, the gleaming sabre, the lace and fringes. He seemed to have taught him, further, his own strange mixture of piety and ferocity.[80]

During his early years in the army of Frederick the Great, Blücher had no opportunity to distinguish himself, and seems to have spent a large part of his time drinking, duelling, making love, and gambling. Reported for misconduct he was passed over for promotion and immediately sent in his resignation to the King who replied, "Captain Blücher can take himself to the devil."

He took himself instead to East Prussia where he became a farmer until the death of Frederick the Great in 1786. He was then, at the age of forty-five, reinstated in his former regiment and given the rank that he would have held had he not left the army thirteen years before.

Save for the bloodless campaign of 1787 in Holland Blücher saw no active service until the coalition wars against the French Revolution. In the meantime his duties were often of a most sordid and trivial kind. It was later counted among the great abuses in the Prussian army that the head of a regiment or of a squadron was obliged to eke out his salary by mixing in matters of a purely commercial nature: to provide shirts, collars, hair-ribbons, and shoes for his men and reap what profit he could from the transaction; to draw emolument, too, from the cleaning of weapons and repairing of uniforms, from the fodder and physic of horses, from the hiring of recruits and the granting of leave of absence to the soldiers. Another age was to invent the word "graft" for such dealings; as yet they were perfectly and openly permissible.

In 1793 Blücher was ordered to join with his squadron of which he was now colonel, the forces of Duke Ferdinand of Brunswick. He took part in a number of sieges and skirmishes which, though not of great importance in themselves, afforded excellent training to the future opponent of Napoleon. In May 1794, he achieved what he himself called the "goal of his desires," being advanced to the rank of major-general. He was already gaining a reputation for boldness and was likened to the famous General Ziethen of Frederick the Great's army. He was praised for the swiftness of his decisions, the energy of his actions, his indefatigability. We are told by a contemporary that "from drilling his squadron, which was quartered at a distance, he would proceed to a hare hunt or a gay dinner and that same night, perhaps, to a surprise attack on the enemy, or to the laying of an ambush for the next morning. Having temporarily silenced the enemy he would enjoy himself at Frankfort gambling or going to the theatre." The games Blücher played were, some of them, forbidden by law; and we have it on very good authority that he "indulged in them to a truly immoderate degree." What Blücher really craved was excitement; and, when, later, he was afforded a sufficiency of that in the Napoleonic wars we find him able altogether to renounce his gambling for many months at a time.[81]

The Peace of Basel, concluded in 1795, banned Prussia behind a line of demarcation and condemned her to ten years of ignominious neutrality. But during these years Blücher gradually emerged as one of the most influential of those men who urged Frederick William to declare war on France.

Halfheartedly the King gave way to these urgings and declared war in September 1806. The immediate results were the crushing defeats of Jena and Auerstädt, an immense fine levied on the Prussian provinces, and the occupation of Berlin.

Blücher, the courageous dashing cavalry general, was one of the few men who came out of this short and disastrous campaign with credit. And when war broke out once more he was the man fixed upon to lead the Prussian armies. It seemed to many a surprising choice for, apart from his professional limitations, he was seriously ill at the time.

Not only was his body affected but his mind was a prey to the wildest delusions.

He actually believed (writes Boyen), that he was pregnant with an elephant… Another time he imagined that his servants, bribed by France, had heated the floor of his room very hot so as to cause him to burn his feet. When he was sitting therefore, he kept his legs raised from the ground, or else he would jump round on tiptoe!

One night the house was roused by sounds of a fearful struggle; it was Blücher, fighting the phantom of an officer for whose dismissal from the service he had been responsible. Still again we hear of his imagining that his head was made of stone and asking those about him to smite it with a hammer.

Boyen attributed Blücher's troubles in great part to his grief at the condition of public affairs, but in part also to habits of dissipation. Scharnhorst, indeed, during the brave retreat with Blücher to Lübeck had discovered qualities in him that made him refuse to consider for a moment the idea of having any one else at the head of the army: "You are our leader and our hero," he wrote, "even should you have to be carried before or behind us on a litter." And again, "he must lead though he have a hundred elephants inside of him."[82]

This, indeed, was the case; and by the time the spring campaign of 1813 was over, Blücher was recognized as being the only possible choice for the leadership of the Prussian armies.

Blücher had made a great impression by his bravery at Lützen, Bautzen, and Haynau; and the force of his personality outweighed the arguments that had been brought against his appointment: he was too old, he had been mentally unsound, his military methods were antiquated, he had no experience in commanding large forces; he had little real knowledge either of strategy or of tactics; he was illiterate to a great extent and would not be able to confer with his Russian subordinates either in their own language or in French; he was addicted to drink and to gambling.

These charges were true either in whole or in part: yet Blücher had qualities that compensated for everything. He had an indomitable will and an unfailing courage and hopefulness; friendly and free with his men, he inspired them with absolute devotion and knew how to spur them on to almost impossible efforts; like Frederick the Great he himself was at his best in moments of the greatest need; his presence of mind and the quickness of his decisions were marvellous; if he knew little of planning a battle and abhorred maps, he had the wisdom to commit such matters to those who were competent and then to put their measures vigorously into execution...

We must add to Blücher's other qualifications a hatred of Napoleon that made the latter's overthrow the ruling passion of his life. He had seen him now at close quarters and the result had been to inspire him with contempt:

"Let him do his worst," he said of the world-conqueror after Bautzen, "he is really nothing but a stupid fellow!"[83]

There were those, of course, who would have preferred a more imaginative commander, one who more fully understood the art and science of war. And when Napoleon returned from Elba and Blücher was appointed to the supreme command, it was openly suggested that a better choice might well have been Yorck or Kleist or Bülow, perhaps Müffling and certainly General Count von Gneisenau.

Gneisenau at this time was a disappointed man, and his heart was full of bitterness; for he had expected to be given a separate command. Hardenberg wrote to console him in terms tending to show that Blücher had been chosen more because of his popularity than from any expectation of great achievements:

"Once more you are not in a very agreeable position. The credit for what you accomplish will be claimed by another. But how can it be helped? The King adheres to the system of advancement by age; otherwise it is you who would command the army. At present you actually do command; but old Blücher gives his name. Few will be deceived about that matter."

Müffling, too, once wrote of Blücher:

"All Europe knew that the old Prince, who was past seventy, understood nothing at all about leading an army – so little, indeed, that when a plan was laid before him for his approval, even if it had only to do with some minor operation, it conveyed no clear meaning to him and he could form no judgment whether it was good or bad."

The truth seems to be that Blücher really was ignorant of many of the technicalities of his trade, but that he was, all the same, an inspired commander. Müffling maintains that he was "*merely* the bravest in battle, the most tireless in bearing fatigue, the one who set the example and who through his fiery addresses understood how to rouse enthusiasm."...

Müffling adds to the picture: "You can reckon on it that if the Prince has given his word to engage in a common operation that word will be kept even if the whole Prussian army be annihilated in the process." Surely this is much; and the thought obtrudes itself that those who lay too much stress on Blücher's shortcomings are lacking in the imagination that enables one to appreciate the superiority of genius over mere routine. The immediate future was to prove that the *vox populi* had a truer ring than the voice of the critics.[84]

What at least was certain at the time was that the Prussian army was a far more powerful and efficient force than it had been at the time of Jena.

"Outwardly," wrote an observer in 1805, "there was much shimmer, glitter, and polish. But behind it – worm-eaten wood!"

The manner of recruiting was wrong, the material bad, and the system of discipline one of intimidation, constraint, and suspicion. Every night officers had to stand ready to pursue those who might attempt to desert; cannon stood loaded so as instantly to give the signal for the chase, while even in the barracks the more trusted soldiers had to spy on the new recruits and, if the latter had been acting suspiciously, were empowered to lock up their boots.

The punishments were degrading to the last degree. Scharnhorst, who was to do more than any other man to remedy the evils, tells us that any sixteen-year-old ensign might flog an old soldier half to death for carelessness in drill. For more serious offences there was the running of the gauntlet of two hundred men armed with salted whips. The culprit's hands were bound, his feet fettered, and a ball of lead was placed in his mouth lest he should bite his tongue off in his agony. The sight at times was too horrible for description. Boyen complained that such public putting to shame forever placed the hall-mark of a rogue upon the offender.

The armies that fought at Jena and Auerstadt were composed of men who did not respect themselves because no respect was shown to them. The officers were often proud, arrogant, and incapable, and many of them far too old to be capable of fulfilling the duties of their positions. After the Duke of Brunswick's death the one who should have seized the command, Möllendorf, was eighty-one years of age!

Frederick the Great was indirectly to blame for this; in his will he had urged that none of his faithful old officers should be dismissed. Instead they were placed in command of the fortresses and were given to understand that their posts were sinecures.

Everything about the Prussian army was complicated and cumbersome. Each officer was in the habit of taking with him on the march from one to five extra horses loaded with articles for his comfort: not only a tent but a bed, a table and a chair. There were 32,000 extra horses with the army that marched out to Jena. Blücher had already handed in a report "on lessening the baggage of the army and removing other hindrances to the mobility of the troops."...

This lightening of the baggage was only one of the reforms that Blücher had vainly tried to effect. In a report drawn up in 1805 he had recommended making military service compulsory for all, shortening the length of time the soldiers should be obliged to remain with the army, giving better pay and better treatment to each individual.[85]

After the Peace of Tilsit, however, the Prussian army had been drastically reformed.

The end and aim of the reform was to raise the self-respect of the soldier and make the army, above all, one of patriots. Strange to say more blindness, more stubborn attachment to the old order of things was met with here than in any of the other reforms. The organisation commission, although headed by Scharnhorst, one of the most single-minded and ardent of all the patriots, contained members who were still steeped in the old conservatism... Outside of the commission, too, there was much opposition to the reform. Yorck, who later commanded under Blücher and was one of his bravest generals, could never forget that he himself was a nobleman and that the reformers wished to take away his privileges: "If your Royal Highness take away my rights and those of my children," he once said to Prince William of Prussia, "on what do your own rest?" Yorck was jubilant when he heard that Stein had been disgraced, and he spoke of Scharnhorst and his adherents as a viper brood that would one day dissolve in their own poison.

Scharnhorst was a quiet man but he was possessed of immense force and determination; and he proceeded to get rid of those members of the reorganisation commission who were out of sympathy with its objects and to fill their places with strong, progressive men. It was now that Gneisenau was called in; there were also Grolman of whom Niebuhr said in 1813: "Such a man I have never yet seen; he would be the proper commander for Germany"; Götzen, who had done wonders in organising defence in Silesia, and Boyen who was eventually to succeed Scharnhorst as Minister of War. The reorganisation committee became so powerful a body that the King himself rarely ventured to oppose its decisions.

Frederick William had been forced by his latest convention with Napoleon to promise that his army should not exceed the number of 42,000 men – a galling engagement to have to make but one that, at all events, made speedy reform more possible. A higher standard was at once established both for officers and men, and the old system of recruiting, that amounted to the hiring of mercenaries who had no loyalty whatever to the cause, was abolished…

Under the new régime the whole conception of the officer's duty changed. He was appointed because of merit, not because of high birth; he was to be an example to the soldiers in the matter of patiently bearing the fatigues of the march; he was to go on foot and carry his knapsack on his back; he was always to remember his "honourable calling, that of leader and educator of an estimable part of the nation."

The commanders are to see that their subordinates "neither treat their soldiers roughly nor permit the insults that are still occasionally the custom." The cruelest of the penalties were entirely abolished. Gneisenau had been strong on that point and had published in a Königsberg newspaper an article entitled "Freedom of the Back." Boyen, too, had declared publicly that the best disciplined army would be the one that had the most humane laws and regulations. Detention in a fortress now took the place of running the gauntlet and there began to be talk of rewards as well as of punishments. Grolman wished it introduced as a custom in the churches that the names of all who had fallen in war or had died of their wounds should be written up in gold letter; that their wives should be placed in the front seats; that the seating of the soldiers should be according to the degree of their bravery in the field and that those who had shown any cowardice should be given "the lowest place in the church far back against the wall." The idea was extravagant of course but that a man like Grolman could cherish it shows how the whole conception of what the army was and what it might be expected to accomplish had changed.

Of what use, one may ask, was all this enthusiasm for military reform when by the terms of the convention concluded with Napoleon in September 1808, the army might not, for ten years to come, number more than 42,000 men? What could such a handful accomplish against Napoleon's hundreds of thousands? Scharnhorst, especially, who had become an expert in ruses, had laboured with this problem and had found the solution. While outwardly conforming to Napoleon's conditions he nevertheless long eluded the vigilance of the French. The numbers were always the same, but not the men! A considerable portion of the youth of the land gained at least the rudiments of military training by spending a month in camp while those already trained were given leave of absence. Those who came for this short time worked doubly hard at the simple tasks assigned to them: to move at command, to load quickly, and to fire straight. It meant a great deal to them, this training, for every one of them had come with the grim determination to hasten the day of reckoning with the oppressor![86]

The reformed Prussian army, greatly increased both in size and efficiency, was by 1815 a formidable weapon. Once more it was felt that there could be only one choice for its commander. The German historian Kircheisen has summed up Blücher's qualities and those of his chief of staff Gneisenau and Baron von Müffling, his quartermaster, who in the forthcoming campaign was to act as liaison officer at Wellington's headquarters.

It was not so much his talent for strategy, as his optimism, his belief in the unbroken strength of Prussia, his stubborn will, his daring courage and great presence of mind that enabled him, even in the most critical moments, to overcome every obstacle, and made him the most important leader on the Allied side, one of the very few, moreover, who had no fear in facing Napoleon. Stettens says of him very truly: "Blücher was in every respect unorthodox [*eine inkorrekte Erscheinung*]," and it was precisely this unorthodoxy which constituted his greatness.

Almost all the qualities which Blücher lacked were to be found in his Chief of Staff, Neithardt von Gneisenau, an accomplished officer who was in no way inferior to Blücher in vigour and boldness of ideas, but did not share his powers of decision. His character was a source of many complaints, and it often required all Blücher's authority to settle the disputes that arose between his Chief of Staff and his corps commanders. The third member of the trio was Colonel von Müffling, the Quartermaster, a versatile, efficient and methodical staff officer, who was responsible for the actual organisation at headquarters.

Seldom has a combination of three outstanding personalities been so perfectly adjusted as that of Blücher,

Gneisenau and Müffling. Gneisenau produced the ideas, Blücher made the decisions or remodelled the conceptions, while Müffling saw to the execution of them. It can be said with confidence that the great achievements of the Silesian army are mainly to be ascribed to the activities of these three men.

Blücher was undoubtedly a leader whose imperturbable confidence in his own powers and whose capacity for inspiring enthusiasm in the masses almost rivalled those of Napoleon himself. Such qualities were more valuable than Gneisenau's brilliance or Müffling's efficiency, for in the last resort either of these was easier to replace than Blücher's unique originality.[87]

7

The Battles of Ligny and Quatre Bras

The time had now come for Napoleon to decide definitely on his plan of action. As he once said, "There is no greater coward than I, when I am drawing up a plan of campaign. I magnify every danger, every disadvantage that can be conceived. My nervousness is painful; although I show a calm face to those about me, I am like a woman in the throes of childbirth. When once my decision is made, however, I forget all, except what will successfully carry through my selected plan." Herein the Emperor was right. He never forgot that "In war you see your own troubles, but those of the enemy you cannot see." Consequently he considered, weighed, and appreciated all sides of the situation and every point of view before he came to his final decision. Then he was adamant, and he held to the chosen course despite all the dangers and the difficulties which must invariably beset execution. With this iron resolution, which literally overbore all difficulties, he coupled energy in the conduct of his operations, and a terrific driving force which compelled victory; and once he had drawn his sword, then he was ready to throw away the scabbard; invariably he fought to win, and to win a decisive action.[88]

The choice that faced Napoleon was whether to act offensively or defensively. In 1814, with less than 100,000 men, he had held his far more numerous enemies at bay by operating defensively from a central position, by turning first to one army and then to the next and defeating them in succession. That campaign had been a brilliant achievement. But it had held no hope of ultimate success; for it had amounted to little more than a delaying action, and a delaying action can only be of use to a commander who can expect to build up sufficient strength to strike an ultimately decisive blow. Napoleon had not been able to do this in 1814. Could he in 1815 expect France to provide him with the numbers of men he would need for such a strategy? And could he allow the enemy to advance and overrun the north and east of France and endanger Paris while he was preparing his final stroke?

He decided that he could not. He calculated that by the middle of August – and then only by the reintroduction of conscription – he would have under his command a field army of rather less than 250,000 men, whereas the Seventh Coalition would by then have been able to bring against him a force more than twice as strong. He made up his mind, therefore, to take the initiative, to leave 100,000 men to hold the Alps, the Pyrenees, Alsace, and la Vendée (where a royalist resistance movement had broken out) and to assume an immediate offensive; so he determined to attack the Anglo-Prussian armies in Belgium before the Russian and Austrian armies could come to their assistance.

By destroying, at the very outset, Wellington and Blücher, the two most renowned army commanders of the Seventh Coalition, Napoleon would strike terror into the Allies and also restore confidence to his own nation. Thus only could the critical situation be really relieved; further, Wellington and Blücher were within striking distance of France's northern frontier, therefore a real chance was offered to Napoleon to make a telling entry into the arena.

After much thought, Napoleon decided on this bold plan, and thereby reaffirmed once more his belief in the soundest method of defence – prompt and vigorous attack.

The plan eventually decided on had much to recommend it. It was rendered feasible because Napoleon clearly realised that the Austrians and Russians had far to come, that no immediate danger threatened from the direction of the Rhine frontier, and that the Allies could not take the offensive until July 1. The time to strike first was thus ample, but the moment to open serious hostilities had arrived. Napoleon determined, therefore, to take the field with every available man, and throw himself on the junction-point of the Anglo-Prussian forces in Belgium before they had warning of his stroke, and then proceed to crush them in detail before Barclay de Tolly [commanding the Russian army] and Schwartzenberg [the Austrian commander] had attained the banks of the Rhine. The Emperor calculated that he could open the campaign in Flanders, with the *Armée du Nord*, on June 15; further, that he could collect a force of 125,000 men to conduct this campaign, and that he should still leave amply sufficient forces to form a defensive screen along the eastern and southern frontiers, and to act as garrisons for the fortresses.

The dispersed cantonments of the Anglo-Prussian forces in Belgium stretched from Ghent to Liège; herein Napoleon saw his opportunity, he would mass the *Armée du Nord* opposite to Charleroi, unknown to the Allies, surprise them whilst dispersed, break their front just where they came together, and driving them away before his advance, he would then beat the two armies in detail.[89]

On June 3, Napoleon issued orders for the concentration of the Army of the North in the area bounded by Maubeuge, Avesnes, Rocroi, and Chimay.[90] *The most stringent security measures were adopted; for surprise was essential to the success of the Emperor's plan.*

Communications between Belgium and the Rhine provinces were intercepted; in the sea-ports all vessels were laid under an embargo, even the fishing-boats; and for fear of giving any hint to the enemy's advanced posts, bodies of volunteers and divisions from the National Guard were posted along the frontiers of the north and the east, to replace troops which were summoned to the various meeting-places. When Napoleon, who had left Paris by night, arrived at Laon at twelve on the 12th of June, all the troops were still on the march. Grouchy's troops were an exception; they had not yet stirred, though Grouchy's headquarters were in Laon itself. Summoned to the Emperor's presence, Grouchy stated that he had received no orders. This was the truth, for not till that very day (12th June) did the chief of the staff at headquarters send him Napoleon's instructions from Avesnes! But immediately after seeing the Emperor, Grouchy issued orders to the four cavalry corps that they were to make for the frontier by forced marches; and he himself started off to Avesnes without losing an hour's time. In this way the concentration was not delayed, since the whole Cavalry Reserve were beyond Avesnes on the night of the 13th; but several regiments had been compelled to ride for twenty leagues without drawing rein – wretched preparation indeed for horses at the opening of a campaign! The misfortune was that this incident, which foreboded evil, failed to arouse the attention of Napoleon to the negligence of the chief of the staff at headquarters.

On the 13th of June the Emperor slept at Avesnes; on the evening of the 14th he moved his headquarters to

Beaumont, the centre of his army. That night, in spite of bad weather, all the troops bivouacked in order to keep well together. At the sound of the *réveil* the Emperor's order of the day was read out to them; "Soldiers, today 14th is the anniversary of Marengo and Friedland, which twice decided the fate of Europe. We were too generous then, as we were too generous after Austerlitz and Wagram. And now, banded together against us, the sovereigns we left on their thrones, conspire against the independence and the most sacred rights of France. They have begun by the most iniquitous aggression. Let us march to meet them; are we not the men we were then?"[91]

The positions of the army were as follows: The 1st Corps (20,731 men under Drouet d'Erlon), forming the extreme left, between the road from Avesnes to Maubeuge and Solre-sur-Sambre; the 2nd Corps (25,179 men under Reille), between Solre-sur-Sambre and Leers; the 3rd Corps (18,105 men under Vandamme); and the 6th Corps (10,821 men under Lobau) between Beaumont and the frontier; the 4th Corps (15,404 men under Gérard) between Philippeville and Florenne; the Cavalry Reserve (13,144 men under Grouchy) at Valcourt, at Bossus, and at Gayolle; the Imperial Guard (20,755 men) before and behind Beaumont. This army had 370 pieces of heavy artillery. The ground covered by the bivouacks did not exceed 24 miles in breadth by six miles in length.

In ten days 124,000 men, separated by distances varying from 30 to 200 miles, had assembled on the frontier, within easy cannon range of the enemy's advanced posts, before the Allies had taken a single defence measure.[92]

There was no sense of urgency in the allied lines, no suspicion that within a matter of hours the two armies would be at grips with the French; their normal round of occupations and amusements continued. In the intervals between training and preparing for a succession of reviews Wellington's men passed their time in smoking and drinking, visiting neighbouring villages, wandering through the streets of nearby towns, occasionally quarrelling with the Belgians, but on the whole receiving a generous measure of hospitality. Their officers shared even more in this convivial atmosphere.

They enjoyed an active social round in Brussels, where many of their wives and families had arrived to join them together with English visitors attracted partly by the forthcoming campaign and partly by the novelty of being able to visit the Continent after so many years of confinement. Wellington shared their amusements to the full. Rumours reached the Duke on the 12th that Napoleon was at Maubeuge but he paid so little attention to the possibility that he went off to Enghien for the day. Two letters of the Rev. Spencer Madan, tutor to the young Lennoxes, a family with whom the Duke was particularly friendly, show something of Wellington during the last two days before the storm broke.

> Brussels, 13th June, 1815
>
> "...Though I have some pretty good reasons for supposing that hostilities will soon commence, yet no one would suppose it, judging by the Duke of Wellington. He appears to be thinking of anything else in the world, gives a ball every week, attends every party, partakes of every amusement that offers. (Yesterday) he took Lady Jane Lennox

> to Enghien for the cricket match, and brought her back at night, apparently having gone for no other object but to amuse her. At the time Bonaparte was said to be at Maubeuge, thirty or forty miles off."

Wellington certainly did not think that hostilities would soon commence, and he wrote to Lord Lynedoch to say so, on the 13th, the day after his trip to Enghien, when Napoleon was supervising the final stages of his army's concentration. Fresh rumours of Napoleon's presence near the frontier were brought to Wellington's notice on the 14th, but he still took no action. "In the drawing-room before dinner," wrote Madan that day, "he was playing with the children, who seemed to look up to him as to one on whom they might depend for amusement. When dinner was announced they quitted him with great regret, saying, 'Be sure you remember to send for us the moment dinner is over,' which he promised to do, and was as good as his word."[93]

Wellington's calm was, however, scarcely justified by the quality of his army.

The Duke, indeed, could scarcely be expected to be in high spirits with a discouraging command in which foreigners outnumbered British troops by more than two to one. His dealings with Allies in Spain had made him an expert in the lukewarm; but this time their temperature was more discouraging than usual. His Dutch were poor, his Belgians unreliable; even his Hanoverians were hardly more than willing; and the King's German Legion alone came up to British standards. Not that his British troops were an inspiring spectacle. For out of twenty-five battalions only six had served in the Peninsula; the rest (except the Guards) were neither up to strength nor standard. His cavalry was tolerably abundant, since there had been no need for cavalry in America; but his demand for guns was answered by a grim intimation from the Ordnance that while guns abounded, "men and horses are the only difficulty I have." Even his Staff depressed him, since he inherited the Staff of a small army of occupation already in the Low Countries. But loud protests in his most emphatic manner gradually relieved him of them; the authorities were most obliging though he complained bitterly of being "overloaded with people I have never seen before; and it appears to be purposely intended to keep those out of my way whom I wished to have"; and he ended with a staff of thirty-three of whom thirty-one had considerable Staff experience in the Peninsula. But at the outset it was not surprising that his correspondence rang with indignant outcries. April found him complaining that the British troops were "not what they ought to be to enable us to maintain our military character in Europe. It appears to me that you have not taken in England a clear view of your situation, that you do not think war certain, and that a great effort must be made, if it is hoped that it shall be short." The month passed in a fever of preparations – of friendly correspondence with the Prussians on his left, of visits to the French royalties at Ghent, innumerable tangles of inter-Allied diplomacy, peculiar transactions with foreign potentates for the supply of infantry at a flat rate of £11. 2s. a head, and ingenious rearrangements of the assorted nationalities in his command until the mosaic gave some promise of stability. But he could still write in May that he had "an infamous army, very weak and ill equipped, and a very inexperienced Staff." He was more hopeful now – "for an action in Belgium I can now put 70,000 men into the field, and Blücher 80,000; so that I hope we should give a good account even of Buonaparte." Besides the need might not arise, since he was sometimes tempted to believe that internal politics might keep the Emperor in Paris. But he was haunted by his old desire for 40,000 British infantry; with them "I should be satisfied, and take my chance for the rest, and engage that we should play our part in the game."

That thought was in his mind one day, when he met Mr. Creevey in the Park at Brussels. The pert civilian asked a question.

"Will you let me ask you, Duke, what you think you will make of it?"

The blunt question stopped him in his walk. "By God," the Duke replied, "I think Blücher and myself can do the thing."

"Do you calculate upon any desertion in Buonaparte's army?"

"Not upon a man," said the Duke, "from the colonel to the private in a regiment – both inclusive. We may pick up a Marshal or two, perhaps; but not worth a damn."

Then Mr. Creevey asked him about the French royalists in Belgium.

"Oh!" said the Duke, "don't mention such fellows! No: I think Blücher and I can do the business."

At that moment his eye was caught by a British private in the green alleys of the Park; and as he watched the little scarlet figure staring at the foreign statues under the foreign trees, "There," said the Duke, pointing a long forefinger, "it all depends upon that article whether we do the business or not. Give me enough of it, and I am sure."[94]

-

The June days went slowly by; and when he wrote to Graham accepting membership of a new military club, he added comfortably that the Emperor seemed unlikely to leave Paris at the moment – "I think we are now too strong for him here." But the reports came in – French *feux de joie* were heard at Maubeuge; Valenciennes was full of troops; the gates of Lille were closed; Soult was on the road; Grouchy had been seen reviewing cavalry; the Guard was on the march; the Emperor was everywhere at once. Something was stirring now behind the frontier.[95]

Early on the morning of June 15 that frontier was crossed.[96] *The march began in a thick mist; but soon the sun broke through giving promise of a fine summer's day.*

Only twelve regiments of cavalry led the way. The other mounted troops had directions to advance on the left of the infantry. The sappers of each army corps were to keep together, and to march in each division, behind the first regiment of light infantry. Three companies of pontoniers with fifteen pontoons and fifteen boats, were appointed to follow immediately after Vandamme's corps; the ambulances were to start in the rear of the Imperial staff. Orders were given to burn any vehicle that might try to slip in with the columns, and not to allow the baggage waggons or ammunition waggons to approach the Army within a distance of three leagues till further notice. The generals who commanded the advanced guards were ordered to regulate their march so as to remain always on a line with one another; they were to send out scouts in every position, to seize all letters in the post-offices, and to communicate their information in frequent reports to the Emperor, who would be in person at the head of the central column. The bulk of the Army must have crossed the Sambre before noon.

These orders are justly considered as perfect. Napoleon had never issued marching orders which were more carefully studied or better thought out, even in the happy days of Austerlitz and Friedland. Never had his genius been more brilliant, never had he exhibited to such perfection, his attention to detail, his broad grasp of the whole, his clearness, and his mastery of the science of war.

Unfortunately his orders were not faithfully executed, Drouet d'Erlon preferred to take his own course and started at half-past four, instead of breaking up his camp at three, as he had been ordered. Vandamme, who should have started at three, was at five still awaiting instructions from the Imperial headquarters; during the night, the officer who had been sent with his marching orders, had fallen from his horse and broken his leg, and had lain all night alone and helpless in the open field. Vandamme was warned of the Army's march only by the arrival of Lobau's corps from the rear of his camp. Finally, the troops of Gérard, which should have been on their way at three, did not meet at the gathering-point, which was on the heights at Florenne, till seven o'clock.

Great agitation reigned in the 4th Corps. They had just heard that General de Bourmont, who commanded the head division, had passed over to the enemy's ranks. This desertion confirmed in the most untimely manner, the fears of treachery, the mistrust of their generals, which had been tormenting the minds of the soldiers for the last three months. Murmurs and imprecations arose from the ranks. One of the brigadiers of Bourmont, General Hulot, judging the moment was critical, harangued the two regiments under his orders; sword in hand, he gave them his solemn oath "he would fight with them against the enemies of France to his last breath." Gérard in his turn passed along, in front of his troops and addressed a few words to them; they answered him by loud cheers. Gérard was personally very much distressed by the desertion of his protégé Bourmont, all the details of which were related to him later by Hulot.

Shortly after five o'clock in the morning, at Florenne, Bourmont had mounted on horseback with his whole staff, Colonel Clouet, chief of the Villoutreys squadrons, Captains d'Andigné, de Trélan, and Sourda, and an escort of five lancers. Once beyond the French outposts, he had given the corporal of the chasseurs a letter for Gérard written in Florenne, and had dismissed him with the rest of the escort, and with the other officers had galloped off in the direction of the frontier. In his letter to Gérard he wrote: "I refuse to join in establishing in France, a sanguinary despotism which would ruin my country... I would have resigned and returned home had I thought I should be left free to do so. This seemed so unlikely, that I am obliged to ensure my liberty by other means... I shall never be seen fighting in the ranks of the foreigner... They will get no information from me which could injure the French army, composed of men whom I love and shall ever continue to regard with deep affection."

Two hours after having written this protest that he was a deserter but not a traitor, Bourmont revealed to Colonel von Schutter, commander of the Prussian advanced posts on the Sambre, that the French would attack Charleroi in the course of the afternoon. Shortly after, he told Colonel von Reiche, aide-de-camp to Zieten, that the French army amounted to 120,000 men. Finally, at three o'clock, when he met Blücher at Sombreffe, he would doubtless have shown the same eagerness in answering all questions the latter could ask. But the old warrior, indignant that a man wearing the uniform of a general of division, could desert on the morning of a battle, hardly condescended to speak to him. An officer of the Prussian staff having pointed out to the old Field-Marshal that he should not treat Bourmont so rudely, since the latter wore a white cockade, Blücher, little caring whether he was understood or not by the traitor, who probably knew German, said out loud, "Cockade be hanged! A cur must always be a cur!"[97]

Napoleon entered Charleroi to the cheers of the inhabitants. He dismounted at a small inn called Belle-vue, and sending for a chair, sat down by the side of the road as the troops marched past him, loudly shouting, "Vive l'Empereur!" But soon, in spite of all the noise and excitement, he fell asleep.

He was frequently noticed thus to doze. He had not been used to being so long in the saddle, and he had worked hard all the 15th. It is perhaps a little thing to do, but it is an indication that the Emperor was no longer physically equal to the conduct of a very difficult military operation. At Ratisbon in 1809 he had failed to pursue; in 1812 he had shown signs of physical weakness; in 1813 he frequently made other things yield to his personal comfort; in 1814 he had borne up against the desperate conditions with wonderful vigor; but the life at Elba had not increased his power of continuous work. He had long had some kidney trouble; hemorrhoids now annoyed him, and since his stay in Fontainebleau after the French campaign, he had suffered from still another disease, says Charras, making all physical exertion, and especially riding, difficult and painful.

"He no longer subdued, as formerly, distractions, sleep, fatigue. His power of application seemed to have reached its limit," says Constant. As he himself said of Ney, he was not the same man. "In the latter years the Emperor had grown fat," we are told by Foy; "he ate more, slept longer, and rode less; but he retained all the vigor of his mind, and his passions had lost little of their strength."

He no longer subordinated his bodily ailments to the demands of the occasion; many things had to yield to his own comfort. Unlike Frederick, whose activity during a severe attack of the gout and its accompanying fever, in October 1759, was the same as ever, Napoleon was now guilty, at the very inception of the campaign, of little lapses in time, the sum of which during the coming four days made up a tale of neglect that ruined an operation which in conception and opening is equal to any he ever conducted. While in speed and conduct he was quite equal to his opponents, this did not suffice to win the campaign against such overwhelming odds. At St. Helena he acknowledged that he could not see as clearly or work as actively: "It is certain that I felt conscious that something had gone from me."[98]

Soon after Napoleon awoke, Marshal Ney arrived at Charleroi. The soldiers recognized him and seemed pleased to see him. "All will go well now," they shouted. "Here is 'Redhead!'"

Napoleon received the Marshal frankly, and gave him the command of the left wing, which comprised Reille's II and d'Erlon's I Corps, and the Cavalry of Lefebvre-Desnouëttes. The orders that Ney received were verbal (naturally therefore they have been a matter of hot dispute), but probably the Marshal was commanded to "Go and drive the enemy before you along the Brussels road." But Napoleon must have said something more to Marshal Ney, in explanation of his general plan of campaign, than the very brief orders which he is usually credited with issuing; and General Pollio assumes very naturally and very properly that Ney must have been made *au fait* with the situation, for he had only just reached the front. Further, the fact that no written orders were sent after the Marshal, on June 15, is a distinct proof that Napoleon had explained matters sufficiently to his subordinate before the latter left the Imperial presence to take over his new command – at any rate so far as June 15 was concerned.[99]

–

On the ground, in presence of the enemy, the grand strategical plan conceived in Paris by Napoleon, grew into shape and developed. He had only expected on this, the first day, to bear down towards the supposed point of junction of the Allied armies, and if possible to get in advance of it. But now, since his adversaries gave him time, he would extend his field of action, and make it impossible for them to unite at all. As the bulk of the English forces was coming from Brussels, and that of the Prussians from Namur, the two armies must necessarily effect their junction by the high-road from Namur to

Nivelles which runs to Sombreffe, and crosses the road from Charleroi to Brussels at Quatre-Bras. The Emperor desired, therefore, to post his left wing at Quatre-Bras, and his right at Sombreffe. He himself would establish his quarters at Fleurus, the summit of the triangle formed by these three points, and on the following day, he would swoop down with his Reserve on that portion of the enemy's forces which should first come up. If both of them retreated, he would gain Brussels without firing a cannon-shot.[100]

–

As Ney rode off to take over his command Grouchy joined the Emperor. Napoleon gave him the right wing of the army, the IIIrd and IVth Corps, with instructions to push the Prussians he should encounter towards Sombreffe. Grouchy set about the task so slowly that after a couple of hours the Emperor rode forward to hurry him on. An engagement with Zieten's outnumbered corps ensued, and in accordance with his instructions, the Prussian general fell back to Fleurus, Here the French right wing halted for the night. Ney moved even more slowly than Grouchy, and whatever the difficulties he found in taking charge of a wing of the army at such short notice, it is hard to understand the reasons for his delay when speed was at such a premium. He drove some Prussians out of Gosselies, three and a half miles from Charleroi, and there halted his infantry; thus he compromised his chances of taking Quatre-Bras...

If Ney had taken Quatre-Bras Wellington would have arrived at the front next day in time to withdraw his forces, for by then the fate of Blücher's army would have been sealed, and the French left free to turn their superior numbers on the English.

Having halted his infantry at Gosselies, Ney sent Lefebvre-Desnouëttes' cavalry division along the road. A squadron of Polish lancers which had left the body of the advanced guard rode up to Quatre-Bras to find the cross roads unoccupied. The squadron commander decided to return to the main force; the position was too far from the rest of Ney's troops to be held with so few men, especially in so thoroughly confused a situation, where the enemy's outposts were falling back and his other troops coming forward to support them. He wheeled his squadron round and made off down the road to report to Ney. The Polish horsemen had not long left Quatre-Bras before Prince Bernard of Saxe-Weimar appeared at the cross roads with 4,500 infantry and a battery of six guns. He had heard accidentally at Genappe that the French had crossed the Sambre that morning, and it was on his own initiative that he ordered his small force to occupy Quatre-Bras in face of the French. As Ney rode up to the front to look at the situation, Saxe-Weimar's men were occupying the buildings of the hamlet and the roads which ran past them.

Small though Saxe-Weimar's numbers were, Ney had only 1,700 cavalry and a solitary battalion of infantry within call. He abandoned any thought of taking Quatre-Bras that evening, and a little after seven turned back towards Gosselies, where he was to pass the night.[101]

–

Colonel Heymès, Ney's aide-de-camp during this campaign, has urged as a possible explanation of the Marshal's conduct, that "there was not one chance in ten of seizing Quatre-Bras." And certainly, when they arrived within sight of Quatre-Bras, not at ten in the evening, as asserted by Heymès, but at seven at the latest, he could hardly hope to carry this position with two regiments of cavalry and a single battalion. But if at five o'clock, while at Gosselies, he had dispatched on the road to Brussels, a mere quarter of the troops entrusted to him by the Emperor – let us say, two divisions of infantry, two of cavalry, and four batteries of artillery by nine o'clock, with the help of this force of 14,000 men, he might have annihilated Prince Bernard of Saxe-Weimar s 4,500 infantry, most of whom had only ten cartridges in their belts. In halting Reille's corps at Gosselies, Ney, for the first time in his life, yielded to motives of prudence. He had given up all thoughts of occupying Quatre-Bras, unless as a cavalry post in case this point were not defended. In his opinion it would be endangering his army to transfer it at a distance of twelve miles from the right wing, to a position where it might come in contact with the whole body of Wellington's forces. Authorities on strategy have declared that Ney acted according to the strict principles of the art of war. This may possibly be true. But had Prince Bernard adhered as strictly to these principles, he would never have acted on his inspiration of marching on Quatre-Bras, with four battalions, at the risk of being utterly crushed by the whole French Army.[102]

Despite Ney's failure to occupy Quatre Bras, however, and despite Grouchy's failure to reach Sombreffe, by the evening of June 15, the chief aim of Napoleon's maneuver had been attained. With little loss Napoleon had succeeded in crossing the Sambre, in overcoming the stiff resistance of Zieten's corps, in penetrating seven miles into the enemy's territory and thrusting his army into the very center of the Allies' cantonments.

The Allies appeared to be

thrown into disorder. In the course of the day not a single English uniform had been seen, neither had the Prussians appeared in any great numbers; they had feebly contested the passages of the Sambre, and their lack of perseverance in the defence of Gilly and Gosselies, skilful and courageous though it was, favoured the assumption that their object was rather to protect a retreat, than to cover a concentration.

Therefore, when the Emperor, who returned to Charleroi for the night, examined the reports sent him by Grouchy and Ney he concluded that the Allies were disconcerted by his unexpected aggression, and had resolved to fall back on the base of their operations, the Prussians in the direction of Liège and Maëstricht, the English and Belgians towards Ostend and Antwerp. The route taken by the Prussian outposts, from Thuin to Marchienne, from Fontaine-L'Evêque and Marchienne to Gosselies, from Charleroi and Gosselies to Fleurus, tended to confirm this presumption. If the Prussians had manoeuvred with the design of immediately joining the English, they would have withdrawn towards the north, whereas they had retreated towards the north-east, thus leaving the road to Brussels unprotected. This resolution, which, judging from appearances, Napoleon attributed to Wellington and Blücher, seemed to ensure the victory to him. The further the Allied armies were separated from one another, the easier it would be to beat them in detail. It was one thing to attack the English when the Prussians were within a single march of them, and another to do so when Wellington and Blücher were separated by fifty or sixty miles.

The Emperor drew out his plan of action on the morning of the 16th of June, probably about six o'clock or a little earlier. With Grouchy and the right wing he meant to march towards Sombreffe and Gembloux. Should a Prussian corps happen to be in either of these two positions, he would attack it. Having reconnoitred and cleared the ground to the east, he would call up the Reserve, temporarily stationed at Fleurus, and with it, he would join Ney and the left wing at Quatre-Bras. From thence he would march on Brussels by a forced night-march. He calculated that the head of the column would reach Brussels on the 17th of June at seven o'clock in the morning.

The orders for the execution of this double movement were dispatched by the chief of the staff between seven and eight in the morning; orders to Kellermann to proceed on Gosselies and place himself at the disposal of Marshal Ney; orders to Drouot to start the Guard on its road towards Fleurus; orders to Lobau to push on the 6th Corps midway between Charleroi and Fleurus; orders to Vandamme and Gérard to march on Sombreffe with the 3rd and 4th Corps, and then to carry out the instructions of Marshal Grouchy, commanding the right wing.[103] Soult wrote to Ney to take up his position at Quatre-Bras, with six divisions of infantry and Kellermann's cuirassiers, and to lead his two other infantry divisions, one to Genappe (five kilometres beyond Quatre-Bras) with Piré's cavalry, and the other to Marbais with the cavalry of Lefebvre-Desnoëttes, in order eventually to support the movements of the right wing. Lastly, Ney was to push his reconnoitring bodies as far as possible on the Nivelles and Brussels roads. As for Grouchy, he received the order to take possession of Sombreffe, whence he was to send an advanced guard to Gembloux and scouts in every direction.

At the Imperial headquarters, all were busied with the dispatch of these orders, when the Emperor received a letter from Grouchy, notifying that strong columns of the enemy, which had apparently come up by the Namur road, were proceeding towards Brye and Saint-Amand. Though he believed the Prussians were retreating, Napoleon had recognized the possibility of a collision with them at Sombreffe; but he had not the remotest idea that they would come and take up positions at the entrance of the approach to Fleurus. This movement indicated that, far from withdrawing his troops and forsaking the English Army, as might have been inferred the night before from the direction taken in retreat by his outposts, Blücher was manoeuvring to give battle together with Wellington on that very day. Instead of the French having merely to dislodge from Sombreffe or Gembloux, the rearguard or an isolated corps, it was evident they had to encounter on the north of Fleurus the entire Prussian Army, and, as Blücher and Wellington evidently meant to operate in concert, the English would probably be encountered in force on the road to Brussels.

This meant the complete ruin of the plan conceived by the Emperor. He could not possibly beat Blücher's army to his right during the day, destroy Wellington's army to his left in the evening, and then march on Brussels that same night. However, Napoleon was in no wise disconcerted. With him, presumptions quickly changed into certainties. When he had once imagined a thing, that thing had to be as he fancied. Indeed, how many times had not fortune justified his previsions! On the morning of the 16th of June he believed that Blücher was retreating and that the road to Brussels was clear; therefore Blücher must be retreating and the road to Brussels *was* clear. The manoeuvres notified by Grouchy were merely demonstrations intended to put him on the wrong scent. It would be mere child's play to settle this handful of Prussian regiments, which was only as it were a screen, to mask the retreat of the bulk of their army. Besides, these views were evidently shared by Grouchy himself; for in the letter in which he mentioned the appearance of the enemy's columns towards Saint-Amand, he also announced that he was mustering his own troops to march on to Sombreffe, in accordance with the orders of the preceding night.

If at five that morning, Grouchy had suspected that the whole of Blücher's army was concentrating to the west of Sombreffe, he would not have prepared for a movement on this village, at the risk of sustaining a disastrous flank attack.

The Emperor did not modify his orders in any way. Far from changing anything, he wrote to Ney and Grouchy towards eight o'clock to reiterate his commands and to hasten their execution.[104] Knowing that his own aides-de-camp were better mounted than the officers of the chief of the staff, he entrusted one of the letters to La Bédoyère, the other to Flahaut, hoping that in this manner, his two lieutenants would receive his reiterated instructions even before those he had just dispatched through Soult. In these duplicates, the Emperor insisted on certain executive details, and disclosed, what Soult had concealed, that the object of this double movement on Sombreffe and on Quatre-Bras, was a night march on Brussels.

Between nine and ten in the morning, as Napoleon was about to start for Fleurus, an officer of lancers arrived from the left wing, to announce that the enemy was massing in great force in the direction of Quatre-Bras. Fearing lest the presence of these supposed masses should cause Ney to hesitate, as on the previous evening, the Emperor thought it necessary to reassure him and to repeat his orders once more. He directed the chief of the staff to write to him immediately to this effect; "As Blücher was in Namur yesterday, it is not likely that he has marched his troops towards Quatre-Bras. Therefore you need only attend to what comes from Brussels. Unite together the divisions of Counts Reille and d'Erlon, as well as the corps of Count de Valmy [Kellermann]; with these forces you are to beat and destroy all the enemy's corps which may happen to come in your way." In case of any eventuality occurring, the Emperor commanded Lobau to remain for the time being at Charleroi, so as to march the 6th Corps to the assistance of Ney if necessary. In pursuance of these orders Adjutant-Commandant Janin, deputy commander on Lobau's staff, was sent to Frasnes to ascertain the position of matters.

The Emperor arrived at Fleurus shortly before eleven o'clock. Here he found Grouchy, and this was no small surprise, as he imagined him to be already marching towards Sombreffe. The Marshal easily explained that in presence of the hostile masses which were taking up their positions to the north of Fleurus, he had been obliged to confine himself to the occupation of this village, which had been evacuated by the Prussians towards dawn. Napoleon passed along the line of outposts. At the end of Fleurus stood a brick mill, built in the shape of a tower and commanding the whole plain. He ordered his sappers to open a breach in its circular roof and to contrive a kind of *loggia* or balcony, which he ascended to inspect the positions of the enemy.[105]

From this platform Napoleon could clearly see that Blücher was solving the problem of separating the Allied armies for him, that he was committing the elementary error of concentrating in a forward area close to enemy troops massed for attack. The Emperor came down from his observation spot with grounds for hope that the campaign would soon be over.

At the first alarm, Blücher had hurriedly left Namur, and by four o'clock on the afternoon of the 15th of June he was at Sombreffe. He was confident he could get his four army corps drawn up behind the little stream of Ligny, by the early morning of the 16th; his attention had been directed to this position two months before by Major von Gröben, and from that time he had resolved he would fight the French at that very place, should they cross the Sambre at Charleroi. He was full of ardour and deemed himself invincible. "With my 120,000 Prussians," he wrote to his wife, "I would engage to take Tripoli, Tunis, and Algiers, if there were not the sea to cross!" However, on account of the inordinate extension of his cantonments, the Field-Marshal experienced some disappointments. At eleven a.m. on the 16th, Zieten's corps, which was reduced to 28,000 men by the losses of the previous evening, was the only one in line. The corps of Pirch I[106] (31,000 men) did not arrive at Sombreffe before noon; it was followed at a short distance by the corps of Thielmann (24,000 men). As for the 4th Corps, a letter from Bülow reached the general headquarters in the night, announcing that this corps could not possibly muster at Hannut (42 kilometres from Sombreffe) before the middle of the day. This meant a difference to Blücher of 30,000 bayonets. Nevertheless, he was determined to accept battle, especially as he counted on the cooperation, more or less effective, of the Anglo-Dutch army. Had not the two Commanders-in-Chief, at the interview of the 3rd of May at Tirlemont, agreed to lend each other mutual support, were Napoleon to take the offensive? And in the evening of the 13th June had not Wellington himself said to Blücher's emissary, Colonel von Pfüell: "My army will be concentrated at Nivelles or Quatre-Bras, according to circumstances, twenty-two hours after the first cannon-shot"?

There was something of diplomacy in these promises given by Wellington. The effect of Blücher's retreat on Liège would be to leave the English Army alone before Napoleon; in this case there would be no alternative for it but to accept battle, with vastly inferior forces, or to fall back on its base of operation, leaving Brussels unprotected. It was therefore most important that Blücher should remain in his position, and as an inducement to that end, Wellington could not but promise him his support. This promise of support he certainly hoped to give, but, practical Englishman as he was, Wellington meant to do so at his own time, and his own convenience, without imperilling in the least, the safety of his own army for the common cause. But might not the offensive movement of the French towards Charleroi be a mere demonstration calculated to draw off in that direction the masses of the Anglo-Prussians? Might not the Emperor, at the same time, bear down on Brussels with the bulk of his army, either by Maubeuge, Mons, and Hal, or by Lille, Tournay, and Ath? Such were Wellington's apprehensions, and fearing he might be decoyed into a false manoeuvre, he was determined not to move horse or man before he knew on which precise spot Napoleon would direct his principal attack.

Although on the 12th, 13th, and 14th of June numerous warnings respecting the concentration of the French Army on the frontier had reached the headquarters at Brussels; although on the 15th, as early as eight in the morning, Wellington had been informed through a letter from Zieten, that the Prussian outposts had been attacked at daybreak, at three in the afternoon that same day he had not issued a single order.

Müffling, the Prussian commissary attached to the English headquarters, having received a private letter from Zieten confirming these previous warnings, hastened to communicate it to the Duke. "If all is as Zieten thinks," replied Wellington, "I will concentrate on my left wing so as to act in concert with the Prussian Army; but should a portion of the enemy's forces march on Mons, I shall be compelled to concentrate on my centre. Therefore, before coming to any decision or taking any step, I must await news from my outposts at Mons. However, as the destination of my troops remains uncertain, while their departure is certain, I will give orders that they should be in readiness to march at any moment."

After such orders, which were not issued till the 15th of June, between six and seven in the evening, the troops had merely to assemble by divisions at Ninove, Ath, Grammont, Brussels, Braine-le-Comte, Nivelles, and to hold themselves in readiness to march at daybreak on the following day. The result was that when the French left wing had already gone beyond Gosselies, and its right had arrived within sight of Fleurus, Wellington, instead of directing his troops to the threatened point, was content to assemble them in isolated divisions within a parallelogram of thirty miles by twenty-seven. It seemed indeed as if he were bewildered and paralysed by the vision of Napoleon attacking in person at all points at once. At twelve o'clock, Blücher wrote to Müffling to say that Pirch's division was retiring on the left bank of the Sambre, and that he was going to concentrate at Sombreffe, where he intended to accept battle from the enemy. He added: "I am awaiting early news of the Duke of Wellington's concentration." This letter, which arrived about seven in the morning, was immediately laid before Wellington; it had no more power to influence him than the two previous despatches from Zieten. "The dispositions of the Field-Marshal are excellent," he said, "but I cannot decide anything till I know what is going on in the direction of Mons." At last he received the desired assurance that all was quiet there. A letter of General Dornberg, delivered between nine and ten o'clock, set his mind at rest on that score. He then determined on a partial concentration towards Nivelles, and not, as is claimed by his apologists, on a movement of the whole army upon Quatre-Bras.

After giving these orders, which could not possibly be executed before daybreak, owing to the lateness of the hour and the immense distance between the various cantonments, Wellington said to Müffling: "My troops are on the point of marching. But here in Brussels the partisans of Napoleon are beginning to agitate. We must reassure *our* friends. Therefore let us show ourselves at the Duchess of Richmond's ball, and we will be in the saddle by five to-morrow morning."

In Brussels, though there had been entertainments every night, this long-expected ball was as much a topic of interest as the impending campaign. It was known that the

Duchess of Richmond had made great preparations, that a vast barn which adjoined her palace or villa had been transformed into a sumptuous hall, where the guests were to dance to the sound of military music, and to which the *élite* of the British staff and of the cosmopolitan society in Brussels – Russian and German diplomatists, English peers, French *émigrés* – had been invited.[107]

One of the guests at this ball, Lady Hamilton Dalrymple, remembered that:

Although the Duke affected great gaiety and cheerfulness, it struck me that I had never seen him have such an expression of care and anxiety on his countenance. I sat next to him on a sopha a long time, but his mind seemed quite pre-occupied; and although he spoke to me in the kindest manner possible, yet frequently in the middle of a sentence he stopped abruptly and called to some officer, giving him directions, in particular to the Duke of Brunswick and Prince of Orange, who both left the ball before supper. Despatches were constantly coming in to the Duke.[108]

Another guest, Captain William Verner of the 7th Hussars recalled:

On the day appointed for the Ball, Captain Standish O Grady and I proceeded to Brussels in a cabriolet, we went in our usual uniform, taking with us Evening Dress for the Ball. We put up at an Hôtel de Swede in the lower town, which was at no great distance from the Duke of Richmond's residence, and having dined and dressed, we proceeded to the Ball.

Just as we entered the State room, and before we had time to go into the ball-room, we were met by

Lord George Lennox, who, knowing me intimately from having been brother Aide de Camp with his father, said, "Verner, the Prussians have been attacked and defeated, and I am going to order the Duke's horses, who is going off immediately." Hearing this startling news, I turned to O'Grady, saying: "Let us go into the room, to have it to say we were in the ball-room." It is scarcely necessary to say that the room was in the greatest confusion and had the appearance of anything but a ball-room. The officers were hurrying away as fast as possible, in order that nothing might prevent their joining their regiments. At this moment Lord Uxbridge came to the door and said, "You gentlemen who have engaged partners had better finish your dance, and get to your quarters as soon as you can." Turning to my companion I observed, "Standish, this is no time for dancing, let us try and secure a cabriolet without loss of time, and be off as soon as we can."[109]

Just as the Duke of Wellington sat down at the supper table, the Prince of Orange, who had been called away by an aide-de-camp, came back suddenly,

and whispered some minutes to his Grace, who only said he had no fresh orders to give, and recommended the Prince to go back to his quarters and go to bed. The Duke of Wellington remained nearly twenty minutes after this, and then said to the Duke of Richmond, "I think it is time for me to go to bed likewise"; and then, whilst wishing him good night, whispered to ask him if he had a good map in his house. The Duke of Richmond said he had, and took him into his dressing-room (his study), which opened into the supper-room. The Duke of Wellington shut the door and said, "Napoleon has *humbugged* me, by G—! he has gained twenty-four hours' march on me." The Duke of Richmond said, "What do you intend doing?" The Duke of Wellington replied, "I have ordered the army to concentrate at Quatre-Bras; but we shall not stop him there, and if so, I must fight him *here*" (at the same time passing his thumb-nail over the position of Waterloo). He then said adieu, and left the house by another way out.[110]

Wellington arrived at Quatre Bras at about ten o'clock on the morning of the 16.

He found Perponcher's division intrenched there instead of the advanced guard of Marshal Ney. His Grace apparently forgot that this was in direct contradiction to his own orders, and he condescended to congratulate General Perponcher on the step he had taken, as well as the Prince of Orange, who had had no hand in the matter. Then, after advancing near enough to Frasnes for a thorough inspection of the French outposts, he dispatched orders to Picton's division and the Brunswick corps, posted at Waterloo, to resume their march, and he wrote to Blücher that Quatre-Bras was occupied by a division of the Prince of Orange, and that the English Army was making for that point. The letter ended with these words: "I do not see many of the enemy in our front, and I await news from Your Excellency to decide my operations."

Wellington very soon changed his views. Thinking justly or unjustly, that ere several hours had elapsed he would be attacked at Quatre-Bras, he concluded that, instead of waiting for news which he could not control, he had better go and see things for himself, and arrange with Blücher by word of mouth. Towards one o'clock he joined the Field-Marshal on the heights of Brye.[111]

The Prussian dispositions did not impress Wellington, and years later Earl Stanhope recalled a conversation he had had on this point with the Duke and Lord Hardinge.

It is a curious thing, said Hardinge, that those who have written about Waterloo in poetry or prose, don't seem to be aware that the Duke came over before the battle to Quatre Bras and examined the Prussian position. I saw you, Sir, in the distance as horsemen, and I thought you must be English by the cut tails. You had, I think, several of your staff with you.

"Only William Gordon," interrupted the Duke.

Aye, but several orderlies, said Hardinge. When I saw the horses' cut tails I galloped towards you, trusting, if ever you should prove French, to the quickness of my horse to bear me off. When you had examined the Prussian position, I remember you much disapproved of it, and said to me, if they fight here they will be damnably mauled.

"I told them so myself, but of course in different terms. I said to them, everybody knows their own army best; but if I were to fight with mine here, I should expect to be beat."

Turning to me, and marking the back of one hand with the fingers of the other, he added: – "They were dotted in this way – all their bodies along the slope of a hill, so that no cannon-ball missed its effect upon them; they had also undertaken to defend two villages that were too far off, only within reach of cannon-shot. Now here is a general rule. Never attempt to defend a village that is not within reach of musketry. It was just that way the French lost the battle of Blenheim. They sent troops into places beyond the reach of musketry, and then couldn't get them back again."[112]

Wellington's discussions with the Prussian staff lasted rather more than an hour, and at the end of them the Duke promised Gneisenau that he would come to his assistance if he was not attacked himself at Quatre Bras. But when Wellington returned to Quatre Bras, his troops were in a dangerous position. They had come up to the front in the most appalling confusion – some had received orders, others had not; several regiments were marching in accordance with the original orders they had received and were not recalled in time to take part in the battle. Many officers had not even had time to change out of the uniforms they had worn at the Duchess of Richmond's ball.

Ney, however, was slow to take advantage of his opponents' disorganization; and it was not until a quarter to twelve that he acted in obedience to the despatch he had received from the Emperor three quarters of an hour before.

In an attempt to realize the instructions contained in this despatch, Ney sent General Reille's corps along the road to Quatre Bras; and at two o'clock he ordered him to clear the enemy out of the woods south of the crossroads; but Reille, who had served in the Spanish campaign, knew Wellington's habit of screening his men from view and warned Ney that they might well be facing the whole of the English army. Since he had not sent out patrols that morning Ney had no means of knowing that his 19,000 infantry, 3,000 cavalry, and 60 guns faced an Allied force of less than 8,000 infantry, 50 cavalry, and 14 guns. He could easily have overwhelmed Wellington; but he decided to approach the enemy with caution, and by the time the armies were actively engaged Wellington's reinforcements had come up to prevent Ney from breaking through the Allied front.

Napoleon anxiously listened for the opening roar of Ney's cannonade, which would assure him that Wellington's troops were held at Quatre Bras, before beginning his own attack on the main body of the enemy under Blücher. His plan was simple enough.

The Emperor determined to fix Blücher by a tremendous frontal attack, designed especially to wear down all Prussian resistance, attract Blücher's reserves to the front, and force the Prussian Marshal to engage them. Then, when Blücher's last closed body of troops was thrown in, the Prussian Army would become "the fixed point," around which Napoleon could manoeuvre his reserve masses and deal the exhausted Prussians a "knock-out" blow. Blücher's left would then become involved and entangled in the rout of his broken centre and right; and the terror-struck Army, a mere horde of rudderless fugitives, would steam away in panic-flight towards the Meuse. Thus he planned it.[113]

Napoleon would have liked to put this plan into immediate operation, but he had to await the arrival of Gérard's IV Corps.

As he was resolved to attack immediately, the Emperor was much perturbed to learn that Gérard's corps was not even in sight. He waited. Doubtless at the time, he believed that he had only a single army corps to deal with, and he had at his disposal Vandamme's corps, the 1st and 2nd Cavalry Corps, and in the second line, behind Fleurus, the Imperial Guard. He feared, reasonably enough, that during the course of the battle, they might be interrupted by the arrival of the bulk of the Prussian Army, which was then probably marching on Sombreffe.

Shortly after twelve, Gérard, who had preceded his army corps, reached the line of outposts with a small escort. Whilst seeking the Emperor, he came within musket-range of the enemy's cavalry. The Prussians charged; Gérard, thrown from his horse, was in imminent danger of being captured; he was saved by one of his aides-de-camp… Not before one o'clock did the head of Gérard's column appear…

It appears the Emperor had thought at first of attacking by Wagnelée and Saint-Amand, so as to throw the Prussians back on Sombreffe. But the position of their right suggested the idea of surrounding them, instead of driving them back. On this account he modified his previous orders to Ney. According to the instructions forwarded in the morning, the Marshal should have planted his men at Quatre-Bras and beyond it, and awaited the order to march on Brussels. At two o'clock Soult was commanded to write to him thus: "The Emperor bids me warn you that the enemy has assembled a body of troops between Sombreffe and Brye, and that Marshal Grouchy with the 3rd and 4th Corps will attack them at half-past two. His Majesty's desire is that you should also attack the forces in *your* front, press them closely and with great vigour, then draw back in our direction to help us to surround the corps I have just alluded to."…

"It is possible that three hours hence, the fate of the war may be decided," the Emperor said to Gérard. "If Ney executes orders properly, not a single piece of artillery of this army can escape him!" At a quarter past three, a second order was sent to Ney; it was more peremptory, more imperative than the first. "An hour ago," said Soult, "I wrote to you that the Emperor was about to attack the enemy in the position he has taken up between Saint-Amand and Brye, and now the engagement has become very decided. His Majesty charges me to say to you, that you are to manoeuvre immediately, so as to surround the enemy's right, and fall on his rear with might and main. This army is lost if you act vigorously. The fate of France is in your hands. Therefore do not hesitate one instant to execute the manoeuvre enjoined on you by the Emperor, and make for the heights of Saint-Amand and Brye."

As Soult was dispatching this order, Napoleon received a letter from Lobau informing him that, according to Colonel Janin's report, Ney had about 20,000 enemies before him at Quatre-Bras. The Emperor reflected that were these 20,000 men to defend themselves obstinately, it might prevent the Prince of the Moscowa from executing the desired movement against the Prussian Army at the proper time. Evidently his grand tactical combination might prove abortive. He did not flatter himself, as he has been unjustly accused of doing, that he could win two battles in the same day. The important point for him, was not to win a partial victory over Blücher and a partial victory over Wellington, but to hold the English in check, while he annihilated the Prussians. The Emperor thought that Reille's corps was all that Ney needed to overawe the English, and that d'Erlon's corps was amply sufficient to turn the Prussian right. He resolved to entrust to d'Erlon, the charge of executing the movement which he had previously entrusted to Ney, and from which he expected such momentous results. There was not an instant to lose. He sent directly to Count d'Erlon, the order to march with his army corps to the rear of the Prussian Army's right. Colonel de Forbin-Janson, who was told to transmit this order to him, was also directed to communicate it to Ney.

At the same time the Emperor, wishing to have all his forces well in hand, sent a message to Lobau, who was temporarily stationed at Charleroi, ordering him to march on Fleurus.

The battle was now in full force. Towards three o'clock, three cannon-shots fired at regular intervals by the battery of the Guard, gave the signal for attack. Vandamme did not even deign to prepare the way for the assault with his artillery, but hurled Lefol's division on Saint-Amand. To the tune of "*La victoire en chantant*," played by the band of the 23rd, the division marched forward in three columns, each of which was preceded by a swarm of tirailleurs. The ground in front of the enemy had been swept of every tree and hedge, and was now a sheet of ripening corn four or five feet high. The march through this surging mass was slow and difficult, and though the ears of wheat afforded cover to the tirailleurs, the columns were perfectly visible. It was on the latter, therefore, that the batteries directed their fire; cannon-balls ploughed down files of men eight deep. The Prussians were well under cover, ambushed in the houses or behind the embankments, and the dense hedges which surrounded the orchards. Fifty yards from the village, Lefol's soldiers sprang up to the first enclosures. Even point-blank discharges failed to check their rush; in less than a quarter of an hour's furious fighting, the enemy was driven from the orchards, the houses, the cemetery, and the church. But Jagow's Prussians rallied on the left bank of the brook, and soon after, supported by four battalions under Steinmetz, they prepared for a counter-attack. The battery of Steinmetz's division turned its fire upon Saint-Amand, where several buildings were seen bursting into flames, and the 24th Regiment crossed the stream at La Haye to take the French in flank. Vandamme ordered Berthézène's division to deploy to Lefol's left, and in accordance with the Emperor's previous instructions he ordered Gérard's division, stationed on the north of Wangenies, to attack Le Hameau and La Haye.

Whilst Lefol had been working towards Saint-Amand, Pécheux's division had advanced on Ligny in three attacking columns, under the fire of the Prussian batteries. The left and the central column carried the hedges and the fences at the entrance to the village; then they were repulsed, their ranks being terribly thinned by the fusillade which poured thick and fast, from the old castle and the nearest houses. The right column of the 30th of the line pushed forward. They fought up the hollow road, at the end of which rose the farm of La Tour, a building with walls like those of a fort, from which poured a perfect hailstorm of bullets; it penetrated as far as the square of the church. Here the regiment, literally surrounded by the enemy, concealed in the houses, in the cemetery, and behind the clumps of willows by the brookside, found itself the centre of a square of crossing fires. In a second the whole head of the column was overwhelmed, 20 officers and nearly 500 men fell, killed or wounded. Those who survived retired in disorder and strove to regain their original positions.

Two fresh attacks proved equally unsuccessful. Batteries from the 12th of the Guard came to reinforce Gérard's artillery, which until that time had merely answered the artillery of the enemy. They opened fire on Ligny. Cannonballs shattered the houses and ricochetted in the streets, the thatched roofs took fire and fell in; the conflagration burst out in ten different points at once. For the fourth time Pécheux's division, seconded now by a brigade from Vichery, marched against the Prussians. After an obstinate struggle and a succession of assaults on each several house, the French gained possession of nearly the whole upper portion of the village.

Ligny was formed of two streets which ran parallel to the Ligne, and were separated by it; the "rue d'En-Haut to the south, the rue d'En-Bas to the north." Between the two streets there were a few straggling cottages, the square of the church, and a vast common which sloped down to the Ligne in the form of a glacis. Expelled from the farm of La Tour and the rue d'En-Haut, the Prussians resumed their positions in the cemetery, in the church, in the houses, and on the square. Pécheux's soldiers advanced valiantly under crossing fires. Some dashed into the houses, others climbed the embankment around the cemetery. Thereupon a great body of the enemy which had rallied under shelter of the church, charged the French, who were thrown into great disorder owing to these repeated assaults. The little square, too narrow for such a number of combatants, became the scene of a terrific contest, a hand-to-hand struggle with no quarter given or sought, a frightful carnage! They shot at one another point-blank, they charged with their bayonets, with the butt ends of their muskets, and even fought with their fists. "The men," says a Prussian officer, "slaughtered one another as if they were impelled by personal hatred. It seemed as if each of them felt he was struggling with his own mortal enemy, and rejoiced that he had at last met with an opportunity of avenging himself. No man thought of flight or of asking for quarter."

The Prussians at last gave way. They abandoned the houses, the church, and the cemetery, and retired in disorder across the two bridges of the Ligne, and were pursued at the point of the bayonet. More than one was thrown into the muddy bed of the brook beneath. Still, on the left bank, the enemy, reinforced by the two last battalions of Henckel's division, re-formed and made a determined stand. The Prussians fired from the hedges and the fringe of willows that bordered the brook, whilst others fired over the heads of their comrades from the houses of the rue d'En-Bas, and from loop-holes opened in the walls of the large farm on the left bank. In spite of this terrible ladder of fires, the soldiers of the 30th and the 96th crossed the bridges and forced back the tirailleurs on to the houses. But Jagow brought up four battalions to the help of Henckel. The Prussians repulsed their assailants on to the right bank; they even attempted to cross to the other side by the two bridges. It was now the turn of the French to defend the brook. From either bank, the soldiers shot at each other at a distance of only four yards, through dense clouds of smoke. A threatening storm hung heavy in the air, and its sultry heat increased that of the continuous firing and of the flames kindled by the falling shells. Ligny became a fiery furnace. Amid the roar of the battle rose the piercing cries of the wounded who were being burnt alive beneath the flaming ruins.

Grouchy, on his side, had commenced his attack against the Prussian left. His cavalry had driven the enemy's posts from Boignée; and Hulot's division from Gérard's corps, which had passed under his direct command, threatened Tongrinelle and exchanged shots in front of Potriaux with Luck's Prussians.

On all points new batteries were being brought into action, and the firing waxed hotter and hotter. From La Haye to Tongrinelle, the fight waged on both banks of the Ligne, from which rose a curtain of fire and smoke, as if from a river in hell itself.[114]

At Quatre Bras Ney was meeting stiffened resistance from the gradually swelling numbers of Wellington's force. He decided to wait for d'Erlon's corps which he had been told was marching to his support. When, therefore, Colonel de Forbin-Janson arrived with Napoleon's message recalling d'Erlon for the operations against the Prussians, Ney was dismayed. He refused to accept the Emperor's decision, and dispatched an order to d'Erlon instructing him to return to Quatre Bras. D'Erlon was in sight of the Ligny battlefield when the order reached him, and he did not get back to Quatre Bras till darkness had fallen when he could serve no useful purpose.

Ney was left with the problem of fighting Wellington without the help of d'Erlon's troops; and while his reinforcements were marching away from him, Wellington's continued to arrive. By now Ney had committed all the men he had with him, except for Kellermann's cuirassiers and the cavalry of the Guard. He resolved to strike a decisive blow with these last reserves. Kellermann was sent for and told that the safety of France was at stake; nothing short of an overwhelming attack could retrieve the situation. Kellermann was to take his cavalry, continued Ney, and charge the English infantry, trampling them underfoot. Ney could not have chosen a man less disposed to dispute an order to charge, but he was beside himself with anger, and Kellermann was not. The general pointed out that the English could not be far short of 25,000, and that three of his four brigades had been left several miles in the rear on Ney's own instructions. Ney was adamant. "Charge with what you have," he replied, "I will send after you all the cavalry I can muster." It was now Kellermann's turn to be blinded by emotion. Enraged that his courage should be questioned, and made desperate by the nature of the order, to charge the English lines with 900 men, he quickly formed his brigade into a column. "I used great haste," he wrote in his report after the battle, "so as not to allow my men time to shrink, or to see the whole extent of the danger in front of them." Kellermann gave the order to charge, and led the way himself, sword unsheathed, at full gallop, 20 yards in front of the leading squadrons.

This supreme effort, this heroic sacrifice, might have turned the day if it had been properly supported. But Kellermann had launched his troops too suddenly for assistance to reach him, and Ney was slow in supporting the charge; he had, moreover, completely forgotten the cavalry of the Guard lying idle near Frasnes.

The 69th Regiment, who occupied a valley to the south of the cross roads, were the first to meet the cuirassiers. Halkett, the brigade commander, had noticed the French cavalry form up for the attack, and sent the 69th the order to form squares. Another officer, on the spot, was unable to see the French, and once more instructed the regiment to deploy in line; the 69th were doing this as the cavalry came upon them. They preserved their ranks in silence and fired when the charging horsemen were thirty yards away. The impetus of the cuirassiers was so great that they swept through the smoke and bullets without stopping, scattered the ranks of the infantry and captured their colours. Beyond the debris of the 69th was the square of the 30th, which Kellermann's troops charged without breaking. Next they dislodged the 33rd, which had not had time to form properly. Having penetrated Wellington's first and second lines, the horsemen swept up the slope of the valley without pausing to reform, cut down the gunners of a battery, broke through a square of Brunswickers, and finally arrived at the cross roads of Quatre Bras itself. Here they paid the penalty of their success; greatly outnumbered, they lay in the centre of the English positions, whose fire poured in on them. No support was sent to distract the enemy and when Kellermann's horse was shot beneath him, the cuirassiers panicked. In vain Kellermann rose from the ground and attempted to rally his men. The system of command, always so difficult to preserve in a cavalry charge, collapsed as the survivors wheeled round, deaf to Kellermann's shouts, and spurred their horses through the disordered but vehement fire of the infantry they had passed on their way to the cross roads. They reached their own lines out of control, and dragged several battalions of infantry after them in their flight. Fresh cavalry were sent forward, but they could make no impression on the English squares without the support of their own infantry.[115]

A young officer in one of these squares, Ensign Edward Macready of the 30th, has described this fighting:

The roaring of great guns and musketry, the bursting of shells, and shouts of the combatants raised an infernal din, while the squares and lines, the galloping of horses, mounted and riderless, the mingled crowds of wounded and fugitives (foreigners), the volumes of smoke and flashing of fire, struck out a scene which accorded admirably with the music. As we passed a spot where the 44th, the old chums of ours in Spain, had suffered considerably, the poor wounded fellows raised themselves up and welcomed us with faint shouts, "Push on old three tens – pay 'em for the 44th – you're much wanted, boys – success to you, my darlings." Here we met our old Colonel riding out of the field, shot through the leg; he pointed to it and cried, "They've tickled me again, boys – now one leg can't laugh at the other."

Hamilton showed us where our regiment was, and we reached it just as a body of lancers and cuirassiers had enveloped two faces of its square. We formed up to the left and fired away. The tremendous volley our square, which in the hurry of formation was much overmanned on the sides attacked, gave them, sent off these fellows with the loss of a number of men, and their Commanding-Officer. He was a gallant soldier, and fell while crying to his men, "*Avancez, mes enfants – courage – encore une fois, Français.*" I don't know what might have been my sensations on entering this field coolly, but I was so fagged and choked with running and was crammed so suddenly into the very thick of the business, that I can't recollect thinking at all, except that the poor Highlanders (over whom I stumbled or had to jump almost every step) were most provokingly distributed.

On our repulse of the cavalry, a General outside the square (said to be Sir Thomas Picton) thanked us warmly, and some seconds after, in still louder terms, damned us all for making such a noise, and asked if we had no Officers amongst us. We were half a minute in the square laughing and shaking hands with all about us, when we were ordered to pursue, and dashing out, were soon brought up by a line of tirailleurs, with whom we kept up a briskish fire… The cannonade and skirmishing were lively on both sides, while the heavy fire from the wood in our rear showed that the Guards and the enemy were hotly disputing it.[116]

–

Ney had hoped to make Kellermann's charge the preliminary to capturing Quatre Bras, but the sole result was that his hard-pressed line became weaker. The enemy began to exploit the French reverse, and Wellington was bringing up reinforcements to press the advantage home when Major Badus approached Ney with a verbal message from the Emperor.

Napoleon insisted that his orders to d'Erlon must be obeyed, whatever the circumstances at Quatre Bras. The fighting there was of small importance compared with the task of defeating the entire Prussian army. If Ney could do nothing more, he must be content with holding the English army to its present positions. Ney's face turned red with anger at this, and he flourished his sword in the air as he shouted at Badus. He ignored the Major's pleadings to countermand the order to d'Erlon, and breaking off the conversation abruptly, rushed into the middle of his disintegrating infantry, rallied them, and led them in a counter-attack.

It was Wellington's habit to advance only when sure of success, and although the French fought stubbornly to hold the ground they had won that afternoon, the numbers against them were too great to be withstood. The French began to fall back slowly until at nightfall the armies occupied the ground they had held at mid-day. Wellington had lost 4,700 killed and wounded and Ney 4,300.[117]

Neither commander had distinguished himself; less than half Wellington's army had arrived by the end of the battle, and Ney, who had known better than the Duke what was afoot, had concentrated only 22,000 of the 43,000 under his orders. Wellington's mistakes were not confined to his miscalculation and delay on the 15th, for he found himself at Quatre Bras with insufficient cavalry and artillery for the infantry that did arrive.

The task of housing and feeding the army had obliged the Duke to scatter his cantonments over a wide area, but there had been months in which to make sure that each detachment of infantry was established in the neighbourhood of enough guns and horsemen to constitute a balanced force. Yet when the fighting at Quatre Bras died down on the evening of the 16th Wellington had only a third of his artillery and a seventh of his cavalry.[118]

Ney, however, was not entirely to blame for the failure of the French command at Quatre Bras. As Harold Kurtz has said:

One might almost say that Napoleon knocked the weapons out of Ney's hands. The reason why after his first encounter with the Prussians Napoleon quickly felt the need for reinforcements is to be found in his own and nobody else's dispositions, for before setting out from Charleroi in the morning Napoleon had left the whole of the Sixth Army Corps under Lobau in that town, and had therefore to draw on his Left Wing for reinforcements since the distance between Charleroi and Ligny is ten miles. Like the First Corps, Lobau's Sixth did not fire a shot that day, but unlike the d'Erlon calamity this fatal omission was not due to the accidents of battle. Napoleon's estimate of his opponents bordered on contempt. He had never encountered Wellington in the field whereas Ney and Reille had, and it was only because Ney exerted himself to the limit of his abilities throughout the afternoon that Wellington was unable to give the Prussians any support. This and his orderly withdrawal to the Frasnes position in the face of superior forces were Ney's considerable achievement in the day's conflict. It meant that the aim of cutting off the Prussians from the British was still feasible if on the next day sufficient reinforcements reached Frasnes, and the Prussians were forced to retreat towards Lière and points east.

For the rest, the arrangements for the day show clearly that Napoleon had reverted to his old system of personal command which reduced initiative of Corps and Divisional Commanders to a minimum, making everything strictly subordinate to the Emperor's own movements and needs. It was typical of both Wings of the Army of the North that nobody moved without specific orders, an inhibition which caused delays at more than one vital moment. Ney himself was infected with this, as it were, pedestrian spirit which again was the result of the Emperor's express wishes; only when his own battle was fully developed did he take it on himself impetuously to ignore Napoleon's orders.[119]

So Ney had, at least, prevented Wellington from going to the aid of Blücher; and Napoleon had consequently been able, even without the help of the peripatetic d'Erlon, to give a severe mauling to the Prussian army.

Blücher's regiments fought bravely, but many of them were in battle for the first time and were not a true match for the French veterans.

An idea of the inexperience of many of the Prussian troops is given by Franz Lieber of the Colberg Regiment:

Presently the colonel rode up to us and said, "Riflemen, you are young, I am afraid too ardent: calmness makes the soldier; hold yourselves in order"; then he turned round: "March!" – and the dull half-suffocated drum, from within the deep column, was heard beating such delicious music. Now, at last, was all to be realized for which we had left our homes, had suffered so many fatigues, had so ardently longed. The bugle gave the signal of halt; we were in front of the village of Ligny.

The signal was given for the riflemen to march out to the right and left of the column, and to attack.

Our ardor now led us entirely beyond the proper limits; the section to which I belonged ran madly, without firing, towards the enemy, who retreated. My hindman fell; I rushed on, hearing well but not heeding the urgent calls of our old sergeant. The village was intersected with thick hedges, from behind which the grenadiers fired upon us, but we drove them from one to the other. I, forgetting altogether to fire and what I ought to have done, tore the red plume from one of the grenadiers' bearcaps and swung it over my head, calling triumphantly to my comrades. At length we arrived at a road crossing the village lengthwise, and the sergeant-major had now succeeded in his attempt to bring us somewhat back to our reason. There was a house around the corner of which he suspected that a number of French lay. "Be cautious," he said to me, "until the others are up," but I stepped round and a grenadier stood about fifteen paces from me; he aimed at me, I levelled my rifle at him. "Aim well, my boy," said the sergeant-major, who saw me. My antagonist's ball grazed my hair on the right side; I shot and he fell; I found that I had shot through his face; he was dying. This was my first shot ever fired in battle.[120]

Captain von Reuter, in command of a battery of Prussian artillery supporting Zieten's corps, indicates how desperate the afternoon's struggle was.

I had just returned to the right flank of my command, when our surgeon, Zinkernagel, called my attention to the red tufts on the shakos of the sharpshooters. I at once bellowed out the order, "With grape on the skirmishers!"

At the same moment both their lines turned upon us, gave us a volley, and then flung themselves on the ground. By this volley, and the bursting of a shell or two, every horse, except one wheeler, belonging to the gun on my left flank, was either killed or wounded. I ordered the horses to be taken out of one of my ammunition waggons, which had been emptied, and thus intended to make my gun fit to move again, while I meanwhile kept up a slow fire of grape, that had the effect of keeping the marksmen in my front glued to the ground. But in another moment, all of a sudden, I saw my left flank taken in the rear, from the direction of the Ligny brook, by a French staff officer and about fifty horsemen. As these rushed upon us the officer shouted to me in German, "Surrender, gunners, for you are all prisoners!" With these words, he charged down with his men on the flank gun on my left, and dealt a vicious cut at my wheel driver, Borchardt, … who dodged it, however, by flinging himself over on his dead horse. The blow was delivered with such good will that the sabre cut deep into the saddle, and stuck there fast. Gunner Sieberg, however, availing himself of the chance the momentary delay afforded, snatched up the handspike of one of the 12-pounders, and with the words, "I'll soon show him how to take prisoners!" dealt the officer such a blow on his bearskin that he rolled with a broken skull from the back of his grey charger, which galloped away into the line of skirmishers in our front.[121]

By early evening Blücher had been obliged to commit his reserves. But Napoleon was waiting only for the sound of Ney's cannon thundering in the rear of the Prussian army, before throwing his reserves, which were still intact, at its center.

The Guards on foot and on horseback, with Milhaud's cuirassiers, were already preparing for the attack, when an aide-de-camp from Vandamme arrived with grave tidings. Three miles to the left, a column of the enemy's forces, numbering from twenty to thirty thousand men, had been sighted; they appeared to be proceeding towards Fleurus with the intention of turning the Army's flank. Vandamme added that, on discovering these troops were hostile, Gérard's troops had abandoned La Haye and that he himself would be forced to evacuate Saint-Amand and to beat a retreat, unless the Reserve arrived in time to arrest this column.[122]

Vandamme was convinced that the column was an enemy one. But Napoleon felt that it must be French, though the only French troops it could have contained were those of Ney or d'Erlon, both of whom had been ordered to approach the battlefield through Saint-Amand and not Fleurus. Nevertheless, he felt compelled to suspend the attack of the Guard while awaiting the return of an aide whom he dispatched to identify the mysterious column. In the meantime, at the sight of the column closing in on their rear, General Lefol's division fled in panic and had to be forced back into position by their own artillery.

Blücher seized the opportunity to take advantage of the confusion and ordered a heavy attack; but the Guard beat him back, and Lefol rallied his men for the recapture of Saint-Amand.

Towards half-past six, the aide returned with the welcome news that the column approaching Fleurus was in fact d'Erlon's. It was marching in the wrong direction for its orders had arrived through an aide-de-camp who had misread the Emperor's penciled scrawl. At last Napoleon felt free to act.

The conclusive victory he had dreamed of the whole afternoon had escaped him; but for all that he might still win the battle and separate Blücher far from Wellington. He gave his orders for the final assault.

The reserve batteries opened fire upon the little hills above Ligny; the Old Guard deployed in columns; the squadrons of service, the 2nd Cavalry Division of the Guard, and Milhaud's cuirassiers prepared for the attack; Lobau's corps poured out of Fleurus. The cannonade ceased, the drums beat the charge, the seething mass moved off under the warm rain of the storm, with cries of "*Vive l'Empereur!*" The first column of the Guard (2nd, 3rd and 4th Grenadiers) penetrated to the west of Ligny; the second (1st Chasseurs and 1st Grenadiers) attacked the village to the east. Led on by Gérard, the soldiers of Pécheux and Vichery crossed the brook of La Ligne; and at last wrested from the Prussians, the farm of En-Bas and all the houses on the left bank. The fragments of Jagow's and Krafft's divisions attempted to re-form on the nearest slopes above the ravine. But Pécheux rushed from the midst of Ligny followed by Vichery and the first column of the Guard; from the right of the village deployed the 1st Grenadiers and the 1st Chasseurs, followed by Milhaud's cuirassiers; while up from the left with the Emperor himself advanced the service squadrons and the heavy cavalry of the Guard. The Prussians gave way at every point. Describing the rapidity and the effect of this irresistible attack, Soult wrote to Davout, "It was like a scene on the stage."

Blücher arrived at full gallop from La Haye. The rain had ceased and the wind was dispersing the straggling clouds. In the last rays of the setting sun, as they lit up for a minute the hills of Brye, he watched the disastrous retreat of his troops; and in the wide breach made in his line of battle, he saw the shaggy helmets of the Old Guard, the mounted dragoons towering above the rest, the dragoons turning round for a fresh charge, and in a glittering mass, Milhaud's 3,000 cuirassiers.

The veteran Blücher, as Major von Grolemann aptly said, "never considers himself vanquished, so long as he can continue the fight." He counted on Röder's cavalry, in reserve between Brye and Sombreffe; on the remnants of Henckel's division, which had been relieved at Ligny at six; on the Stülpnagel and Borcke divisions, which Thielmann ought to have detached from his army corps, to hold the French in check. But his orders had been misinterpreted; Henckel was already very close to Sombreffe, while Stülpnagel was still far from Ligny. As for Borcke's troops, Thielmann could not afford to diminish this his last reserve, so closely was he pressed in front by Grouchy; Hulot's division had carried Potriaux and was threatening Sombreffe; Exelmans' dragoons (Burthe's brigade) had routed Lottum's cavalry, had taken its cannon, and were advancing towards the Namur road. Röder's 32 squadrons alone were at his disposal. Blücher rode up to them and commanded them to charge. Lützow, the celebrated "partisan" leader in the war of 1813, hurled the 6th Uhlans against a square which he believed to be composed of the uniforms worn by the men. It was the 4th Grenadiers of the Guard. The uhlans were received by a line of fire at close quarters, and 83 of their men fell to the earth. Lützow was thrown from his horse and made prisoner. A charge of the 1st Dragoons and of the 2nd Landwehr of the Courmache, then a charge of the Brandeburg uhlans and of the Queen's dragoons, then a fourth one in which all the squadrons took part, were equally unsuccessful. The first were repulsed by the Old Guard, which had come to the first line to relieve Gérard's divisions; the others were sternly flung back by the dragoons of the Guard and Milhaud's cuirassiers. Till nightfall, the intermingled French and Prussian squadrons surged and struggled on the slopes of the hills, before the squares of the Guard, which continued their slow but steady advance towards the mill at Bussy.[123]

Blücher was himself almost taken prisoner. His chief of staff reported:

A charge of cavalry led on by himself, had failed; while that of the enemy was vigorously pursuing, a musket-shot struck the Field-marshal's horse; the animal, far from being stopped in his career by this wound, began to gallop more furiously, till it dropped down dead. The Field-marshal, stunned by the violent fall, lay entangled under the horse. The enemy's cuirassiers, following up their advantage, advanced; the last Prussian horseman had already passed by the Field-marshal; an adjutant alone remained with him and had just alighted to share his fate. The danger was great, but Heaven watched over him. The enemy, pursuing their charge, passed rapidly by the Field-marshal without seeing him; the next moment, a second charge of cavalry having repelled them, they again passed by him, with the same precipitation, not perceiving him any more than they had done the first time. Then, but not without difficulty, the Field-marshal was disengaged from under the dead animal and he immediately mounted a dragoon horse.[124]

–

Despite its bad outcome, this last effort by the Prussian cavalry did afford time for the infantry to draw off in squares and for most of the guns to be dragged away. Moreover, on the two wings the French advance was held. Spasmodic firing lasted until after midnight. Two rearguards clung to Brye and Sombreffe for several hours, while the rest of the army retreated on Wavre under Gneisenau's command.

Napoleon did not think it wise to pursue. Of Ney he had heard no news. Bülow's fresh corps must be near at hand. The two Prussian wings might still offer stiff resistance. So, having ordered Grouchy to have the enemy pursued at daybreak, he rode back to Fleurus for the night, and his troops bivouacked among 20,000 dead and wounded on the field of battle. No attempt was made to keep contact with the Prussians or to watch the line of their retreat.

Whereas French casualties totalled some 12,000, the Prussian losses were close on 16,000, and twenty-one guns; and during the night another 8,000 deserted their colours – men who, coming as they did from provinces formerly in the French Empire, were sympathetic towards Napoleon or at least of doubtful loyalty. Yet when Wellington's liaison officer at Prussian headquarters sent a report on the fighting, he was able to say that Blücher's men, though beaten, were ready to fight again.[125]

The decision to retreat on Wavre (whether or not taken solely because the town would serve as a good rallying point and because the Prussians could defend themselves on the far bank of the stream on which it stood) saved the Allied armies. For once at Wavre, sixteen miles to the north, the Prussians would be in a position to support the Duke's army on its establishment in position at Waterloo.

8

The Retreat of the Allied Armies

On the morning of June 16 Napoleon got out of bed at six o'clock and sat down to a leisurely breakfast. He seemed satisfied that the Prussians had been so badly mauled at Ligny the day before that there was no need to pursue them with rigor.

Count Claude-Pierre Pajol, who was in fact following large groups of deserters and stragglers who had lost their way, reported that the Prussians were falling back on Namur and Liège. But the Emperor took no steps to send out more cavalry to cover the retreat. Nor did he make any move to attack Wellington although he learned, while still at breakfast, that the Duke had not moved from Quatre Bras. He appeared to be tired out, sunk in apathy.

When Grouchy came to ask for orders, Napoleon told him to accompany him to the Ligny battlefield. The imperial coach drove away slowly across the furrows, jolting so violently that "tired as he was," says Grouchy, Napoleon got out and mounted a horse.

Having arrived at the height of the Bussy mill, the Emperor passed in front of his troops, which were standing in line, unarmed, at the head of their bivouacs. He stopped to congratulate the heads of the corps, the officers, and the men. So tremendous was the cheering on the part of the latter when they saw their Emperor, that the sound was heard at more than three kilometres' distance by

General von Gröben, who was in observation before Tilly. Having completed his round, the Emperor dismounted and conversed at some length with Grouchy, and several other generals on the state of public opinion in Paris, on the legislative assembly, and Fouché and the Jacobins. Some among his hearers admired the freedom of mind which he preserved under such grave circumstances, but others were slightly disturbed at seeing him waste his time talking politics, allowing his thoughts to wander on irrelevant topics, instead of on those which should have completely absorbed him. Grouchy did not, however, dare to question the Emperor on the operations he had designed for the day. Already, as they were starting from Fleurus, he had asked for his orders, and Napoleon had answered with some temper – "I will give them to you when I see fit."[126]

Orders had by now been given for an infantry division to support Pajol on the road to Namur and for a cavalry reconnaissance of Wellington's position; meanwhile Soult had sent a muddled set of instructions to Ney.[127]

But it was not until after eleven o'clock, when fresh dispatches reached the Emperor, that any constructive steps were taken to follow up the previous day's victory by exploiting the severing of the Allied front. Grouchy was now ordered to pursue the Prussians and report on their movements, while the bulk of the army was to march against the English at Quatre Bras under the Emperor himself.

At two o'clock Napoleon arrived at Quatre Bras.

Marshal Ney had not yet given the slightest sign of life. The Emperor sent orders direct, to the commanders of the corps in position before Frasnes. D'Erlon appeared at last with the head of his column of infantry. As the Emperor reproached him for having arrested his movement against the Prussian right on the previous evening, he answered that, being under the direct command of Marshal Ney, he had been obliged to obey the orders of his immediate chief. The Emperor, feeling time was too precious to be wasted in idle discussion, ordered Count D'Erlon to take the 1st Corps and instantly follow the cavalry on the Brussels road. Shortly after this, Ney arrived. In his letter of eight o'clock, Napoleon had already expressed his displeasure at Ney's extremely unskilful operations of the previous day. He did not return to the subject, but he very drily expressed his surprise that the orders he had forwarded to him that very morning, relative to the occupation of Quatre-Bras had not yet been executed. Ney excused himself on the ground that he believed Wellington's entire army was before him. In that case the Marshal might at least have ascertained the fact by sending out a vigorous offensive reconnaissance. Now he had not pushed forward a single squadron beyond his lines. He had proved as negligent, as heedless, as apathetic as on the morning of the 16th and the evening of the 17th.

It is true that Marshal Ney, through the carelessness of the chief of the staff, had remained all night in complete ignorance of the battle of Ligny. He could not have taken the offensive, until he had received the order of eight o'clock in the morning. Moreover this order was conditional. Even had Ney attacked then, it was likely the English would have effected their retreat with no more confusion than before, thanks to the masses of their cavalry. They would merely have started an hour sooner, and Ney would have occupied Quatre-Bras at noon; a sterile result, indeed. All the same, there would have been the chance that Wellington, under a vigorous assault, might have decided to fight in his positions. And this action Marshal Ney had done nothing whatever to bring about. For this the Emperor reproved him. Far more bitterly, no doubt, did he reproach himself for not having transferred, as early as seven o'clock that morning, the Guard and Lobau's corps from Ligny to Quatre-Bras. He had thus let slip the opportunity of annihilating the English Army. Wellington, with nearly all his troops still in position, with his line of retreat on Genappe endangered, his left over-powered by Napoleon, his front attacked by Ney, would have been forced to accept a battle which he would have virtually lost before it began.[128]

But the delay had given Wellington the chance to evade him, although several hours elapsed before the Duke heard of Blücher's retreat. Major-General Baron von Müffling, liaison officer between Wellington and Blücher, spent the whole night in ignorance of the movements of his chief:

During the night no intelligence reached me, which I attributed to the circumstance of the enemy's having rendered our communication on the chaussée insecure. At daybreak I sent out my aides-de-camp to seek, by crossroads, communication with the Prussian army. It was essential to know whether the Field-Marshal was in a condition to assume the offensive, which the Duke was now able to do, his whole army, including the corps of Prince Frederick of the Netherlands, being now assembled.

The Quartermaster-General of the English army had ridden out with the same object with which I had charged my aides-de-camp; he came back with the news that Field-Marshal Blücher had quitted the battlefield of Ligny. Of this there could be no doubt, for the Quartermaster-General, Colonel Delaney, had spoken with General von Zieten, who formed the rear-guard. The Duke and I were both much surprised at this news. The Duke looked at me, as if he wished to ask whether I had known the thing and concealed it from him on good grounds. But on my saying quite naturally, "This is probably the account which the officer, who was shot down, was bringing me," and adding, "but now you cannot remain here, my Lord," he immediately entered with me as usual on the measures to be taken.

As we knew nothing farther of the Prussian army but the direction of their retreat upon Wavre, – moreover that Bülow with his corps had taken no part in the battle, – and that Napoleon had not pursued, – I argued thus: "Things cannot be so bad; the Duke must retreat to a point on a line with Wavre. We shall then have intelligence of the state of Blücher's army; and until we have, nothing can be decided." This was quite the Duke's opinion: he had selected the position of Mont St. Jean; meanwhile came the question whether he should make his troops, weary with their preceding day's march, break up at once, or first let them rest and cook. He preferred the latter, but was apprehensive that his rearguard might in consequence be involved in severe fighting. I could not share this apprehension. The enemy had only bivouacked on the 16th (the previous day), in the dusk of the evening; and in such cases it was always Napoleon's custom in his wars in Germany, to allow his troops first to cook, and to break up at ten the next morning.

The English cavalry, part of which had only arrived that morning at Quatre Bras, must at any rate feed first;

and could then, together with the whole of the horse-artillery, form the rear-guard, for which the ground was well adapted.

The Duke allowed his people to cook, at the risk of sharp fighting on the part of his rear-guard. At nine o'clock an officer arrived from Wavre, with verbal messages to me, just as I was sitting with the Duke on the ground. I knew that this officer spoke French and English, and therefore indicated to him by a motion of my hand that he might say to the Duke what he had to report to me. He did so. The Duke put some questions, received sensible and satisfactory replies, and by these was induced to declare to me that he "would accept a battle in the position of Mont St. Jean, if the Field-Marshal were inclined to come to his assistance even with one corps only."[129]

By ten o'clock the Allied infantry had skillfully broken contact behind a cavalry screen and had marched away unmolested. At first their retreat had been easy enough. But by eleven Napoleon at Quatre Bras had realized how much time he had wasted. He had the vision of a lost victory before his eyes.

He wished to seize it still. He imagined that by hastening his march, he might be able to join Wellington and compel him to make a stand. Finally, he gave orders that Reille, then Lobau, then the Guard should rapidly follow the 1st Corps and the light cavalry up the Brussels road; they were to be flanked by the chasseurs of the Domon and the cuirassiers. He himself, with the service squadrons and the mounted battery of the Guard, galloped to the head of the column to kindle fresh vigour in the pursuit.[130]

How different the retreat became once Napoleon had roused his army is well shown by Captain Mercer, whose battery was with Lord Uxbridge, commander of the cavalry that formed the rear guard.

The sky had become overcast since the morning, and at this moment presented a most extraordinary appearance. Large isolated masses of thundercloud, of the deepest, almost inky black, their lower edges hard and strongly defined, lagging down, as if momentarily about to burst, hung suspended over us, involving our position and everything on it in deep and gloomy obscurity; whilst the distant hill lately occupied by the French army still lay bathed in brilliant sunshine. Lord Uxbridge was yet speaking, when [Napoleon], immediately followed by several others, mounted the plateau I had left at a gallop, their dark figures thrown forward in strong relief from the illuminated distance, making them appear much nearer to us than they really were. For an instant they pulled up and regarded us, when several squadrons, coming rapidly on the plateau, Lord Uxbridge cried out, "Fire! – Fire!" and, giving them a general discharge, we quickly limbered up to retire, as they dashed forward supported by some horse-artillery guns, which opened upon us ere we could complete the manoeuvre... The first gun that was fired seemed to burst the clouds overhead, for its report was instantly followed by an awful clap of thunder, and lightning that almost blinded us, whilst the rain came down as if a waterspout had broken over us. The sublimity of the scene was inconceivable. Flash succeeded flash, and the peals of thunder were long and tremendous; whilst, as if in mockery of the elements, the French guns still sent forth their feebler glare and now scarcely audible reports – their cavalry dashing on at a headlong pace, adding their shouts to the uproar. We galloped for our lives through the storm, striving to gain the enclosures about the houses of the hamlets, Lord Uxbridge urging us on, crying, "Make haste! – make haste! for God's sake gallop, or you will be taken!" We did make haste, and succeeded in getting among the houses and gardens, but with the French advance close on our heels... Away we went, helter-skelter – guns, gun-detachments, and hussars, all mixed *pêle-mêle*, going like mad, and covering each other with mud, to be washed off by the rain which, before sufficiently heavy, now came down again as it had done at first in splashes instead of drops, soaking us anew to the skin, and, what was worse, extinguishing every slow match in the brigade. The obscurity caused by the splashing of the rain was such, that at one period I could not distinguish objects more than a few yards distant. Of course we lost sight of our pursuers altogether, and the shouts and halloos, and even laughter, they had at first sent forth were either silenced or drowned in the uproar of the elements and the noise of our too rapid retreat; for in addition to everything else the crashing and rattling of the thunder were most awful, and the glare of the lightning blinding.[131]

This appalling weather did not, of course, favor a fast pursuit.

The French historian Commandant Henry Lachouque, in emphasizing Grouchy's difficulties, has described the conditions on the road to Gembloux:

The track (for it could not be called a road in 1815) is a river of slush: the sappers go in front of the artillery, which sinks in the mud, and struggle to drag it forward.

As for the infantry, whose shakos are sodden, they march across fields, take two steps forward and one back in the rye already trampled down by the Prussians.

The men, soaked to the skin, slip, lose their shoes, fall, grumble, swear. If this is the condition of the men one can imagine the plight of the horses as under the whip of the drivers they try to drag the guns, the ammunition wagons and the rickety old carts. Painfully they cover no more than two and a half kilometres an hour.[132]

–

Again fate was against the Emperor; for rarely has this storm been given sufficient credit for the part it played in retarding the Emperor's fiery, if tardy, pursuit of his foe. Given good weather, then June 17 might have seen very different happenings – even in spite of Ney's early and disastrous failure. For the sodden roads and fields delayed the French advance tremendously; otherwise Wellington would probably have been attacked towards evening, so as to ensure that he was immobilised; and then by 8 a.m., on June 18, at latest, the great battle would have been begun. It might have been as bloody as Eylau, but it would have been far more decisive, and a French victory.[133]

The weather, which had reduced the roads to quagmires, brought Grouchy's pursuit of the Prussians to a halt two hours before dark. This pursuit had never been carried on with the dash of Napoleon's. Instead of pressing on to locate Blücher's main force and interposing his men between it and the Emperor's right wing. Grouchy covered less than ten miles during the whole of that day. Very different was the behavior of his quarry, Field-Marshal

Blücher, as an officer in the Westphalian Landwehr squadron reported:

In very bad weather we set off again in the morning to cross the Dyle. The mood of the troops was certainly grave, but not in the least disheartened, and even if one could have detected that we were on a retreat rather than a victory march, the bearing of all but a few isolated units was still very good. "We have lost once, but the game is not up, and to-morrow is another day," remarked a Pomeranian soldier to his neighbour who was grumbling, and he was quite right. The firm bearing of the army owed not a little to the cheerful spirit and freshness of our seventy-four-year-old Field-Marshal. He had his bruised limbs bathed in brandy, and had helped himself to a large schnapps; and now, although riding must have been very painful to him, he rode alongside the troops, exchanging jokes and banter with many of them, and his humour spread like wildfire down the columns.[134]

Zieten and Pirch I reached Wavre first. Thielmann's corps arrived at eight o'clock and took up positions to the north of the town. Bülow established himself to the east. At 11 o'clock a dispatch from Müffling confirmed the news that Wellington had taken up his line of battle at Mont-Saint-Jean, a ridge to the south of the village of Waterloo, and would fight Napoleon there provided he could count on the assistance of one Prussian corps.

Gneisenau still hesitated. "If the English should be defeated," he objected judiciously enough, "they themselves would be utterly destroyed." Blücher succeeded at last in convincing his all-powerful chief of the staff. "Gneisenau has given in!" he said with a triumphant expression to Colonel Hardinge, the English military attaché. "We are going to join the Duke." To Wellington he wrote; "Bülow's corps will set off marching to-morrow at daybreak in your direction. It will be immediately followed by the corps of Pirch. The 1st and 3rd Corps will also hold themselves in readiness to proceed towards you. The exhaustion of the troops, part of which have not yet arrived, does not allow of my commencing my movement earlier."

This letter reached Wellington toward two o'clock in the morning, at his headquarters at Waterloo, a village situated a league in the rear of the first English lines. Now that he could rely on the assistance of the Prussians, Wellington determined to accept battle.[135]

-

Thus Blücher had answered Wellington's request for assistance, by pledging himself to send two corps to Mt. S. Jean; this was double the force asked for originally by Wellington.

There can be no doubt now that Wellington gravely underestimated his task; and the result achieved by Napoleon at Ligny should have enlightened him on this point. For had Blücher sent only one corps, as he was actually asked to do, this reinforcement would not have changed the issue of the big battle, and the supporting troops must have shared in Wellington's rout, and contributed to the magnitude of the disaster. Marshal Blücher's previous personal experience of Napoleon's powers was almost invaluable. The Prussian Marshal realised that the task which the Duke of Wellington had consented so loyally to undertake, was one that was likely to prove far more arduous and trying than the Duke could possibly conceive. Also the drubbing which the Emperor, handling inferior numbers, had administered in an afternoon to the Prussian Army at Ligny, had burned the impression even more deeply into Blücher's mind. It was no time to run any further risk; a decision must be obtained, and as soon as possible. Fortunately therefore, for the Allies, Blücher rose to the height of the situation, and decided to send every available man to co-operate at Mt. S. Jean. Further, despite the injuries he had received at Ligny, the indomitable Marshal intended to march at the head of his army to Mt.-S.-Jean; and he meant to drive his corps against Napoleon's open and exposed right flank, should the latter attack Wellington on June 18. But if the 18th passed without any fighting then Blücher suggested (through Müffling, the Prussian Attaché on Wellington's Staff) that the two combined armies should attack the French on June 19. Such invincible determination, on the part of the commander of a beaten army, was well nigh without parallel, and indeed requires no comment.[136]

Wellington's troops took up their positions at Mont-Saint-Jean, dirty, wet, and hungry. William Gibney, Assistant Surgeon of the 15th Hussars, thought:

There was no choice; we had to settle down in the mud and filth as best we could, and those having any provisions about them were fortunate. As I had obtained a bit of tongue (but whether cooked, or only smoked and salted, I know not) in the morning, and had a thimble-full of brandy in my flask, I was better off than many, and finishing the somewhat queer-tasting food; with others I looked about for a drier place to lie down and rest the weary limbs. It was all mud, but we got some straw and boughs of trees, and with these tried to lessen the mud and to make a rough shelter against the torrents of rain which fell all night; wrapping around us our cloaks, and huddling close together, we lay in the mud and wooed the drowsy god, and that with tolerable success. For, notwithstanding rain, mud, water, cold, and the proximity of the enemy, most of us managed to sleep. As for myself, I slept like a top, but I had become seasoned to the work, and was young and strong.[137]

Captain Mercer, however, with the rain pouring through his tent in streams, could not sleep, so he got up and found that his resourceful men

had managed to make a couple of fires, round which they were sitting smoking their short pipes in something like comfort. The hint was a good one and at that moment my second captain joining me, we borrowed from them a few sticks, and choosing the best spot under the hedge, proceeded to make a fire for ourselves. In a short time we succeeded in raising a cheerful blaze, which materially bettered our situation. My companion had an umbrella (which, by the way, had afforded some merriment to our people on the march); this we planted against the sloping bank of the hedge, and seating ourselves under it, he on one side of the stick, me on the other, we lighted cigars ... Whilst so employed a rustling in the hedge behind attracted our attention, and in a few minutes a poor fellow belonging to some Hanoverian regiment, wet through like everybody else, and shivering with cold, made his appearance, and modestly begged permission to remain a short time and warm himself by our fire.

He had somehow or other wandered from his colours, and had passed the greater part of the night searching for them, but in vain. At first he appeared quite exhausted, but the warmth reinvigorating him, he pulled out his pipe and began to smoke. Having finished his modicum and carefully disposed of the ashes, he rose from his wet seat to renew his search, hoping to find his corps before daylight, he said, lest it should be engaged. Many thanks he offered for our hospitality; but what was our surprise when, after fumbling in his haversack for some time, he pulled out a poor half-starved chicken, presented it to us, and marched off. This was a god-send, in good truth, to people famished as we were; so calling for a camp-kettle, our prize was on the fire in a twinkling. Our comrades in the tent did not sleep so soundly but that they heard what was going on, and the kettle was hardly on the fire ere my gentlemen were assembled round it, a wet and shivering group, but all eager to partake of our good fortune – and so eager that, after various betrayals of impatience, the miserable chicken was at last snatched from the kettle ere it was half-boiled, pulled to pieces, and speedily devoured. I got a leg for my share, but it was not one mouthful, and this was the only food I had tasted since the night before.[138]

The French were in even worse straits than the Allied soldiers. Many of them came into the lines in the early hours of the morning. A sergeant of the guard complained:

The tracks were so deep in mud after the rain that we found it impossible to maintain any sort of order in our columns. In looking for easier paths a large number of men went astray, and not until daybreak did they all manage to rejoin the columns.

The Emperor had selected the farm of Le Caillou, right on the main road itself, as Headquarters. One by one the regiments of his Guard came up, but each arrived there in a state of exhaustion. During all the marches and countermarches of that frightful night there was a real helter-skelter. Regiments, battalions, even companies became muddled; and in complete darkness and drenching rain people were hunting vainly for their generals or their officers. We had constantly to push our way through thick hedges or deep ravines. Furthermore, grumbles and curses were levelled on all sides against the generals on whom was laid the blame, quite unjustly, for all this hardship. In fact, discontent rose to such a pitch that repeated shouts of "*A la trahison!*" were heard.

Driven to the limit of their patience even more than of their strength, a crowd of grenadiers and light infantry dashed into any buildings they came across, some seeking shelter from the dreadful ordeal, others a bivouac where they could dry themselves and rest for a few hours.

At about midnight the bulk of our regiment arrived, despite everything, in an orchard in which stood a farm only just converted into the headquarters of the Guard. This was definitely our bivouac. And about time too! What a day and a night!

Our greatcoats and our trousers were caked with several pounds of mud. A great many of the soldiers had lost their shoes and reached the bivouac barefoot.[139]

The farm at Le Caillou, where Napoleon had established his headquarters, was a mile and a half south of La Belle Alliance. Here, at dawn, he was shown a dispatch from Grouchy which indicated that not all the Prussian army was retreating on Liège. At least part of it was making for Wavre: "perhaps it may be inferred that this part is going to join Wellington."[140] *But still convinced that the Prussians were in no condition to fight and that even if they were, Grouchy's 30,000 men would certainly keep them at bay while he disposed of Wellington, Napoleon awaited the coming day with confidence.*

9

Waterloo: Morning

Dawn found both armies in a pitiable state. From the Allied side Sergeant-Major Cotton reported:

The rain descended in torrents, succeeded, as the morning advanced, by a drizzling shower which gradually ceased. Soon after the break of day, all who were able were on the move. Many, from cold and fatigue, could not stir for some time; fortunately, on most of us the excitement was too powerful to allow this physical inconvenience to be much felt... Some were cleaning arms, others fetching wood, water, straw, etc., from Mont-Saint-Jean... Some trying, from the embers of our bivouac, to light up fires, many of which had been entirely put out by the heavy rain. At this time there was a continual irregular popping along the line, not unlike a skirmish, occasioned by those who were cleaning their firearms, discharging them when practicable; which was more expeditious and satisfactory than drawing the charges. Our bivouac had a most unsightly appearance: both officers and men looked blue with the cold; and our long beards, with our wet and dirty clothing drying upon us, was anything but comfortable.[141]

Only a few regiments enjoyed an adequate breakfast. Most men had nothing but biscuits, rum stirred up in oatmeal, or perhaps a little soup. They began to take up their positions about six o'clock. Wellington rode along the front refreshing his memory of the ground.

The plateau of La Belle Alliance and of Mont-Saint-Jean, each with an average elevation of 400 feet, run nearly parallel to each other from west to east. They are separated by two twin valleys, which the main road from Charleroi to Brussels crosses perpendicularly from south to north. These two valleys are narrow and not very deep; from La Belle Alliance inn to the ridge of Mont-Saint-Jean there is only the distance of 1,300 yards as the crow flies, and the lowest levels of the valley are computed at 300 feet. East of the main road, lies the valley of Smohain, which is very broken and grows continually narrower until it becomes a ravine and is lost in the bed of the brook of Ohain; the other valley, that of Braine-L'Alleud, stretches to the west with numerous undulations, and crosses the Nivelles road, cutting it obliquely. This second road runs from S.S.W. to N.N.E. Having gained the plateau of Mont-Saint-Jean, it branches off at an acute angle to the hamlet of the same name on the main road, which three miles farther up, passes through the village of Waterloo, built in a hollow of the forest of Soignes; then it continues towards Brussels, through the wood.

Seen from La Belle Alliance, the main road to Brussels which goes down and up again in a straight line, seems very steep. But this is an illusion of perspective. In reality the inclination of the slope is not great. A horseman can ascend it at an even gallop, without straining his horse or putting it out of breath. However, to the right as well as to the left of the road, the ground is extremely uneven, and, in many places, becomes steep. It is an infinite succession of mounds and hollows, of depressions and banks, of furrows and hillocks. Nevertheless, when viewed from a height, the double valley has the aspect of a plain extending without any marked depressions between two low hills. It is necessary to walk over the ground, to perceive the constantly undulating formation of the ground, similar to the billows of a swelling sea.

The road from Ohain to Braine-L'Alleud, which skirts the ridge of the plateau of Mont-Saint-Jean where it cuts the Brussels road at a right angle, covers, with a line of natural obstacles, nearly the entire line of the English positions. To the east of the main road, this road is on a level with the ground, but a double border of high, thick hedges renders it inaccessible to cavalry. To the west the ground rises sharply, the Ohain road winding between two embankments of from five to seven feet in height; it forms thus, for a distance of 400 yards, a formidable covering trench. Then it regains its level and continues its course without presenting any further obstacles save a few scattered hedges. Behind the ridge, which forms a screen, the ground declines northward, a tendency favourable to its defence. The troops of the second line and the reserves were thus hidden from the telescopes of the enemy and were partly sheltered from their fire.

Scattered over a radius of two miles, half-way up the hill and in the levels beneath – the chateau of Hougoumont with its chapel and its vast dependencies, its park surrounded by walls, its orchard enclosed by a barrier of hedges, and the copses which guarded its approach from the south; the farm of La Haye-Sainte, a stone building flanked by a hedge-girt orchard and a terraced kitchen-garden; the hillock overlooking the excavation of a sand-pit which was protected by a hedge; the Papelotte farm; the large farmhouse of La Haye; and last of all the hamlet of Smohain – formed so many bastions, "covered lodgments and small forts," in front of the position.[142]

–

The English commander's defensive position, some three miles long, was chosen with fine tactical judgment, and every part of it had been long before studied and charted. There were no field-works, except some abatis across the two chaussées, but the slope formed a natural glacis, peculiarly well adapted to artillery fire; and from the elevated-English position could be observed all the movements of the French forces, while the reverse slope of the crest enabled Wellington to hide his troops and markedly protect them from the French guns.

Wellington was well aware in what a deadly manner Napoleon could use artillery, and his screening his troops behind the crest of the hill showed keen appreciation of tactical values. He had made his right the stronger flank and posted his reserve near by it, because he continued to fear an attack from there; and his left remained the weaker, because he expected Blücher to sustain it.

As Napoleon claimed, the British position was subject to the defect of having its line of retreat along a single road through a forest; and though the woods were open enough for foot and horse to march on either side of the road, yet in case of disaster, this was manifestly a peril. Some accounts state that the road was much clogged up by the oncoming train and by broken-down wagons and ambulances; and at some stage of the battle this was altogether probable. In later days Wellington said that the road was ample, and that he could also have retired by his right towards the coast; that the French could not have followed him, as he could have defended the outlet of the forest, and this especially as the Prussians would have been upon the enemy's heels. But none the less, Wellington had never yet felt the impact of Napoleon's tremendous blow, and as the 18th of June might have opened clear, and with ground hard enough for Napoleon to move to the attack shortly after daylight, the Prussians being eliminated, the position must be said to have had the defect mentioned. Although the question is a pure hypothesis, the risk did exist…

On the English left, were Picton's and part of Cole's British divisions, and Perponcher's Belgian division, with the British cavalry of Vivian and Vandeleur on the extreme left, partly deployed, partly in column; one hundred twenty guns were on this wing, of which Picton seems to have exercised the command. The villages in front of the left were held by Bernard, with over three thousand men. The infantry was behind the crest, fairly covered from the fire which would open the battle, except Bylandt's [Dutch-Belgian] brigade which was badly posted near the chaussée on the front slope, where the French artillery could reach it.[143]

It had been posted there due to a misunderstanding of Wellington's order to his unit commanders to dispose their troops according to the usual practice, Bijlandt's brigade had taken this to mean the usual continental practice, that is to say, on the forward slope of the ridge.

Behind the left wing near the chaussée was Ponsonby's cavalry. The auxiliaries held several places in the line. The centre, under Orange, was protected by the sunken road, and began at the chaussée with Alten's division, La Haye Sainte being well prepared for the battle. On Alten's right came Cooke's division, a part of whose troops were in Hougoumont. The right was under Hill, and Clinton's division and the Brunswickers ran from Merbe Braine westerly, Chassé's Dutch-Belgian division out as a flying right wing at Braine l'Alleud. Behind the centre were Somerset's heavy cavalry near the chaussée, mostly in close column, and the Dutch-Belgian cavalry on his right rear. This made a heavy mass of cavalry behind the right. The artillery was distributed all along the line. The reserve was of foot, thirteen thousand strong.[144]

–

By holding the well-situated posts of Hougoumont, La Haye Sainte, and the sand-pit in his immediate front, and down the forward slope of the hill, the Duke expected to gain further time and also to embarrass the attack; for until these advanced posts were mastered a serious attack on the whole of the main position would be very difficult to deliver. Hence Wellington told off a garrison to each of these posts. Hougoumont he considered to be the most important (in truth, he was still obsessed with covering Brussels from the direction of Mons, and his line to the sea possessed great attractions), hence he garrisoned the Château with seven companies taken from the three regiments of English Guards, a company of Hanoverians, a battalion of the Nassau Regiment, and one hundred men from the Lüneburg Battalion (Kielmansegge's Brigade), all being placed under the command of a trusted Guards' officer – Colonel Macdonnell.

But the real tactical key to the position, in a frontal action, was undoubtedly the farm of La Haye Sainte. It was placed but a very short distance in front of the Allied centre, the spot Napoleon most desired to reach, and practically afforded a covered way to within one hundred yards of the crest of the ridge. The post was a large and important one, and would have accommodated quite one thousand men. However, its importance was not recognised; for at the outset Major Baring and only the 2nd Light Battalion of the King's German Legion (some 376 men in all) were allotted to it for its defence.[145]

This, however, was a minor tactical error. Otherwise, apart from Bijlandt's brigade, Wellington's dispositions were admirable. In leaving 17,000 men and 30 guns eight miles from the battlefield, however, he had made a strategical mistake that nearly all military historians have condemned. Still so concerned for his lines of communication with the sea, he had preferred to detach a fifth of his army to prevent a movement by the French that would have contradicted the whole purpose of Napoleon's strategy.

As General Brialmont observed:

It is inconceivable that Wellington should have credited his adversary with a plan of operation which could only tend to hasten the junction of the Allied Armies, because from the outset of the campaign, Napoleon had been evidently manoeuvring to prevent this junction.[146]

These 17,000 troops Wellington could ill spare. For not only was he (with 67,661 men and 156 guns) outnumbered by Napoleon's 71,947 men and 246 guns, but the quality of most of his troops was inferior. Even the British battalions were, in general, a scratch collection of 2nd battalions, while the well-officered battalions of the King's German Legion were all under strength since the non-German troops had been discharged in 1814. Thousands of the Dutch and Belgians had previously served under Napoleon and were to give way or desert during the course of the battle.

We were, take us all in all, a very bad army. Our foreign auxiliaries, who constituted more than half our numerical strength, with some exceptions, were little better than a raw militia – a body without a soul, or like an inflated pillow, that gives to the touch and resumes its shape again when the pressure ceases – not to mention the many who went clear out of the field, and were only seen while plundering our baggage in their retreat.[147]

Napoleon seemed to have no doubt that this battle would easily be won.

About eight o'clock the Emperor had breakfasted at the Caillou farm with Soult, the Duke of Bassano, Drouot, and several general officers. After the meal, which had been served on silver plate with the Imperial arms, the maps of Ferrari and Capitaine were spread out on the table. The Emperor said; "The army of the enemy is superior to ours by more than one-fourth. We have nevertheless ninety chances in our favour, and not ten against us."[148]

Some of his generals appeared to doubt this, but when Soult repeated his belief that part of Grouchy's force should be recalled if they were to win,

Napoleon, exasperated, replied to him roughly: "Because you have been beaten by Wellington, you consider him a great general. And now I tell you that Wellington is a bad general, that the English are bad troops, and that this affair is nothing more serious than eating one's breakfast."

"I earnestly hope so," said Soult.

Shortly after, Reille and Jérôme entered Le Caillou. The Emperor asked Reille his opinion of the English Army, which this general was in a position to give, since he had had many a contest with it in Spain. Reille answered; "Well posted, as Wellington knows how to post it, and attacked from the front, I consider the English Infantry to be impregnable, owing to its calm tenacity, and its superior aim in firing. Before attacking it with the bayonet, one may expect half the assailants to be brought to the ground. But the English Army is less agile, less supple, less expert in manoeuvring than ours. If we cannot beat it by a direct attack, we may do so by manoeuvring." For Napoleon, who had never personally fought a pitched battle against the English, the opinion of a veteran of the Spanish wars was worthy of consideration. But he was probably irritated with Reille for having spoken so freely, without reflecting that the generals who heard him might be discouraged, and therefore he did not appear to attach the least importance to his opinion. He broke off the conversation by an exclamation of incredulity.

The weather had cleared, the sun was shining, a rather brisk wind, a drying wind as sportsmen call it, was beginning to blow. Artillery officers came to report that they had inspected the ground, and that it would soon be possible to manoeuvre the pieces. Napoleon called for his horses...

The Emperor, skirting at full trot the flank of the columns which were still debouching from Genappe, rode to the front of La Belle Alliance, in the very line of the tirailleurs, in order to observe the enemy's positions. His guide was a Fleming named Decoster. This man owned a little inn on the roadside between Rossomme and La Belle Alliance; he had been taken in his own house at five o'clock in the morning and brought before the Emperor, who required some native of the country. The maps which Napoleon used in his campaigns indicated the features of the ground only in a very general and summary way, and Napoleon nearly always took a guide. Decoster had been carefully kept in sight, for he seemed anxious to escape; on departing from Le Caillou he had been hoisted on to a charger whose saddle was attached by a long strap to the saddle-bow of a chasseur of the escort. Naturally he cut a very sorry figure during the battle and amid the flying balls and bullets. He wriggled in the saddle and kept ducking his head and bending over his horse's neck. The Emperor said to him once; "Now, my friend, do not be so restless. A musket-shot may kill you just as well from behind as from the front, and will make a much worse wound." According to local traditions, either through imbecility or through malice, Decoster gave false information throughout the whole day. Another guide as well, was brought to the Emperor, a certain Joseph Bourgeois, from the hamlet of Odeghien. He stuttered with fear and kept his eyes obstinately fixed on the ground; Napoleon sent him away. Whenever he was asked what the Emperor was like he would answer; "If his face had been the face of a clock, nobody would have dared to look at it to tell the time."

The Emperor remained some time before La Belle Alliance. After dispatching General Haxo of the Engineers to ascertain whether the English had raised any entrenchments, he took up his post about three-quarters of a mile in the rear, on a bank which rises near the Rossomme farm. From the farm were brought out a chair and a little table upon which the maps were spread.[149]

At this table, Napoleon dictated a letter to Grouchy at ten o'clock, ordering him merely to direct his movements upon Wavre.[150] *For the Emperor still discounted the Prussian danger.*

At Le Caillou, Jérôme had acquainted his brother with a report he had heard the day before, in the Inn of the "Roi d'Espagne." The waiter who served him at supper, and who had previously waited on Wellington at breakfast, related that an aide-de-camp of the Duke had spoken of a junction agreed on between the English and Prussian Armies, at the entrance of the forest of Soignes. This Belgian, who seemed well informed, even added that the Prussians would march by Wavre. The Emperor treated this as mere nonsense. "After such a battle as Fleurus," he said, "the junction between the English and Prussians is impossible for at least two days; besides, the Prussians have Grouchy on their heels."[151]

When he had dictated his letter to Grouchy. Napoleon left Rossomme to review his troops as they deployed for battle.

The whole plateau was furrowed by the marching columns. D'Erlon's corps closed up on its right, to allow the corps of Reille to establish itself on the left. On the flank and rear of these first lines of infantry … eight divisions of cavalry began to deploy, their swords and their cuirasses shining in the sun, the pennons of their lances waving in the breeze. It was a kaleidoscope of vivid hues and metallic flashes…

By the Brussels road other troops debouched. Men, horses, and cannon were coming up as far as the eye could reach; the numerous battalions of Lobau, Domon's chasseurs, Subervie's lancers, the foot artillery in its plain dark blue uniform with touches of red, the horse artillery in "dolmans," the front of them covered with scarlet braid; the Young Guard, tirailleurs with red epaulettes, voltigeurs with green epaulettes; the foot artillerymen of the guard, with bearskin helmets, marching by the side of those terrible twelve pounders which the Emperor called his "most beautiful daughters." Far in the rear advanced the dark columns of the Old Guard; chasseurs and grenadiers wore the campaigning-dress – blue trousers, long blue greatcoats with a single row of buttons, bearskin helmets without either plume or braid. Their parade uniforms for their triumphal entrance into Brussels, they carried in their knapsack, which brought the weight that each man carried, including equipment, arms and fifty cartridges, to a load, weighing sixty-five pounds! The grenadiers could only be distinguished from the chasseurs by their greater height, the brass plate on their bearskins, and their epaulettes which were entirely red, while those of their comrades were green with red fringe. Both grenadiers and chasseurs wore powdered queues and massive gold earrings half a crown in diameter.

The drums beat, the trumpets blew, the bands struck up, "*Veillons au salut de l'Empire*"… Passing before Nanoleon the eagle-bearers inclined their standards – the standards of the "Champ de Mai," the new standards already baptized at Ligny by fire and blood – the horsemen brandished their sabres, the infantry waved their shakos on the points of their bayonets. The cheers overpowered and drowned the sounds of the drums and trumpets. The cries of "*Vive l'Empereur*" followed each other so lustily and so rapidly, that they prevented the words of command from being heard. "Never," says an officer of the 1st Corps, "were the words '*Vive l'Empereur*' shouted with more enthusiasm; it was like frenzy. And what made this scene even more solemn and more affecting was the fact that facing us, only a thousand yards distant perhaps, stood the dark red line of the English Army, distinctly visible."

The infantry of d'Erlon and the infantry of Reille deployed in the first line on the height of La Belle Alliance; the four divisions of d'Erlon, arranged two deep, the right opposite Papelotte, the left resting on the Brussels road; the three divisions of Reille in the same order, the right upon this road, the left not far from the road to Nivelles. The light cavalry of Jacquinot and the light cavalry of Piré, arranged in battle array three deep, flanked the right of d'Erlon and the left of Reille. On the second line, the infantry of Lobau posted itself in double column by divisions, along and to the left of the Brussels road, and the cavalry of Domon and Subervie were placed in compact columns by squadrons, along and to the right of the same highroad. Prolonging the second line, the cuirassiers of Milhaud and of Kellermann stood in battle order and two deep – the former to the right, the latter to the left. The Imperial Guard remained in reserve near Rossomme; the infantry (Young Guard, Middle Guard, Senior Guard) upon six lines, each of four battalions, deployed on both sides of the Brussels road; the light cavalry of Lefebvre-Desnoëttes (lancers and chasseurs) on two lines six hundred feet behind the cuirassiers of Milhaud; the reserve cavalry of Guyot (dragoons and grenadiers) also on two lines, six or seven hundred feet behind Kellermann's cuirassiers.

The artillery of d'Erlon was in the intervals between the brigades, Reille's artillery before the front, Lobau's artillery on the left flank. Each cavalry division had its battery of horse artillery by its side. The batteries of the Guard were placed quite in the rear between Rossomme and La Maison de Roi. The highroad to Brussels and the roads which crossed it, were left clear purposely, so as to allow of the rapid transit of artillery reinforcements to all points.[152]

At eleven o'clock Napoleon dictated his brief instructions for the plan of battle. Of the courses open to him General Jomini believed that he chose the right one.

To manoeuvre by the left, in order to overthrow their right, was a difficult matter, and led to nothing decisive; this was not a good strategic direction, as it would be entirely removed from the centre of operations, which was naturally connected by the right, with Grouchy, and with the road to Lorraine: besides this, the enemy's right wing was protected by the farm of Hougomont, and by the two large boroughs of Braine la Leud and Merbe-Braine.

To attack with the right, in order to crush the English left, was much more preferable, as this would maintain a direct relation, or an interior line with Grouchy, and would prevent the junction of the two hostile armies: but to gain, *en masse*, this extreme left, it would be necessary to extend beyond Frischermont, leaving open the line of retreat and venturing into the obstructed country of St. Lambert, where a defeat had been without remedy.

It remained for Napoleon to take a middle course, that of renewing the manoeuvre executed at Wagram and Moscowa, (Borodino,) that is, to assail the left at the same time that he drove in the centre. It was the best plan of battle he could have adopted, and with him, it had often proved successful. To force the centre only is difficult and dangerous, unless it happens to be a weak and unfurnished point, as at Austerlitz, Rivoli, and Montenotte; but we do not always find an enemy sufficiently complaisant, as to allow us such an advantage, and it would be absurd to expect it from an army following a good system, or, rather, that understands the principles of war. But to make an attack upon a wing, overthrow it, and at the same time fall upon the point, where this wing joins the centre, with a large force, is an operation always advantageous when well executed.

Napoleon resolved, then, to attempt it. However, instead of concentrating the bulk of his masses against the left, as at Borodino, he directed them on the centre; the extreme left was not to be assailed, but by the division forming the right of Erlon's corps, which would attack Papelotte and La Haye; Ney was to lead the three other divisions on the right of La Haye Sainte; Reille's corps would support this movement on the left of the Mont-St.-Jean causeway; Bachelu's and Foy's divisions, between this causeway and the farm of Hougomont; Jerome's, led in fact by Guilleminot, was to attack this farm, the salient point of the enemy's line, the chateau and park wall of which, Wellington had crenelled, and where he had posted the English guards. Count Lobau, with the 6th corps and a mass of cavalry, would follow the centre in a third and fourth line, on the right and left of the causeway, to support Ney's attack on La Haye Sainte;

lastly, twenty-four battalions of guards and de Valmy's cuirassiers, were to second the decisive shock, wherever needed, in a fifth and sixth line.

Such was the plan that many incidents deranged, and which Napoleon can leave, without fear, to the scrutiny of the masters of the art. It could not be bettered, unless moving his reserves a little nearer his right, thus giving more vigor to the effort between Papelotte and the Charleroi causeway.[153]

A more recent historian of the battle, however, believes that Napoleon's plan could certainly have been improved.

These tactics were barbarously unsubtle, for they envisaged smashing the centre of the English front, doubtless at heavy cost, after which the rest of the army would rapidly exploit the breach in the enemy's line.

When Napoleon began his career as a general in Italy he was already a past master in the art of taking calculated risks in battle; by the time he ended it in Belgium nineteen years later his tactics were more those of a gambler than a soldier. He retained his skill as a strategist to the end – the opening of his last campaign was brilliant – but on the battlefield he now exchanged stratagem for brute force. In his choice of frontal assault on Wellington's lines are all the gambler's compulsive refusal to face realities and capacity for self-delusion. On the morning of the 18th of June he wrote off the Prussians on the slenderest of evidence, he disparaged the English army and its commander although his generals had warned him to respect them, and he ignored the strength of the position Wellington had chosen to defend. At breakfast time he told his officers that he thought that his chances of victory were ninety out of a hundred, although he believed, erroneously, that the English outnumbered him. Frontal attacks had won quick victories before, at a heavy price, but these had been against unreliable troops, and although some of Wellington's regiments were poor material, the best of them could be expected to hold their ground stubbornly. Yet the Emperor refused to manoeuvre as Reille urged him to do in the light of French experience in the Peninsula; doubtless he rejected the idea because it seemed less likely to bring him the decisive victory he so desperately needed. The facts of the situation scarcely justify his decision; the English stood a strong chance of holding him at bay for many hours, possibly till nightfall. If he failed to carry their lines his reverse would be so great that there might not be a second opportunity to win the campaign, while if he decided to manoeuvre and failed to turn Wellington's front, his army would be left virtually intact, and his position would still not be beyond redemption. Had Napoleon been able to make a dispassionate appreciation of his situation before Mont-Saint-Jean he would have realised that if he succeeded in battering his way through the English centre it would be by such a small margin that he would have risked all to gain all; there was at least as much chance of winning the battle by manoeuvre, and far less risk attached to it. He denied himself his army's greatest strength, its mobility, he gave away the enemy's weakest point, its lack of flexibility, when he chose a frontal assault. He could not have placed more faith in his star and his troops' willingness to sacrifice their lives.[154]

Napoleon had hoped to begin his attack at nine o'clock;[155] *but the sloshy ground not yet dried by the sun and the late arrival of the last of his troops had led him to abandon his plans for an early start. The battery of 80 guns to the right of La Belle Alliance was ordered to open its cannonade at noon, an hour before d'Erlon's troops assaulted the Allied center.*[156] *As a preliminary diversion, which it was hoped would induce Wellington to take troops from his center to strengthen his right, Reille was ordered to send one of his divisions into a simulated attack on Hougoumont. Prince Jérôme, to whom this duty was assigned, was not content, however, with misleading the enemy and turned what was intended to be a diversion into a full-scale assault. Fierce fighting went on there for most of the day. But the Guards successfully defended the château and, when that was set on fire, the walls and yards of the farm, with splendid courage and panache.*

While the struggle way still raging at Hougoumont, Napoleon was handed a message from Ney saying that the battery was ready to open its cannonade. Before giving the order to fire, which would fill the air with smoke, the Emperor had one last look through his telescope at the surrounding skyline.

At a distance of about six miles to the north-east, he perceived what appeared to be a black cloud emerging from the woods of Chapelle-Saint-Lambert. Though his practised eye made it impossible for him to doubt, he hesitated at first to acknowledge these were troops. He consulted with the officers around him. All the glasses of the staff were turned upon this point. As usually occurs, opinions differed. Some officers contended that there were no troops there at all, but only a clump of trees or the shadow of a cloud; others saw a marching column, even discerned French uniforms, or Prussian uniforms. Soult said he could plainly distinguish a numerous body of troops which had piled arms.

It was not long before the point was fully settled. As a detachment of cavalry galloped off to reconnoitre these troops a subaltern of the 2nd Silesian Hussars whom Colonel Marbot's hussars had just captured near Lasne, was brought before the Emperor. He was the bearer of a letter from Bülow to Wellington, announcing the arrival of the 4th Corps at Chapelle-Saint-Lambert. This hussar, who spoke French, made no difficulty about telling all he knew. "The troops just perceived," he said, "are the advanced guard of General von Bülow. Our whole army passed last night at Wavre. We have seen no French, and we suppose they have marched on Plancenoit."

The presence of a Prussian corps at Chapelle-Saint-Lambert, which would have confounded the Emperor a few hours before, when he treated as "nonsense" the account brought by Jérôme with regard to the proposed junction of the two armies of the allies, now only surprised him in a slight degree, for during the interval he had received this letter from Grouchy, dated Gembloux, six o'clock in the morning:

"Sire, all my reports and information confirm the fact that the enemy is retiring upon Brussels, either to concentrate there, or to give battle after uniting with Wellington. The first and the second corps under Blücher appear to be marching, the former upon Corbais and the second upon Chaumont. They must have started from Tourinnes yesterday evening at half-past eight, and have marched all night; fortunately, the weather in the night was so wretched that they cannot have advanced very far. I am going to start immediately for Sart-a-Walhain whence I shall proceed to Corbais and to Wavre."[157] This despatch was far less reassuring than the one of the previous day. Instead of the retreat of two Prussian corps in two columns, the one upon Wavre and the other upon Liège, Grouchy announced that these two columns were marching concentrically upon Brussels, with the probable design of joining Wellington. He no longer spoke of preventing their junction; and though it was natural to conjecture he intended manoeuvring to that effect, by marching to Wavre, he used but little haste in so doing, for at six o'clock in the morning he had not yet left Gembloux.

No doubt the Emperor might hope that the Prussians would march straight upon Brussels; but it was also very possible that they would join the English Army by a flank movement.

To parry this probable danger, the Emperor did not think of sending fresh instructions to Grouchy till very late. Except in the event of a delay, which was possible but highly improbable, the Marshal's letter ought to have reached the Imperial headquarters between ten and eleven o'clock; and it was only at one o'clock, a few minutes before perceiving the Prussian corps on the heights of Chapelle-Saint-Lambert, that the following message from the Emperor was written to Grouchy: "Your movement from Corbais to Wavre agrees with His Majesty's arrangements; nevertheless, the Emperor requests me to tell you that you must keep manoeuvring in our direction, and to seek to draw nearer to the army, so as to be able to join us before any corps places itself between us. I do not indicate to you any special direction. It is for you to ascertain the point where we are, to act accordingly, and to keep up our communications, and to see that you are constantly in a position to fall upon and annihilate, any of the enemy's troops which might try to molest our right."[158]

This order had not yet been dispatched when the Prussian columns appeared in the distance. A few minutes later the Emperor, after questioning the captive hussar, had this postscript added: "A letter which has just been intercepted tells us that General Bülow is to attack our right flank. We believe we can perceive this corps on the heights of Chapelle-Saint-Lambert. Therefore do not lose a minute to draw nearer to us and to join us and crush Bülow, whom you will catch in the very act [*en flagrant délit*]."

The Emperor was then not otherwise disconcerted. Though he realised that his situation had seriously altered, he did not consider it compromised. Indeed, the reinforcement that had reached Wellington only consisted after all of a single Prussian corps, for the prisoner had not mentioned that the whole of the army was following Bülow. This army must be still at Wavre. Grouchy would either come up with it there, attack it, and consequently hold it back at a great distance from Bülow; or else, giving up the pursuit of Blücher, he was already marching on Plancenoit by Mousty, as the hussar supposed, and would bring to the bulk of the French Army, a reinforcement of 33,000 bayonets. The Emperor, who easily deluded himself by his own fancies and wished above all things to impart them to others, said to Soult: "This morning we had ninety odds in our favour. We still have sixty against forty, and if Grouchy repairs the terrible fault he has made in amusing himself at Gembloux, and marches rapidly, our victory will be all the more decisive, for Bülow's corps will be completely destroyed."

In any case, as Grouchy might delay, and Bülow's advanced guard was in view, the Emperor immediately took measures to protect the flank of the army. The light cavalry divisions under Domon and Subervie were detached to the right to observe the enemy, to occupy all the outlets, and to connect themselves with the heads of Marshal Grouchy's columns as soon as they appeared. Count Lobau received orders to move up the 6th Corps behind this cavalry, to a good intermediate position which would enable him to hold the Prussians in check.

It was now about half-past one. The Emperor gave Ney the orders to attack. The battery of eighty pieces began with the roar of thunder to pour forth a sudden storm of fire, which was at once answered by the English artillery. After half an hour's cannonading, the main battery suspended its fire for a minute, to allow of the passage of d'Erlon's infantry. The four divisions were marched in echelons by the left, with intervals of 400 yards between each echelon. The Allix division formed the first echelon, the Donzelot division the second, the Marcognet division the third, and the Durutte division the fourth. Ney and d'Erlon led the assault.

Instead of arranging these troops in columns of attack, that is to say in columns of battalions by divisions, at half or at full distance, a manoeuvre which is very favourable for rapid deployments, such as the forming of squares, each echelon had been arranged by battalion, deployed, and in close ranks. The divisions of Allix, Donzelot, and Marcognet (Durutte on his own responsibility would not consent to this manoeuvre) thus presented three compact phalanxes of a front of 160 to 200 files, with a depth of twenty-four men. Who had ordered such a formation, perilous under any circumstances, but specially unfortunate on this uneven ground? Ney, or rather d'Erlon, commander of the army corps. At any rate it was not the Emperor, for in his general order of eleven o'clock, nothing of the sort had been specified; there was not even any question of attacking by echelons. On the battlefield, Napoleon wisely left his lieutenants to take the initiative in all details of execution.

Irritated at not having fought on the previous day, the soldiers were burning to attack the enemy. They rushed forward with cries of "*Vive l'Empereur!*" and descended into the valley under the fiery vault of French and English shells which crossed over their heads.[159]

Donzelot's division fell on La Haye Sainte, poured into the orchard and sealed the boundary walls. The divisions of Allix and Marcognet in the center pushed up the slope towards Bijlandt's brigade, already much weakened by the French artillery, and drove it back. While on the left Durutte's division captured Papelotte. It seemed, as the greater part of Donzelot's division bypassed La Haye Sainte and assaulted the lines behind it, that the whole Allied line would collapse.

But Major Baring's companies of the King's German Legion, defending the buildings of La Haye Sainte, brought the rest of Donzelot's division under a murderous fire and held them back. And then as the main mass of the division clumsily attempted to deploy just below the crest of the slope, Sir Thomas Picton's 5th Division, stretched out in line far on either side of them, fired a concentrated volley into the ranks. Picton gave the order to charge and died almost immediately, shot through the head. His men came on, however, rushed down the slope, driving the confused French troops before them.

Before the French cavalry came up in support, forcing the Allied infantry to form squares, Lord Uxbridge gave his own cavalry the order to charge.

Vandeleur's dragoons, aided by French dragoons and Belgian hussars, charged down into Papelotte as Durutte's division withdrew. And in the center d'Erlon's great masses of infantry were *too densely packed to defend themselves against the horsemen's sabres. One of d'Erlon's officers, Captain Duthilt of the 45*^{me} *de Ligne, tried to*

establish some sort of order and to reform the platoons, since a disordered group can achieve nothing. Just as I was pushing one of our men back into the ranks I saw him fall at my feet from a sabre slash. I turned round instantly – to see English cavalry forcing their way into our midst and hacking us to pieces.

Just as it is difficult, if not impossible, for the best cavalry to break into infantry who are formed up in squares and who defend themselves with coolness and daring, so it is true that once the ranks have been broken and penetrated, then resistance is useless and nothing remains for the cavalry to do but to slaughter at almost no risk to themselves. This is what happened. In vain our poor fellows stood up and stretched out their arms: they could not reach far enough to bayonet those cavalrymen mounted on powerful horses, and the few shots fired in this chaotic mêlée were just as fatal to our own men as to the English. And so we found ourselves defenceless against a relentless enemy who, in the intoxcation of battle, sabred even our drummers and fifers without mercy.[160]

The reaction of the British cavalry was hysterical, as the account of a corporal in the Scots Greys shows:

I felt a strange thrill run through me, and I am sure my noble beast felt the same, for, after rearing for a moment, she sprang forward, uttering loud neighings and snortings, and leapt over the holly-hedge at a terrific speed. It was a grand sight to see the long line of giant grey horses dashing along with flowing manes and heads down, tearing up the turf about them as they went. The men in their red coats and tall bear-skins were cheering loudly, and the trumpeters were sounding the "Charge." Beyond the first hedge the road was sunk between high, sloping banks, and it was a very difficult feat to descend without falling; but there were very few accidents, to our surprise.

All of us were greatly excited, and began crying, "Hurrah, Ninety-Second! Scotland for ever!" as we crossed the road. For we heard the Highland pipers playing among the smoke and firing below, and I plainly saw my old friend Pipe-Major Cameron standing apart on a hillock coolly playing "Johnny Cope, are ye waukin' yet?" in all the din.

Our colonel went on before us, past our guns and down the slope, and we followed; we saw the Royals and Enniskillens clearing the road and hedges at full gallop away to the right.[161]

The Highland infantry were determined not to be left out of it.

Many of the Highlanders grasped our stirrups, and in the fiercest excitement dashed with us into the fight. The French were uttering loud, discordant yells, just when I saw the first Frenchman. A young officer of Fusiliers made a slash at me with his sword, but I parried it and broke his arm; the next second we were in the thick of them. We could not see five yards ahead for the smoke…

The French were fighting like tigers. Some of the wounded were firing at us as we passed… Then those in front began to cry out for "quarter", throwing down their muskets and taking off their belts. The Gordons at this rushed in and drove the French to the rear. I was now in the front rank, for many of ours had fallen…

We had now reached the bottom of the slope. There the ground was slippery with deep mud. Urging each other on, we dashed towards the batteries on the ridge above, which had worked such havoc in our ranks. The ground was very difficult, and especially where we crossed the edge of a ploughed field, so that our horses sank to the knees as we struggled on. My brave Rattler was becoming quite exhausted, but we dashed ever onwards.

At this movement Colonel Hamilton rode up to us crying, "Charge! charge the guns!" and went off like the wind up the hill towards the terrible battery that had made such deadly work among the Highlanders. It was the last we saw of our colonel, poor fellow! His body was found with both arms cut off. His pockets had been rifled…

Then we got among the guns, and we had our revenge. Such slaughtering! We sabred the gunners, lamed the horses, and cut their traces and harness. I can hear the Frenchmen yet crying "*Diable*" when I struck at them, and the long-drawn hiss through their teeth as my sword went home. Fifteen of their guns could not be fired again that day. The artillery drivers sat on their horses weeping aloud as we went among them; they were mere boys, we thought.[162]

A sergeant of the Scots Greys captured the eagle of the 45me de Ligne.

I took the Eagle from the enemy; he and I had a hard contest for it; he thrust for my groin – I parried it off, and I cut him through the head; after which I was attacked by one of their Lancers, who threw his lance at me, but missed the mark by throwing it off with my sword by my right side; then I cut him from the chin upwards, which cut went through his teeth. Next I was attacked by a foot soldier, who, after firing at me, charged me with his bayonet; but he very soon lost the combat, for I parried it, and cut him down through the head; so that finished the contest for the Eagle.[163]

The excitement of the British cavalry could not be contained. Ignoring Uxbridge's orders to return, Lord Edward Somerset's and Sir William Ponsonby's brigades galloped up the slope, sabred all in their path, charged headlong at the enemy's guns, silenced thirty of them and cut down their crews. It was an expensive affray. Of 2,500 cavalry who, took part in the charge, 1,000 did not return.

But by three o'clock the only French troops on the slopes were the dead and wounded. Then at Hougoumont the battle died away – and the Prussians drew ever nearer.

10

Waterloo: Afternoon and Evening

Napoleon now found himself committed to an impending battle on a second front, to avert or postpone which he was forced to detach, under Lobau, the very reserve of infantry which was to have followed up D'Erlon's expected success. With the Prussians approaching from the other side, he dared not commit this now to a left-hook against the British centre, the vital approach to which was still untaken. Apart from the small portion of Reille's corps still uncommitted to the unending fight round Hougoumont, he had no infantry left for a new attack on the ridge, except the twenty-four battalions of the Imperial Guard. And these, in view of the growing threat to his flank and the, to him, unexpected revelation of British defensive striking-power, he was not yet prepared to commit. For the Guard was the last card that stood between him and ruin. He kept it, 13,000 strong, the apple of his eye, unused beside him.

For about half an hour there was a pause in the battle, except at Hougoumont, where Jérôme and Foy threw ever more troops into the inferno round the blazing but still defiant buildings. Wellington took advantage of the lull to readjust his dispositions. Pack's brigade took the place vacated by Bylandt's Netherlanders, Lambert's brigade came up from the second line to strengthen Picton's battered division, and two more companies of the King's German Legion were thrown into La Haye Sainte. The Prussians were taking far longer to arrive than the British commander had expected. There had been a delay in their start, aggravated by a fire in the narrow streets of Wavre and the fact that Bülow's as yet unused corps in the van had the farthest distance to march. After the rains, the cross-country lanes were almost impassable for transport, and Gneisenau, the Prussian Chief of Staff, was reluctant to attack Napoleon, with Grouchy's troops in his rear, until he knew for certain that Wellington was standing fast. Only Blücher's insistence – for the old man, oblivious of his injuries, was with Bülow's advance guard by midday – carried the tired and hungry troops forward through the soggy defiles of the Lasne and the dense woods that lay between it and the battlefield. "I have promised Wellington," he told them as they dragged the guns axle-deep through mire, "you would not have me break my word!"

Meanwhile, the French gunners had taken up their position again on the central ridge and, soon after three o'clock, reopened their fire. It was more intense than anything the oldest Peninsular veteran had experienced. The range was so accurate that almost every shot told, and after a quarter of an hour Wellington withdrew his infantry a hundred yards farther back from the crest. Under cover of the bombardment, La Haye Sainte in the centre was again surrounded. But Baring's handful of German Legionaries continued to hold the walls, and with Kempt's and Lambert's men standing firm on the plateau above, D'Erlon's mangled infantry refrained from pressing home their assault. They seemed to fear a renewal of the storm of cavalry that had struck their comrades.

Suddenly the battle took a novel and spectacular form. For, mistaking the partial withdrawal of Wellington's infantry for the beginning of a general retirement, Marshal Ney decided to take a short cut to victory by sweeping the ridge with heavy cavalry. Of these – the finest in the world – his master had almost as many as Wellington's British infantry. He therefore ordered forward 5,000 of them, including eight regiments of cuirassiers, drawing them up in the plain immediately to the west of the *chausée* where the slope was easiest.

Wellington watched the splendid spectacle with amazement. It seemed unbelievable that the French would dare to assail a line of unbroken British infantry with cavalry alone. But such was plainly their intention, and, with his own heavy cavalry too weakened to counter-charge in strength, there was a danger that, if Napoleon was able to bring up infantry and guns behind them, the defenders, forced to remain in square, might be blasted out of existence by case-shot. The two divisions to the west of the Brussels road – the 3rd and 1st – were ordered to form battalion squares or oblongs in chequer-wise pattern across the gently swelling, corn-covered plateau. They were aligned so that every face of every square had a field of fire free of the next. Until the attackers appeared over the crest Wellington ordered the men to lie down. Behind the twenty squares his cavalry, including the remnants of the two British heavy brigades, were drawn up in support.

Between and a little in advance of the squares Wellington placed his guns, bringing up his last two reserve batteries of Horse Artillery to inflict the utmost damage on the advancing cavalry.[164]

Captain Mercer brought his men galloping up:

Away we flew, as steadily and compactly as if at a review. I rode with Frazer, whose face was as black as a chimneysweep's from the smoke, and the jacket-sleeve of his right arm torn open by a musket-ball or case-shot, which had merely grazed his flesh. As we went along, he told me that the enemy had assembled an enormous mass of heavy cavalry in front of the point to which he was leading us (about one-third of the distance between Hougoumont and the Charleroi road), and that in all probability we should immediately be charged on gaining our position. "The Duke's orders, however, are positive," he added, "that in the event of their persevering and charging home, you do not expose your men, but retire with them into the adjacent squares of infantry." As he spoke, we were ascending the reverse slope of the main position. We breathed a new atmosphere – the air was suffocatingly hot, resembling that issuing from an oven. We were enveloped in thick smoke, and, *malgré* the incessant roar of cannon and musketry, could distinctly hear around us a mysterious humming noise, like that which one hears of a summer's evening proceeding from myriads of black beetles; cannon-shot, too, ploughed the ground in all directions, and so thick was the hail of balls and bullets that it seemed dangerous to extend the arm lest it should be torn off. In spite of the serious situation in which we were, I could not help being somewhat amused at the astonishment expressed by our kind-hearted surgeon (Hutchins) who heard for the first time this sort of music.

He was close to me as we ascended the slope, and, hearing this infernal *carillon* about his ears, began staring round in the wildest and most comic manner imaginable, twisting himself from side to side, exclaiming, "My God, Mercer, what *is* that? What *is* all this noise? How curious! How very curious!" And then when a cannon-shot rushed hissing past, "*There! There!* What *is* it all?" It was with great difficulty that I persuaded him to retire: for a time he insisted on remaining near me, and it was only by pointing out how important it was to us, in case of being wounded, that he should keep himself safe to be able to assist us, that I prevailed on him to withdraw. Amidst this storm we gained the summit of the ridge, strange to say, without a casualty; and Sir Augustus, pointing out our position between two squares of Brunswick infantry, left us, with injunctions to remember the Duke's order, and to economise our ammunition. The Brunswickers were falling fast – the shot every moment making great gaps in their squares, which the officers and sergeants were actively employed in filling up by pushing their men together and sometimes thumping them ere they could make them move. These were the very boys whom I had but yesterday seen throwing away their arms, and fleeing, panic-stricken, from the very sound of our horses' feet. Today they fled not bodily, to be sure, but spiritually, for their senses seemed to have left them. There they stood, with recovered arms, like so many logs, or rather like the very wooden figures which I had seen them practising at in their cantonments. Every moment I feared they would again throw down their arms and flee; but their officers and sergeants behaved nobly, not only keeping them together, but managing to keep their squares closed in spite of the carnage made amongst them. To have sought refuge amongst men in such a state was madness – the very moment our men ran from their guns I was convinced, would be the signal for their disbanding. We had better, then, fall at our posts than in such a situation. Our coming up seemed to reanimate them, and all their eyes were directed to us – indeed, it was providential, for, had we not arrived as we did, I scarcely think there is a doubt of what would have been their fate. Our first gun had scarcely gained the interval between their squares, when I saw through the smoke the leading squadrons of the advancing column coming on at a brisk trot, and already not more than one hundred yards distant, if so much, for I don't think we could have seen so far. I immediately ordered the line to be formed for action – *case-shot!* – and the leading gun was unlimbered and commenced firing almost as soon as the word was given: for activity and intelligence our men were unrivalled. The very first round, I saw, brought down several men and horses. They continued, however, to advance. I glanced at the Brunswickers, and that glance told me it would not do; they had opened a fire from their front faces, but both squares appeared too unsteady, and I resolved to say nothing about the Duke's order, and take our chance – a resolve that was strengthened by the effect of the remaining guns as they rapidly succeeded in coming to action, making terrible slaughter, and in an instant covering the ground with men and horses. Still they persevered in approaching us (the first round had brought them to a walk,) though slowly, and it did seem they would ride over us. We were a little below the level of the ground on which they moved – having in front of us a bank of about a foot and a half or two feet high, along the top of which ran a narrow road – and this gave more effect to our case-shot, all of which almost must have taken effect, for the carnage was frightful.[165]

–

As the case poured into them, the leading ranks went down like grass before a skilled mower. Again and again, when the French charged, the same thing happened, and the Brunswickers who, before the battery's arrival, had stood like soulless logs in their agony and had only been kept at their posts by the gallantry of their officers, recovered heart.

Elsewhere, where the gunners obeyed Wellington's orders, the French cavalry, crowded in a dense mass into the half-mile gap between Hougoumont and La Haye Sainte, rode over the abandoned guns and swept round the squares beyond. They did not gallop like English foxhunters, but came, as was their wont, at a slow, majestic pace and in perfect formation, their horses shaking the earth. As they appeared the British infantry rose at the word of command, their muskets at the ready and their bayonets bristling like massed gigantic *chevaux de frise.* If the cavalry of the Empire were Atlantic breakers, the British squares were the rocks of an iron coast. The men, many of them rosy-faced youngsters from the plough, were much impressed by the splendid appearance of the hordes of legendary horsemen who suddenly encircled them and even more by their courage, but they were not intimidated by them, as Ney had intended. As their experienced officers and N.C.O.s seemed to regard the newcomers as harmless, in their stolid, unimaginative English way they did so too. The cuirassiers and lancers made a great deal of noise and glitter, brandishing their weapons like pantomine giants and shouting "*Vive l'Empereur!*" but they seemed infinitely preferable to the continuous hail of shot and shell which had poured from the French batteries till they arrived on the ridge.

Short of impaling their horses on the hedges of bayonets, Ney's cavalry tried every device to break the squares. Occasionally little groups of horsemen, led by frantic officers, would dash for the face of one, firing off carbines and pistols and hoping to draw sufficient fire to enable their comrades behind to break in on a line of unloaded muskets. But the British and Hanoverian squares preserved perfect discipline, withholding their fire until they received the word of command and then, with their volleys, bringing down everything before them. The loss of horses was prodigious; the poor creatures lay dead or dying in hundreds, their riders, many of them wounded, making their way in a continuous stream back down the hill, or sprawling in their heavy cuirasses in the mud, looking, as Wellington afterwards recalled, like overturned turtles.

Whenever he judged that the intruders were sufficiently worn down and wearied, Wellington endeavoured to push them off the plateau with his cavalry, or, in default, by edging forward his squares in echelon towards the abandoned guns. He did not hurry, for he was playing for time, and he could not afford to let his light British and King's German Legion cavalry encounter the heavier armed cuirassiers until the latter were too exhausted and reduced to retaliate. The foreign Horse which he had brought up from the flanks and reserve to take the place of Ponsonby's and Somerset's lost squadrons proved, most of it, worse than useless, refusing repeated appeals from

Uxbridge to charge. One regiment of Hanoverian hussars, led by its colonel, fled as far as Brussels.

Even the British cavalry showed a reluctance at times to charge home in the face of such overwhelming weight and numbers, though several regiments, particularly the 13th Light Dragoons and the 15th Hussars, behaved with the greatest gallantry. The shock felt by men encountering for the first time the sights and sounds of battle – and such a battle – had in the nature of things a more paralysing effect on cavalry than on infantry whose men in square had the close support of officers and comrades. Once Uxbridge, whose energy and initiative throughout this critical time was beyond praise, was driven into exclaiming that he had tried every brigade and could not get one to follow him, and then, as he rode up to the 1st Foot Guards, "Thank God, I am with men who make me not ashamed of being an Englishman." One of the officers recalled how, while Wellington was sheltering in his square, the men were so mortified at seeing the cuirassiers deliberately walking their horses round them that they shouted, "Where are our cavalry? Why don't they come and pitch into these French fellows?" Such resentment failed to take into account the hopeless numerical inferiority of the Allied cavalry after its earlier losses, and was based on an incomplete view of the battlefield. All the hard-pressed infantrymen could see, amid clouds of thick, eddying smoke, was the outer face of the square on either side, and the hordes of encircling French Horse. They could not realise that the very presence of the decimated English squadrons in their rear helped to sustain the wavering morale of the Netherlanders and Brunswickers, and that the memory of their earlier, and heroic onslaught accounted for Napoleon's failure to follow up his cavalry with infantry and subject their squares to case-shot at close range.

Five times in two hours the French horsemen were driven from the plateau; five times, after rallying in the plain they returned. Whenever they disappeared the British gunners ran out of the squares and reopened fire, while Napoleon's guns resumed their cannonade.[166]

The plight of the Allied troops in the squares during these cannonades was pitiable.

Our situation, now, was truly awful; our men were falling by dozens at every fire. About this time, also a large shell fell just in front of us, and while the fuze was burning out, we were wondering how many of us it would destroy. When it burst, about seventeen men were either killed or wounded by it; the portion which came to my share, was a piece of rough cast-iron, about the size of a horse-bean, which took up its lodging in my left cheek; the blood ran copiously down inside my clothes, and made me feel rather uncomfortable. Our poor captain was horribly frightened; and several times came to me for a drop of something to keep his spirits up. Towards the close of the day, he was cut in two by a cannon shot.

The next charge the cavalry made, they deliberately walked their horses up to the bayonet's point; and one of them, leaning over his horse, made a thrust at me with his sword. I could not avoid it, and involuntarily closed my eyes. When I opened them again, my enemy was lying just in front of me, within reach, in the act of thrusting at me. He had been wounded by one of my rear rank men, and whether it was the anguish of the wound, or the chagrin of being defeated, I know not; but he endeavoured to terminate his existence with his own sword; but that being too long for his purpose, he took one of our bayonets, which was lying on the ground, and raising himself up with one hand, he placed the point of the bayonet under his cuirass, and fell on it.

The next time the cuirassiers made their appearance on our front, the Life Guards boldly rode out from our rear to meet them, and in point of numbers, they seemed pretty well matched. The French waited, with the utmost coolness, to receive them, opening their ranks to allow them to ride in.

It was a fair fight, and the French were fairly beaten and driven off. I noticed one of the Guards, who was attacked by two cuirassiers, at the same time; he bravely maintained the unequal conflict for a minute or two, when he disposed of one of them by a deadly thrust in the throat. His combat with the other one lasted about five minutes, when the guardsman struck his opponent a slashing back-handed stroke, and sent his helmet some distance, with the head inside it. The horse galloped away, the headless rider sitting erect in the saddle, the blood spurting out of the arteries like so many fountains.[167]

Ensign Gronow of the 1st Foot Guards said afterward that not a man who survived could ever forget the awful grandeur of those cavalry charges.

You perceived at a distance what appeared to be an overwhelming, long moving line, which, ever advancing, glittered like a stormy wave of the sea when it catches the sunlight. On came the mounted host until they got near enough, whilst the very earth seemed to vibrate beneath their thundering tramp. One might suppose that nothing could have resisted the shock of this terrible moving mass. They were the famous cuirassiers, almost all old soldiers, who had distinguished themselves on most of the battlefields of Europe. In an almost incredibly short period they were within twenty yards of us, shouting "*Vive l'Empereur!*" The word of command, "Prepare to receive cavalry," had been given, every man in the front ranks knelt, and a wall bristling with steel, held together by steady hands, presented itself to the infuriated cuirassiers.

I should observe that just before this charge the Duke entered by one of the angles of the square, accompanied only by one aide-de-camp; all the rest of his staff being either killed or wounded. Our Commander-in-Chief, as far as I could judge, appeared perfectly composed; but looked very thoughtful and pale...

Again and again various cavalry regiments, heavy dragoons, lancers, hussars, carabineers of the Guard, endeavoured to break our walls of steel. The enemy's cavalry had to advance over ground which was so heavy that they could not reach us except at a trot; they therefore came upon us in a much more compact mass than they probably would have done if the ground had been more favourable. When they got within ten or fifteen yards they discharged their carbines, to the cry of "*Vive l'Empereur!*" but their fire produced little effect, as is generally the case with the fire of cavalry. Our men had orders not to fire unless they could do so on a near mass; the object being to economise our ammunition, and not to waste it on scattered soldiers. The result was that when the cavalry had discharged their carbines, and were still far off we occasionally stood face to face looking at each other inactively not knowing what the next move might be.

When we received the cavalry, the order was to fire low so that on the first discharge of musketry, the ground was strewed with the fallen horses and their riders, which impeded the advance of those behind them, and broke the shock of the charge. It was pitiful to witness the agony of the poor horses, which really seemed conscious of the dangers that surrounded them. We often saw a poor wounded animal raise its head, as if looking for its rider to afford him aid…

During the battle our squares presented a shocking sight. Inside we were nearly suffocated by the smoke and smell from burnt cartridges. It was impossible to move a yard without treading upon a wounded comrade, or upon the bodies of the dead; and the loud groans of the wounded and dying was most appalling.

At four o'clock our square was a perfect hospital, being full of dead, dying, and mutilated soldiers. The charges of cavalry were in appearance very formidable, but in reality a great relief, as the artillery could no longer fire on us: the very earth shook under the enormous mass of men and horses. I shall never forget the strange noise our bullets made against the breastplates of Kellermann's and Milhaud's cuirassiers, six or seven thousand in number, who attacked us with great fury.[168]

–

Some time after five o'clock Ney brought up the last cavalry from the second line – Kellermann's two divisions of cuirassiers and the heavy squadrons of the Imperial Guard. At one moment more than 9,000 Horse assailed the ridge in a compact phalanx. This immense body was packed in the 800 yards front between the *chausée* and the

British bastion at Hougoumont, where the ground was a morass piled with dead horses. The front ranks, including most of the senior officers, were completely wiped out by the English batteries, and the weary mounts could only proceed at a walk. Yet they still continued to return.

Throughout this time and during the bombardments which preceded each assault, the British infantry patiently endured their fate. They seemed in their steady squares to be rooted to the ground. Though it would have been hazardous in the extreme to have manoeuvred with some of the young second British and Hanoverian *landwehr* battalions, they showed themselves, under their fine officers and N.C.O.s, as capable of standing fire as the oldest veterans. Theirs, as Harry Smith said, was no battle of science; it was a stand-up fight between two pugilists, milling away till one or the other was beaten. Inside each suffocating square, reeking with the smell of burnt cartridge and powder, it was like a hospital, the dead and dying strewing the ground. The sufferings of many of the wounded were indescribable; one rifleman had both legs shot off and both arms amputated, but continued to breathe as he lay amid his comrades. Few cried out in their pain, and when they did so, their officers immediately quieted them; it was a point of pride with Englishmen of all classes to take punishment without murmuring. Their stoicism was equalled by that of the French cavalry, who won the ungrudging admiration of the entire British army...

During the last hour of Ney's cavalry attacks the sound of the Prussians' guns had been audible on the British ridge in the lulls of firing, though few yet realized its import. By four o'clock, the two leading divisions of Bülow's corps had reached the western edge of Paris wood, just over two miles east of La Belle Alliance. Half an hour later, in view of the urgency of Wellington's messages, they went into action without waiting for their supports. Soon after five, when they had advanced to within a mile and a half of the Brussels road, Lobau counter-attacked and drove them back. But at six o'clock, two more Prussian divisions having emerged from the wood, Bülow again attacked, striking round Lobau's southern flank at Plancenoit, a village less than a mile from the French lifeline.

The situation was growing grave in the extreme for Napoleon. His troops had been marching and fighting almost continuously for four days; their losses during the afternoon had been heavier than in any engagement of comparable scale in his career. Again and again they had seemed on the point of carrying the ridge and sweeping Wellington's international flotsam and jetsam down the Brussels road. Yet whenever the smoke cleared, the stubborn redcoats were seen to be still standing. The Prussian shot, already playing on the *chausée*, brought home to the Emperor that, unless he could break Wellington's line in the remaining hours of daylight, his doom was certain.

The Emperor descended from the mound on which he had so long watched the battle.[169]

In the earlier hours of that day Napoleon had been seen at times walking up and down restlessly with his hands behind his back, or sitting slumped in his chair, morose and silent.

One of Soult's staff officers, Colonel Auguste-Louis Pétiet, thought how sadly changed he was from the dynamic figure he had admired at Austerlitz.

During his stay on Elba, Napoleon's stoutness had increased rapidly. His head had become enlarged and more deeply set between his shoulders. His pot-belly was unusually pronounced for a man of forty-five. Furthermore, it was noticeable during this campaign that he remained on horseback much less than in the past. When he dismounted, either to study maps or else to send messages and receive reports, members of his staff would set before him a small deal table and a rough chair made of the same wood, and on this he would remain seated for long periods at a time...

His stoutness, his dull white complexion, his heavy walk made him appear very different from the General Bonaparte I had seen at the start of my career during the campaign of 1800 in Italy, when he was so alarmingly thin that no soldier in his army could understand how, with so frail a body and looking as ill as he did, he could stand such fatigue.[170]

He could not stand such fatigue now, and he had had little sleep in the last few days. But at this critical time, he came once more to vivid life.

[He] roused himself, to snatch, as so often in the past, victory from defeat.

He had to fight on two fronts. To the south-east 30,000 Prussians were striking at his communications; to the north 20,000 Britons and as many or more Germans and Netherlanders were still barring the Brussels road. Despite his casualties he still had between 50,000 and 60,000 veteran troops, though of Grouchy's 33,000, wandering somewhere in space to the east, there was no sign. To clear his flank and gain time for a further assault on the British, he despatched eight young Guard battalions of the Imperial Guard to reinforce Lobau and recover Plancenoit. Simultaneously he gave Ney peremptory orders to throw in infantry and capture La Haye Sainte.[171]

La Haye Sainte had recently been reinforced, but Major Baring's repeated requests for more ammunition had remained unanswered. For some reason or other, the place had not been adequately prepared for defence. "The most important mistake which the Duke of Wellington committed as to the actual fighting of the battle of Waterloo," says Shaw-Kennedy, "was overlooking the vast importance of retaining possession at any cost of the farm and enclosures of La Haye Sainte." Not only had an inadequate supply of ammunition been provided, but all tools and implements with which the defence could have been strengthened had been removed. Taking stock at this time, the defenders found they had only three or four rounds of ammunition each. There was some question of withdrawing to the main position, but the men were so willing to fight to the end that Major Baring decided to hold out as long as he could. The French now assailed the position with resolution; many fell, but gradually the fire of the defenders died down. Their ammunition was spent. Ney's engineers were able to batter down the gates and doors of the farm with their axes and enter the buildings. Stubborn hand-to-hand fighting continued until the heroic garrison was almost wiped out. At last, having delayed the French occupation until the last possible moment, Major Baring struggled up the Brussels road with forty-two of his men, all who remained of the original garrison of 378.

In capturing La Haye Sainte, Ney had gained a great advantage for the French and he followed up his success promptly, bringing up a battery to fire from the position at the Allied troops on the Ohain lane, and placing a French regiment in the gravel pit which the 95th had been forced to abandon. The whole front was in action once more; Reille's infantry were engaged at Hougoumont; a group of cuirassiers had rallied and was forming in the valley, not far from La Haye Sainte; Durutte had driven Prince Bernard's forces out of Papelotte, and the divisions of Quiot and Marcognet, stimulated by Donzelot's success, began to assail Wellington's line anew.[172]

These successes gave the French a chance of victory. Sharpshooters and guns were thrown forward from the captured La Haye Sainte, the key to the Allied center, and a heavy fire was opened up on the 3rd and 5th Divisions. The Prince of Orange, who by this time was close to hysteria, insisted that the 5th Battalion of the King's German Legion should deploy into line and advance to recapture La Haye Sainte.

Colonel Baron von Ompteda protested that such a movement was suicidal in the presence of such strong forces of cavalry. But the Prince insisted that it should be carried out. Lieutenant Wheatley described the consequence.

Colonel Ompteda ordered us instantly into line to charge, with a strong injunction to "walk" forward, until he gave the word. When within sixty yards he cried "Charge," we ran forward huzzaing. The trumpet sounded and no one but a soldier can describe the thrill one instantly feels in such an awful moment. At the bugle sound the French stood until we just reached them. I ran by Colonel Ompteda who cried out, "That's right, Wheatley!"

I found myself in contact with a French officer but ere we could decide, he fell by an unknown hand. I then ran at a drummer, but he leaped over a ditch through a hedge in which he stuck fast. I heard a cry of, "The Cavalry! The

Cavalry!" But so eager was I that I did not mind it at the moment, and when on the eve of dragging the Frenchman back (his iron-bound hat having saved him from a cut) I recollect no more. On recovering my senses, I look'd up and found myself, bareheaded, in a clay ditch with a violent headache. Close by me lay Colonel Ompteda on his back, his head stretched back with his mouth open, and a hole in his throat. A Frenchman's arm across my leg.[173]

–

"The centre of the line was left open," said an aide-de-camp of General Alten. "We were in peril. At each moment the issue of the battle was more than doubtful." In spite of his accustomed confidence, Wellington became uneasy. He could see plainly the black masses of Blücher's troops assaulting the flank of the French Army, but he himself was without any support. He was heard to murmur: "Night or the Prussians must arrive." He had already despatched several aides-de-camp in the direction of Ohain to hasten the march of Zieten's corps. But his resolution was in nowise daunted. Officers arrived to him from every side, describing the situation as desperate, and asking for fresh orders. There was no other order but to stand firm to the last man.

The wavering and the slight move backward of the enemy's line, had not escaped the notice of Marshal Ney. But his soldiers were quite as exhausted as those of Wellington, He realised that the addition of a few fresh troops would have sufficed to give them new spirit and new courage, to overcome the last resistance of the English. He sent Colonel Heymès to the Emperor asking for a few infantry. "Troops!" cried Napoleon, "where do you expect me to get them? Do you expect me to make them?"

The Emperor still had eight battalions of the Old Guard, and six battalions of the Middle Guard left. If, at that very moment, he had sent but half of them to Marshal Ney, we may believe, on the authority of the best informed and most impartial of the English historians, that this reinforcement might have forced the enemy's centre.[174] But Napoleon, who had no cavalry reserve, did not consider that with all his "bear skins" he had too many to preserve his own position. The situation was quite as critical for him as for Wellington. Before a third onslaught from the whole of Bülow's corps, Lobau gave way, and the Young Guard, after a stubborn resistance, allowed Plancenoit to be torn from its grasp. The shells of the Prussian batteries were now ploughing up the ground around La Belle Alliance. Napoleon, already overpowered on his flank, was menaced by an irruption of the Prussians to the rear of his line of battle. He formed 11 battalions of the Guard into as many squares, and posted them opposite Plancenoit along the Brussels highroad from La Belle Alliance as far as Rossomme. The 1st battalion of the 1st Chasseurs was kept at Le Caillou. Generals Morand and Pelet received orders to recapture Plancenoit with the 1st battalion of the 2nd Grenadiers and the 1st of the 2nd Chasseurs. With their drums beating, these old veterans charged forward in close columns of platoons. They outdistanced the Young Guard, which Duhesme was striving to rally, assaulted Plancenoit on two diffierent points, forced their way in, without deigning to fire a shot, overthrew, trampled down, and drove out the mass of the Prussians. The attack was so impetuous, that in twenty minutes the whole village was swept. With their bayonets dyed with blood, these old soldiers followed on the heels of the fugitives, chased them for six hundred yards, and drove them to the opposite hill.[175]

Wellington received the news of the various Allied reverses with his habitual calm.

As all the Allied leaders in the centre had by now been killed or wounded, [Wellington] temporarily took over command there himself. Leading five young Brunswick battalions into the full storm of the French batteries, he rallied them when they broke under that hurricane of shot and brought them steadily back into line. Meanwhile, Vivian, seeing a new force of Prussians moving up from the east, arrived on his own initiative from the left of the ridge. Uxbridge galloped off to fetch Vandeleur's 11th, 12th and 16th Light Dragoons, and Somerset, with the wreck of the Union Brigade extended in single rank to make the utmost show, instilled confidence and pressure from behind into Chassé's Netherlanders.

The bombardment had now reached a new degree of intensity as Napoleon brought up every available gun to reinforce his massed batteries. All along the Allied centre men were going down like ninepins; close by the cross-roads 450 of the 700 men of the Twenty-seventh lay in square where they had fallen. In a neighbouring regiment – the Fortieth – both ensigns and fourteen sergeants had been killed or wounded round the tattered colours. The 5th Division, 5,000 strong when the battle started, seemed to have dwindled to a line of skirmishers. Kincaid with the Rifles began to wonder at that moment whether there had ever been a battle in which everyone on both sides had been killed. The stream of wounded and fugitives towards the rear was so great that a Prussian aide-de-camp, who rode up from Zieten's oncoming corps to investigate, returned with a report that the British were defeated and in retreat. No one knew what was happening outside his own immediate vicinity, for in the windless, oven-like, smoke-filled air visibility was reduced to a few yards.

Yet Wellington's grip on the battle never relaxed. Unlike his imperial adversary he was used to commanding comparatively small armies and to attending to every detail himself. In his grey greatcoat with cape, white cravat, Hessian boots, telescope and low cocked-hat, he rode continuously up and down the line, often alone and seemingly oblivious of the storm of shot. He neither avoided nor courted danger, but, knowing that his presence was necessary to keep his young soldiers to the sticking point, showed himself, placid and unconcerned, wherever the fire was hottest. Everywhere he infected men, near the limit of endurance, with courage and confidence. Almost every member of his staff, including De Lancey, his Quartermaster General, had by now fallen, but, though he looked thoughtful and a little pale, he betrayed no sign of anxiety. Once, chatting with the commanding officer of a square in which he had taken shelter, he was heard to say, "Oh, it will be all right; if the Prussians come up in time, we shall have a long peace." But occasionally he looked at his watch.[176]

An officer of the 30th Foot, Lieutenant Edward Macready, provides a good picture of the Duke's unruffled calm and its effect.

The Duke visited us frequently at this momentous period; he was coolness personified. As he crossed the rear face of our square a shell fell amongst our grenadiers, and he checked his horse to see its effect. Some men were blown to pieces by the explosion, and he merely stirred the rein of his charger, apparently as little concerned at their fate as at his own danger. No leader ever possessed so fully the confidence of his soldiery, "but none did love him"; wherever he appeared, a murmur of "Silence – stand to your front – here's the Duke!" was heard through the columns, and then all was steady as on a parade.[177]

Despite his calm Wellington recognized that he was close to defeat. Even the bravest and strongest of his soldiers were reaching the limits of their endurance.

Unless the Prussians arrived soon, the Duke knew he could not hold on.

The French had enveloped Hougoumont on [Wellington's] right, and had advanced beyond the Nivelles road which runs behind the château; the exhausted regiments in his centre continued to struggle with the troops who had reached the road along the ridge; and on his far left Papelotte remained in the hands of the enemy. Napoleon decided to send the Guard to carry the English front, but although he issued his orders only a few minutes after the recapture of Plancenoit, by the time the column had been brought into action, Wellington had been given a half-hour's respite in which to reorganise his defences, and more important still, Zieten had come up on his left, releasing troops to reinforce the centre of the line, and threatening the Emperor's right wing into the bargain. The issue of the battle, however, had hung by an even slenderer thread than the passage of thirty minutes. Zieten had been delayed at several points on his route to the battlefield, and when his advanced guard reached Ohain at six o'clock, the majority of his troops were still some distance away.

Here Zieten was met by Colonel Freemantle, one of the aides-de-camp the Duke had sent to hasten his approach. The aide explained how desperate the situation had become, and asked for immediate help, if only to the extent of 3,000 men. Zieten was fearful of committing his corps piecemeal lest they should be defeated in detail, and told Colonel Freemantle that he would come to the Duke's assistance once the rest of his force had caught up with him. While Zieten waited to continue his march he despatched an officer to reconnoitre the approaches through which he would pass to join the English. The officer came back with the alarming news that the allied army was in full retreat from Mont-Saint-Jean; he had been deceived by the large numbers of wounded and fugitives leaving the front line. Convinced that his fears had been more than justified, Zieten turned his troops to the left to support Bülow in his struggle with Lobau and the Young Guard. Fortunately for Wellington, Müffling, the Prussian general attached to his staff, had ridden to the heights above Papelotte to watch Zieten enter the English line, and when he saw him turn away to join Bülow he galloped up to the retreating corps. Zieten was unwilling to change his direction again, but Müffling was insistent: "The battle is lost", he said, "if the first corps does not go to the Duke's rescue." Much against his will, Zieten was at last persuaded to counter-march his troops.

The battalions of the Imperial Guard were still making their way to La Haye Sainte to begin their assault when Zieten's column appeared from Smohain, and headed for the junction of the two French fronts. The sight of a fresh body of the enemy bearing down on them was too much for some of the Emperor's exhausted and disheartened infantry, and they began to retreat until Napoleon rode up to them and persuaded them to return to their positions.

If the Guard had been sent forward when Ney asked for reinforcements, they would have found it a simple matter to come up under the cover of the troops already on the ridge and make their way through the remains of Wellington's centre, already engaged with the debris of d'Erlon's corps. By the time they did arrive, the situation had changed out of all recognition. Wellington had called in fresh troops from his right and left, and these, with the brigades already on the spot, cleared the ridge of the French who had held it for so long. Unharassed by skirmishers, the allied batteries were able to resume their fire, quickly silencing the battery at La Haye Sainte which had done such damage to the centre of the English line. The Guard were left to deliver their assault without the support of close artillery and musket fire, and as they approached, the defenders were strengthened by the arrival of Chassé's division of Dutch-Belgian infantry, and six fresh regiments of cavalry under Vivian and Vandeleur which had been relieved above Papelotte by Zieten's arrival…

The battalions of the Guard chosen for the attack were being drawn up across the valley when an officer of the carabiniers rode up to the skirmishers of Leeke's regiment holding his sheathed sword high above him, and shouting "*Vive le Roi!*" He had intended to desert earlier in the day, but had delayed in the hope that he could induce some of his comrades to join him. "Get ready!" he cried, "that scoundrel Napoleon will be upon you with his Guard in less than half an hour." The information was forwarded to Wellington, who rode along his line from the elm tree above La Haye Sainte to the far right above Hougoumont, supervising the deployment of the reinforcements he brought up to meet the Guard's attack. The Emperor sent General de la Bédoyère with a number of officers along the whole of the front to announce Grouchy's arrival. The ingenuous Ney protested at the spreading of such a falsehood, but it served to hearten the troops whose morale had been shaken by the appearance of Zieten's corps. Napoleon intended to support the Guard with a general advance, but the order was not obeyed along most of the front and where it was, evoked only a feeble response; the five battalions of the Imperial Guard marched forward alone to storm the allied positions.[178]

The Guard were moving forward. "A black mass of the grenadiers of the Imperial Guard, with music playing and the great Napoleon at their head, came rolling onward from the farm of La Belle Alliance," as an English observer put it. Posting one battalion on high ground between La Haye Sainte and Hougoumont, Napoleon led the other five onwards towards the English line and appeared to be about to command the assault in person. He had ended his stirring address with the cry: "*Tout le monde en arrière!*" which suggested that he intended to place himself in front. For a time he did, indeed, march at the head of the troops; but as they reached La Haye Sainte he relinquished his place to Marshal Ney and took shelter in the gravel-pit...

Marshal Ney led the Guard into action. Their front being covered by d'Erlon's troops, which were engaged immediately to the west of La Haye Sainte, they turned obliquely to the north-west, aiming at Wellington's right centre. The five battalions advanced in echelon. The 1st battalion of the 3rd Grenadiers took the lead with Marshal Ney and General Friant riding at their head; they were followed on their left by the 4th Grenadiers, then by the 1st and 2nd battalions of the 3rd Chasseurs, who gradually merged into one group, and finally by the 4th Chasseurs who were on the extreme left. The generals rode slowly at the head of their battalions, and the whole body of men moved with admirable precision.

Smoke hung in sulphurous clouds over the field; the light of the declining sun pierced it in gold shafts. Fighting continued above La Haye Sainte where the Duke was directing the Brunswick, Nassau and Hanoverian troops as they fought off d'Erlon's infantry. British Horse Artillery and Field Brigades waited in a concave line along the ridge which ran down from the Ohain lane to the rear of Hougoumont. They now opened fire on the leading battalion of the Guard, taking them in the flank with a double salvo of grape-shot from over thirty guns. Marshal Ney fell from his fifth horse, rose and continued to lead the column on foot. Closing their ranks, the grenadiers moved on, reaching the Ohain lane, driving back some Brunswickers and seizing guns temporarily abandoned. Then, deviating slightly, they attacked Halkett's brigade, and the 30th and 73rd Regiments retired before them. General Friant fell wounded from his horse and was taken to the rear. Pausing at La Haye Sainte, he talked to Napoleon, assuring him that the Guard were breaking through Wellington's line and that victory had been achieved. Napoleon, still in the gravel-pit, awaited the arrival of the three battalions of the Old Guard, due to follow the Middle Guard into action. From time to time, says a contemporary French account, he made as if to go towards the front line, whereupon Bertrand or one of the others would urgently restrain him, telling him that the safety of France and the army depended upon his life. He was easily dissuaded from any rash action, and it was noticed that when any message had to be taken it was sent by one of those who had remained silent, not by one who had reminded him of the value of his life.[179]

-

In the general darkness and confusion, and because of the fire from the guns on the ridge, the leading battalions of the first column struck the British line at two points: where Halkett's battered brigade of the 3rd Division was drawn up in front of Chassis Netherlanders, and immediately to the west where Wellington was waiting with Maitland's 1st Guards. As the huge bearskins suddenly loomed out of the darkness, the waiting British sprang to their feet in the corn and poured from their extended line a volley at point-blank range into the head of the advancing columns. The French tried to deploy but too late, and most of their officers were swept down. Then, while they were still in confusion, the British charged, Wellington himself giving the word to the Guards with a quiet, "Now, Maitland, now's your time!"

But though the Imperial Guard recoiled, it did not break. Both parts of the column re-formed and opened fire on the oncoming British, their guns supporting them with ease. To the east the remnants of the 33rd and 69th were driven back and at one moment almost broke, but were rallied by Halkett. A Dutch battery, behaving with great coolness and gallantry, raked the French column, and Chassé's Belgians, 3,000 strong, came up in support. Gradually the attackers, isolated and without support behind them, began to give ground. Meanwhile those opposed to the 1st Guards, though driven back for some distance, had also rallied. Maitland ordered his Guardsmen back, but his voice could not be heard above the firing, and some of them, mistaking his intention, tried to form square. In the confusion the two British battalions withdrew in disorder, only to re-form at the word of command with flawless and habitual steadiness on regaining their original position.

But before the battle between the rival Guards could be resumed, it was decided by the action of the most experienced regiment on the British side. Wellington always maintained that, if he had had at Waterloo the army with which he crossed the Pyrenees, he would have attacked Napoleon without waiting for the Prussians: "I should have swept him off the face of the earth," he said, "in two hours." The first battalion of the 52nd, commanded by John Colborne, afterwards Lord Seaton, had served in John Moore's original Light Brigade; Colborne himself was Moore's finest living pupil. It had gone into action at Waterloo with more than a thousand bayonets, being one of the very few British battalions which was up to strength – "a regiment," wrote Napier of its Peninsular exploits, "never surpassed in arms since arms were first borne by men." Owing to the skilful way in which Colborne had placed and handled it, its casualties during the French cavalry charges and the long hours of bombardment had been extraordinarily light.

As the second and westernmost column of the Imperial Guard after passing by Hougoumont pressed up the slope towards Maitland's unbroken line, the drummers beating the *rummadum, dummadum, dum*, of the *pas de charge*, Colborne, who was stationed in the center of Adam's brigade to the right of the Guards, took a sudden decision. Without orders either from the Duke or any superior officer, he moved his battalion forward out of the line for a distance of three hundred yards, and then, as it drew level with the leading company of the advancing French column, wheeled it to the left with the order, "Right shoulders forward." He thus laid it on the flank of the French. By doing so he took the risk both of leaving a gap in the line behind and of having his men cut to pieces by cavalry – a fate he had experienced when, as one of Stewart's brigade commanders, he had moved up the hill at Albuera.

The reward of his daring was decisive. The Imperial Guard, taken by surprise, halted and poured a volley into the 52nd which brought down 140 of its men. But the British reply to this grave Roman battalion was decisive. It seemed as though every bullet found its mark. So heavy were the casualties in the dense, astonished column that the Imperial Guard did not wait for the 52nd to charge. It broke and fled. As it did so, the 52nd resumed its advance eastwards across, and at right angles to, the British front, with the two other battalions of Adam's brigade – the 95th and 71st – moving up on Wellington's instructions on either flank. A few hundred yards on they encountered another French column re-forming – the first that had attacked – and dealt it the same treatment and with the same results. Gradually, as the recoiling units of the French army streamed back across their path from the impregnable plateau, the British Light Infantry inclined to the right towards La Belle Alliance. Round them, out of swirling smoke, scattered units of British and French cavalry appeared in charge and counter-charge.

For from the ridge above them, starting from the right, the whole British line had begun to advance as Wellington, hat raised high in air, galloped westwards from one tattered, enduring regiment to another. The time for which he and they had waited had come. "Who commands here?" he shouted to Harry Smith, Lambert's brigade major. "Generals Kempt and Lambert, my Lord." "Desire them to form column of companies and move on immediately." "In what direction my Lord?" "Right ahead, to be sure."

It was now nearly dusk. But, as the French cannonade ceased and the smoke began to drift from the ridge, the setting sun cast a ray of light along the glinting British line, now motionless no more, and on the accoutrements of the defeated columns in the plain. The whole French army was suddenly dissolving with the landscape: entire regiments leaving their arms piled and taking to their heels.[180]

-

Zieten's corps was now pouring over the battlefield. Some of his men had joined Blücher in the region of Plancenoit, some had crossed the Brussels road and were near Hougoumont. In the dusk there was much confusion, and one Prussian battery had settled down about 400 yards from Mercer's troop and proceeded to rake it from end to end with a heavy and incessant fire. Not knowing who was firing on them, the exhausted gunners of G Troop slowly swung round their two left flanks guns and fired back.[181]

Mercer, himself, describes the scene:

We had scarcely fired many rounds at the enfilading battery when a tall man in the black Brunswick uniform came galloping up to me from the rear, exclaiming, "Ah! mine Gott! mine Gott! vat is it you doos, sare? Dat is your friends de Prossiens; an you kills dem! Ah! mine Gott! – mine Gott! vill you no stop sare? – vill you no stop? Ah! mine Gott! – mine Gott! vat for is dis? De Inglish kills dere friends de Proosiens! Vere is de Dook von Vellington? Ah, mine Gott! – mine Gott!" etc. etc., and so he went on raving like one demented. I observed that if these were our friends the Prussians they were treating us very uncivilly; and that it was not without sufficient provocation we had turned our guns on them, pointing out to him at the same time the bloody proofs of my assertion. Apparently not noticing what I said he continued his lamentations, and, "Vill you no stop, sare, I say?" Wherefore, thinking he might be right, to pacify him I ordered the whole to cease firing, desiring him to remark the consequences. *Psieu, psieu, psieu*, came our friends' shot, one after another; and our friend himself had a narrow escape from one of them. "Now, sir," I said, "you will be convinced; and we will continue our firing, whilst you can ride round the way you came, and tell them they kill their friends the English; the moment their fire ceases, so shall mine." Still he lingered exclaiming, "Oh, dis is terreebly to see de Proosien and de Inglish kill vonanoder!" At last darting off I saw no more of him. The fire continued on both sides, mine becoming slacker and slacker, for we were reduced to the last extremity, and must have been annihilated but for the opportune arrival of a battery of Belgic artillery a little on our left, which, taking the others in flank nearly at point blank, soon silenced and drove them off. We were so reduced that all our strength was barely sufficient to load and fire three guns out of our six.

These Belgians were all beastly drunk, and, when they first came up, not at all particular as to which way they fired; and it was only by keeping an eye on them that they were prevented treating us, and even one another... We were all looking out anxiously at the movements below and on the opposite ridge, when [an English officer] suddenly shouted out, "Victory! – victory! they fly! – they fly!" and sure enough we saw some of the masses dissolving, as it were, and those composing them streaming away in confused crowds over the field, whilst the already desultory fire of their artillery ceased altogether. I shall never forget this joyful moment! – this moment of exultation! On looking round I found we were left almost alone. Cavalry and infantry had all moved forward, and only a few guns here and there were to be seen on the position. We were congratulating ourselves on the happy results of the day, when an aide-de-camp rode up, crying "Forward, sir! – forward! It is of the utmost importance that this movement should be supported by artillery!" at the same time waving his hat much in the manner of a huntsman laying on his dogs. I smiled at his energy, and pointing to the remains of my poor troop, quietly asked, "How sir?" A glance was sufficient to show him the impossibility and away he went.

Our situation was indeed terrible: of 200 fine horses with which we had entered the battle, upwards of 140 lay dead, dying, or severely wounded. Of the men, scarcely two-thirds of those necessary for four guns remained, and these so completely exhausted as to be totally incapable of further exertion... Our guns and carriages were, as before mentioned, altogether in a confused heap, intermingled with dead and wounded horses, which it had not been possible to disengage from them. My poor men, such at least as were untouched, fairly worn out, their clothes, faces, etc., blackened by the smoke and spattered over with mud and blood, had seated themselves on the trails of the carriages or had thrown themselves on the wet and polluted soil, too fatigued to think of anything but gaining a little rest. Such was our situation when called upon to advance! It was impossible, and we remained where we were. For myself, I was also excessively tired – hoarse, to making speech painful, and deaf from the infernal uproar of the last eleven hours. Moreover, I was devoured by a burning thirst, not a drop of liquid having passed my lips since the evening of the 16th; but although, with the exception of the chicken's leg last night, I may be said to have eaten nothing for two whole days, yet did I not feel the least desire for food.[182]

–

Napoleon had been engaged in forming the Old Guard in the valley when the rout of his army became apparent. Hastily he ordered the three battalions into squares, with their right on the Brussels road, about 100 yards from La Haye Sainte. Vivian's cavalry surged round them but were driven off; Allied infantry and artillery soon followed, however, and against these the squares could do little: Napoleon therefore ordered them to retreat. He then galloped down the Brussels road with Bertrand and other members of his suite, keeping with him the guide, Decoster. He had left two battalions of grenadiers in position at Rossomme, and these he now joined, taking refuge within one of the squares and hoping to stem the rout from this position. But he had driven the Grand Army beyond endurance, and nothing could now be done.

D'Erlon was trying in vain to control the flood of panic-stricken fugitives pouring down the slope from La Haye Sainte. As he was irresistibly carried back in their midst, Marshal Ney called out to him: "D'Erlon, if you and I get out of this we know what waits us – we shall be hanged!" Then Ney caught sight of Brue's brigade, greatly reduced yet keeping admirable order in the midst of the general chaos. Animated by desperation, he rushed towards them and ordered them to halt and turn. Bareheaded, his face black with powder, his uniform torn and bloodstained, he waved a sword broken to the hilt and placed himself at the head of the small band of men. "Follow me!" he roared, "and I will show you how a marshal of France dies on the battlefield." Dutifully the men followed, once more driving themselves up the muddy slope to face the enemy. But the marshal might have spared them this useless action, for they had nothing to fear from the Bourbons. Most of them perished, while Ney escaped the death he sought and found his way into one of the retiring squares. Durutte, his right hand severed, his forehead gaping, was carried backward on his horse in the midst of a charge of the English cavalry which swept him to La Belle Alliance, and thence he escaped down the Brussels road.

The Young Guard under Duhesme, and two battalions of the Old Guard, under General Pelet, fought valiantly to hold Plancenoit. The village was mostly in flames, but they held on until they fell, thus preventing the Prussians surging over the Brussels road and cutting off Napoleon's retreat.

The three squares of the Old Guard left by Napoleon below La Haye Sainte fought their way slowly back to La Belle Alliance. Reduced by incessant attacks, they could no longer form squares three deep and so changed to triangles, two deep; with their bayonets fixed they kept their formation though continually harassed. English officers, coming close, entreated them to save their lives by surrendering, but received only General Cambronne's famous reply, "*Merde!*" A few moments later this valiant soldier, struck in the forehead by a bullet, fell senseless to the ground. Later in the evening, unconscious and stripped by the peasants even of his underwear, he was carried off the field a prisoner.

Cambronne fell just as the remnant of his battalion reached the heights of La Belle Alliance. Unable to hold together, the men were now merged with the general wave of fugitives where everyone was for himself. Only three battalions of the Old Guard were now in order; they were the two battalions of grenadiers which Napoleon had joined at Rossomme, and the 1st Chasseurs which had been left all day at Le Caillou. Napoleon was within one of the squares at Rossomme; a battery had been brought up at his orders, and trumpets sounded to rally the fugitives. In spite of enemy attacks, the squares of grenadiers did not move, except to close up over those who fell.

Eventually the Prussians broke through in masses upon Rossomme, driving before them those troops on the right – Count Lobau's infantry, the cavalry of Domon and Subervie, the Young Guard in Plancenoit – who had been covering the retreat of the army. These French fugitives were attacked by British cavalry as they reached the heights of Rossomme; seeking refuge in the squares of the Old Guard, they were shot down with others trying to break in. General Duhesme fell severely wounded. His aide-de-camp, assisted by one or two privates, lifted him from the ground, and they carried him with them as they endeavoured to escape.

Between La Belle Alliance and Rossomme there was the most murderous chaos. Cuirassiers who had lost their horses threw down their heavy armour in order to run more quickly, thus adding to the debris that littered the ground. Drivers of vehicles cut the traces of the harness and galloped off; in this way, hundreds of wounded men were abandoned to their fate. Cannon and overturned wagons blocked the way; dead horses, dead men, were strewn on roads and fields; the Allied pursuers sabred and bayoneted the French as fast as they could, and no doubt each other as well as the light failed and the universal madness increased.

In the midst of the débâcle the two squares of grenadiers stood firm and beat off all assailants; never was the courage and self-control of the Imperial Guard better displayed. But Napoleon now ordered them to retreat. He himself galloped back with Soult, Drouot, Lobau and about half a dozen mounted chasseurs. Reaching Le Caillou, he found the personal escort he had posted there, the 1st Chasseurs, and ordered them to proceed with him to Genappe. "I count on you," he said. Keeping to the side of the column, while the two battalions of grenadiers, commanded by General Petit, covered his retreat, Napoleon rode on.[183]

At a quarter past nine Wellington met Blücher in front of La Belle Alliance. Wellington recalled the scene:

"Blücher and I met near La Belle Alliance; we were both on horseback; but he embraced and kissed me, exclaiming, *Mein lieber Kamerad*, and then *quelle affaire!* which was pretty much all he knew of French."[184]

He persuaded Wellington now – whose troops were exhausted, though why more so than Blücher's, which had had the terrible march from Wavre, it is not altogether easy to see – to leave the pursuit in his hands. He personally rode after his victim that night as far as Genappe. Gneisenau called the pursuit a mad chase, *die reine Klapperjagd*, and declared later, "it was the most glorious night of my life!"

Blücher himself found time, before he finally retired to rest, to write to his wife:

"You well remember what I promised you, and I have kept my word. The enemy's superiority of numbers obliged me to give way on the 17th; but on the 18th, in conjunction with my friend Wellington, I put an end to Napoleon's dancing. His army is completely routed, and the whole of his artillery, baggage, caissons, and equipages are in my hands. The insignia of all the different orders he had won have just been brought to me, having been found in his carriage in a casket. I had two horses killed under me yesterday. It will soon be all over with Bonaparte."

In an official letter written the next day Blücher has fresh details to add:

"The victory is the most complete that ever was gained. Napoleon escaped in the night without either hat or sword. I send both sword and hat to-day to the King. His most magnificently embroidered state-mantle and his carriage are in my hands, as also his perspective glass with which he observed us during the battle. His jewels and all his valuables are the booty of our troops…"

A Prussian officer writes on the 24th of Napoleon's seal ring which "now blazes on the hand of the hero,

Gneisenau," and also of the great numbers of diamonds found: "The fusileers sold four or five diamonds as large as a pea, or even larger, for a few francs."[185]

–

As the Prussians went by, the English soldiers saluted them with a threefold cheer of "Hip! Hip! Hurrah!" Then they proceeded to settle down in their bivouacs, despite the heaps of dead around them. From the plateau of Mont-Saint-Jean to the heights of Rossomme, from Hougoumont to Plancenoit, and even as far as Smohain, the ground was covered with dead bodies and slain horses. More than 25,000 French, and 20,000 English, Belgians, and Prussians lay upon the ground, in some places scattered about like fallen trees, in others, lying in long files like rows of wheat cut down by the reapers' sickles. The moon had risen and lit up distinctly their ghastly, blood-stained faces and their mud-stained uniforms smeared with red stains; the weapons that had dropped from their hands, gleaming in the moonlight. Now and again thick, dark clouds, spreading over the sky, veiled this vision, from which the least sensitive among the old warriors turned away their eyes. But soon the vision reappeared in the cold light of the moon. Amidst the agonised moans of the dying and the groans of the wounded, at short intervals, a hoarse cry went up, stifled as it were with horror and dread. It was some officer whom a vile robber of the dead was finishing with the butt-end of a gun in order to rob him of his purse or his cross of honour.

The Prussians carried out their pursuit with the utmost vigour.[186]

–

Such was the issue of this struggle, commenced under such happy auspices, and which resulted more fatal to France than the battles of Poitiers and Azincourt. It must be admitted, that this disaster was the work of a multitude of unheard-of circumstances: if Napoleon can be reproached for certain faults, it must be allowed that fortune dealt cruelly with him in the lesser details, and that his enemies in return, were as fortunate as they showed themselves skillful. However unjust be the spirit of party, we are forced to render homage to the merits of two generals, who, unexpectedly attacked in their cantonments extending from Dinant and Liège to Renaix, near Tournay, had taken such wise measures, as to be in condition next morning for giving battle to equal forces, and for afterwards conquering by an able concentration of the two armies.

As to Napoleon, we have already pointed out the faults in execution, committed the 16th and 17th, as well by himself as by his lieutenants. In the very battle of Waterloo, the French might be censured for having attempted the first attack in masses too deep. This system was never successful against the murderous fire of English infantry and artillery...

There were likewise extraordinary charges of cavalry, which being devoid of support, became heroic but useless struggles. Notwithstanding all this, it is almost certain that Napoleon would have remained master of the field of battle, but for the arrival of 65,000 Prussians on his rear; a decisive and disastrous circumstance, that to prevent was not entirely in his power. As soon as the enemy led 130,000 men on the battle-field, with scarcely 50,000 to oppose them, all was lost.[187]

That is the view of General Jomini. Captain Becke lays more emphasis on Napoleon's declining powers.

This campaign of 1815 is inexplicable on the supposition that Napoleon's powers were not seriously impaired by the life he had led. After giving due weight to Ney's dire failure on June 17, and to Grouchy's wretched manoeuvres on June 17 and 18,[188] yet it must be acknowledged that Napoleon himself was responsible, very largely, for the disaster which overtook the last, and perhaps the most devoted of all the Grand Armies of that heroic age.

Napoleon, the greatest indeed of all historic men, although he achieved immortality, was, nevertheless – a man. He had ended by considering himself something almost superhuman, and thereby he lost all sense of due proportion; and in 1815, owing to his waning mental powers, his ruin and final overthrow were ensured.

In the battle of Waterloo itself, as M. Houssaye has proved, Napoleon was full of energetic action; for even if he did not sleep during the battle, yet he took his rest, and wisely so, during some non-critical period. For during all the other and critical phases of the battle he was wakeful, active and eager. Even though his mind no longer dominated his body as of yore, yet the stimulus of action, and particularly of battle, at once galvanised him into at least a resemblance of his old self. So, in 1815, there came brilliant flashes on occasions, which revealed a trace of the old unsurpassed genius, but they were few and far between and at ever-lengthening intervals.

Thus, without holding either extreme view, the sound conclusion is probably that the Emperor's powers were impaired seriously; but this is far from saying that in 1815 he was palsied, paralysed, or impotent. The battle invariably acted as a tonic to his mind, and stimulated him afresh while it lasted; and, at times, his iron will could gain the mastery over his body to such an extent, that he was still capable of great, but alas! only temporary, energy; and in the conduct of his battle, on June 18, the confirmation of these views, with regard to the withering of his mental powers is only too apparent.[189]

Wellington, too, had made his mistakes, as Colonel Dodge pointed out:

In this Waterloo campaign, Wellington was not at his best as a strategist. He misunderstood Napoleon's opening movements, and was slow in preparing to meet them. He barely escaped defeat at Quatre Bras owing to Ney's slackness. He was open to disaster during the first part of the 17th, and the risk he took during the 18th at Waterloo was scarcely justified. His detachment at Hal was thrown away. How he could have thought that Napoleon would move round between the sea and the British army, so as to permit Blücher and him to retire to a junction, it is hard to say. Had Blücher not been able to get up in time, he would have suffered defeat as a result of his errors. But he fought the battle like a true Briton.

It is claimed that both Wellington and Blücher should have operated to a concentration on June 17, but Wellington showed little disposition to do this. He fell back to his predetermined ground, as if expecting Blücher to do all the manoeuvring. At Wavre and at Waterloo the two armies were further apart than at Quatre Bras and at Sombreffe. If closer cooperation was to be expected, it is of Wellington that the work should be demanded, and not of Blücher, who did more than his share.

Napoleon says that "the Prussian general violated these three great rules in war: 1st, to keep your cantonments close to each other; 2d, to give as assembly to the various cantonments a point where they can all arrive before the enemy; 3d, to operate his retreat on his reinforcements."

This is fair criticism, but as it happens, Blücher helped Wellington win Waterloo by disregarding the third item, after the same fashion that Napoleon himself frequently violated his own maxims, when the risk run was warranted by the probable gain. The only real error made by Blücher was in accepting battle at Ligny; but he was acting, as he supposed, in concert with Wellington.

There can be attributed to Napoleon during the campaign, a series of faults, which in the old days of his almost superhuman activity – as at Ratisbon – he would not have committed. He began by losing time at the very start. Two sets of orders should have been sent to Vandamme. He knew that Ney at Bautzen had failed for lack of orders sufficiently explicit, and he should have made those he sent him on this occasion definite. If he wanted him to capture Quatre Bras, he should earlier and with certainty have told him so. He had the maps, it was his head that devised the manoeuvre, and he knew that Ney had no broad strategic comprehension. He should have seen to it that Ney followed up his orders. He should not have wasted the forenoon of the 16th. He should have given positive orders to Ney to detach Erlon, or when he had Erlon in hand, he should have held on to him. He should have pursued the Prussians after his indecisive victory quickly and sharply. He should have positively ascertained their direction. He should have reckoned on Blücher's tremendous energy and Gneisenau's ability, of which he had had sufficient evidence the two preceding years. He should have given Grouchy clear orders to move on interior lines. After examining the position of the

English with Bertrand at midnight preceding Waterloo, he should at once have called in Grouchy. He should have attacked the Anglo-Dutch earlier than he did. He should have attacked them with all his forces as soon as Bülow was discovered, if he was not ready to retire. Napoleon had said at Austerlitz that there was only a certain time given to the general to do his best work, and that he himself should be good for it only six years more. It was just six years from then to the Russian campaign.

All criticism of Napoleon's conduct of this campaign must be read in the spirit that prompts it, the utmost admiration of his genius, and a desire to inquire why he here failed, when previously, under as difficult conditions, he had won. After all is said, and despite his last four years, Napoleon remains the greatest soldier of modern times; criticism of any kind must always result in evolving this same conclusion; and every word spoken in blame of his laxness here is subject to the knowledge that no failure can rob him of his fame as the best leader and broadest teacher of war of the Christian era.[190]

11

Victors and Victims

The duke reached his head-quarters at Waterloo about ten o'clock at night. He had ridden the same horse all day, yet such was the spirit of the animal, that on his master dismounting, he kicked out in play, and well-nigh struck the duke. The duke entered, and found his dinner prepared with as much regularity as if the cook had expected him home from a review. He ate little, and ate in silence: indeed, grief for the fallen, and anxious thoughts about their relatives, quite broke him down.

The duke retired to bed, worn out with fatigue and excitement. He slept till an hour which was late for him; that is to say, at seven next morning Dr. Hume arrived to make his report, and found that his chief was not yet stirring. Having waited till eight, Dr. Hume took it upon him to knock at the bedroom door, and being desired to enter he did so. The duke sat up in his bed. He was undressed, but had neither washed nor shaved over-night. His face was therefore black with the dust and powder of the great battle, and in that plight he desired the chief of his medical staff to make his report. Dr. Hume read on; but becoming himself deeply affected, he stopped as if to draw breath, and looked up. The tears were running from the duke's eyes, making furrows and channels for themselves through the grime upon his cheek. "Go on," he said, "go on, for God's sake, go on. Let me hear it all. This is terrible." Dr. Hume finished his paper, and withdrew, leaving his great chief in an agony of distress.[191]

Later there were disagreements with the Prussians about the name by which the shared victory should be known. The Prussians wished to call it the Battle of La Belle Alliance; and still, in fact, do so.[192] *There were also disagreements about the fate of Napoleon, the Prussians wanting him to be executed. But Wellington refused to sanction such a measure; and Blücher gave way.*[193] *When Wellington went to say good-bye to him, he found the old Marshal's mind had been affected by his recent experiences. Earl Stanhope remembered a conversation he had had with the Duke about this:*

"When I went to take leave of him [Blücher], he positively told me that he was pregnant! And what do you think he told me he was pregnant of? – An elephant! And who do you think he said had produced it? – A French soldier! That is the human mind.

"It was the last time I ever saw him. I went to him; he could hardly speak French, but he said (striking his side), '*Je sens un elephant là!*'.

"And what could you say to him? I could only say, *Je vous assure que vous vous méprenez!* and that he would soon get better. But he continued to express his surprise at there being a Frenchman in the case. *Imaginez que moi – moi – moi! un soldat Français!* I suppose he had dreamt it the night before.

"He was a very fine fellow, and whenever there was any question of fighting, always ready and eager – if anything too eager."[194]

On the night of his final defeat, Napoleon rode back toward Paris.

Past him already the disorganised army was flowing like a river. He followed it the long night through over sodden roads towards the Dyle bridge, then on to Genappe, Quatre Bras, Charleroi. He was so tired that had not Gourgaud held him up he would have fallen from his horse. Now and again, shaking off his dejection, he would try to halt a few cavalrymen in order to organise a nucleus of resistance. But the flood was too strong. Those were not soldiers any more. They were just human beings paralysed by fright and exhaustion.

At five in the morning he rode through Charleroi and crossed the Sambre. He drew rein in a meadow. Someone had lighted a fire. Slowly he paced around it, his head bowed, his arms folded across his breast. Near by stood his aides-de-camp and members of his staff – Bertrand, Drouot, Flahaut, La Bédoyère, Gourgaud. They watched him in mortal silence.

Fugitives were still rushing past, but in less crowded masses – carabiniers, lancers, now and then an infantryman. Napoleon went out to meet them once more and tried to rally them. They only fled the faster. The Emperor went back to his officers and sat down on a stone, took a bit of food. Then he mounted his horse again and started for Philippeville. He was there two hours later, very tired. Maret and Chaboulon rode up. To the latter he dictated two letters for his brother Joseph. One was to be read to the ministers. It was so worded as to minimise the disaster. The other, confidential, was frank. It announced his return to Paris.

That was a mistake. He should have halted at Philippeville and gathered the remnants of his army. After a few days of panic thousands of men, knowing that the Emperor was holding on at the frontier, would have rallied to his standard. He could have reinforced them with Grouchy's corps which had more freedom of manoeuvring than in Paris, a centre of intrigues which he could not now be sure of controlling. But his old terror of politicians blinded him. He remembered the vote of deposition by a rump Senate with which Talleyrand had stabbed him in the back in 1814 just as he was about to fall upon the Allies. This time, too, if he stayed too far away, Fouché and his friends would combine with the Royalists and overthrow him. He must return to the capital to overawe them. He must appear before the Assembly. His presence would force the Members to concentrate on the defence of the country. Seconded by Davout, by Carnot, he would scrape the provinces clean, get three hundred thousand men together and, repeating the tactics of the Campaign in France, wear the enemy armies down one by one and finally drive them out of the land.

That was what he was hoping for. But it was a hope without wings, a disillusioned faith resting on crumbling foundations. Ever since his return from Elba, triumphal though that had been, he had ceased to believe in his star. His wife and his son had failed him. He sensed around him a France that was too tired, deadly tired. Vainly had he striven to rouse her, force her to take up the burden again. He knew that he was poorly seconded, imperfectly obeyed. Treason was sneaking all about him, ready to draw the snare taut. He had set out for Waterloo in the state of mind of the gambler who throws his dice and waits, motionless, for the result. He had lost. Well – he would try to begin the game again. But he expected to lose everything.

He got into a barouche, alone. Maret and Bertrand, his aides-de-camp, followed in two other carriages. As far as Laon he slept. At the halts for new horses a few cheers would rouse him now and then. He would wave his hand, then let his head fall again upon his chest. He was at the extreme end of his strength. The tremendous strain of those three months of sleepless nights, sustained by a sheer miracle of will up to Waterloo, now suddenly came down upon him with crushing force. He looked worn out, withered, years older.

At Vaux-sous-Laon, whither he arrived on the evening of June 20, he alighted in the courtyard of the post and began pacing back and forth over the straw-littered ground. A timid crowd gazed at him through the door that had been left open.

"Job on his dunghill!" someone whispered.

The Emperor received the prefect, a few magistrates, a number of officers of the National Guard. He issued orders for the provisioning of Laon, where, he thought, his new army might mobilise. Jerome and Ney had followed him at some distance. He received them, then dictated a *communiqué* on the battles of Ligny and Mont Saint-Jean to be published in the *Moniteur*.[195] He set out again for Paris after dark. He gave instructions to drive around the walls so as to enter by the Roule Barrier. It was eight o'clock. The shops were still closed. Slipping unnoticed along the Rue du Faubourg Saint-Honoré, the barouche drew up in front of the Élysée.

Since April 17 Napoleon had not felt in a mood to stay at the Tuileries.

–

Caulaincourt was waiting for him in the doorway. The general ran to meet him and helped him to alight.

Wearily the Emperor dragged himself up the steps.

"Well, Caulaincourt, there we are! Something splendid! How will the nation take this setback?"

Reaching his study he flung himself on a sofa.

"Why, the thing was won! The army had done miracles. Then, at the end of the day, a panic seizes them! I can't understand it! Ney went in like a lunatic. He slaughtered all my cavalry! I'm all in. I must have two hours' rest before I shall be fit for anything."

He had been tortured with a distended bladder ever since the action at Ligny. He put his hand to his chest:

"I am smothering – here. Have them get me a bath ready."

Recovering his composure he remarked to Caulaincourt that he intended to state the situation before the two Houses, ask for their support and be off again at once.

The Duke de Vicenza replied that the Members seemed hostile – Fouché, Lafayette, Lanjuinais, Manuel, had been busy since the night before when the first rumours of defeat began circulating in Paris. The Liberals were raising their voices. The Royalists were thrilling with joy.

"I am sorry to see you in Paris, sire," Caulaincourt concluded. "It would have been better not to leave the army. That is where your strength lies."

"But I have no army left! I have nothing but fugitives! I might be able to find a few men. But how arm them? I have no guns now."

But almost in the same breath he corrected himself:

"I'll find men and guns. There's a remedy for everything. You judge the Members too harshly. Most of them are all right. I have only Lafayette and a few others against me. I am in their way. They would like to work for themselves. I shan't let them!"

He had been in his bath a few moments, chatting with Joseph and Regnault de Saint-Jean d'Angély, when Davout, the Minister of War, arrived at the Élysée. At sight of him Napoleon lifted his arms out of the water and let them fall again with a great splash. Davout's uniform was drenched.

"So then, Davout! So then!" he cried.

He gave a brief account of the battle, venting his irritations, complaining of Ney again. Davout interrupted him:

"He has put his own neck in a halter for your sake."

"What is going to come of it all?" asked the Emperor.

"Nothing is really lost," replied Davout, "but we must take energetic steps."

He suggested the immediate dissolution of the Assembly. He was right, that soldier! With "the lawyers" scattered the Emperor would again be master. But Napoleon refused. He had become, he said, a constitutional monarch. He did not want to seem to be browbeating France.

He dressed and then ate breakfast in company with his brothers – Joseph downcast, Lucien enthusiastic, as in the Brumaire days. Both emphasised the danger of appealing to the Members. Napoleon listened, gazing at them out of large staring eyes, and made no answer.

Before the meeting of the Council he further received Cambacérès, Peyrusse, Rovigo and Lavalette: "The moment he caught sight of me," writes the last, "he came up to me with an epileptic laugh that frightened me. 'Oh, my God!' he cried, rolling his eyes upwards. But that was just a flash. He recovered his self-control almost at once and asked me what was going on in the Assembly."

Shortly after ten o'clock he went with them to the Council Hall. In the gallery, between two rows of anxious faces, amid generals and dignitaries who had hastened to the Elysée at word of his return, he failed to distinguish two chamberlains in red coats: Las Cases, a sometime *émigré*, and Montholon, a young general, but recently in disfavour with him.

The ministers had been summoned by Joseph. They were all present. They had been waiting in fact for a long time, conversing in low tones: Cambacérès as pompous as ever; Carnot and Maret sad, deeply moved, sincere: d'Angély and Decrès sniffing the direction of the wind; Fouché with his white face set, foreseeing and welcoming the catastrophe which, he thought, would mean power for him. Under his feigned deference Fouché was the chief adversary, as Napoleon was well aware. The Minister of Police had been discounting defeat from the beginning of the Hundred Days. In May he said to Pasquier:

"The Emperor will win one of two battles. He will lose the third. Then it will be our turn."

Though he was risking his own head Fouché was not afraid. During all the days that followed he was to act secretly but boldly, stampeding the Liberals with the threat of a military dictatorship and discouraging Napoleon's friends by picturing him as condemned beyond recall by the Allies, by Parliament, and by the country.

The Emperor took his seat and opened the meeting. He ordered Maret to read his *communiqué* on the action at Mont Saint-Jean. Then he said:

"Our misfortunes are great. I have come to remedy them. If the nation rises, the enemy will be crushed. If, instead of taking energetic steps, we waste time arguing, all is lost. To save the country I must have a temporary dictatorship. I could, of course seize it, but it would be wise and more national for the Assembly to confer it on me."

The ministers sat silent. Most of them lowered their eyes, that the Emperor might not read their thoughts. Napoleon called on them one after the other. Carnot spoke like a patriot, in the tone of a man of the Revolution. He was for calling France to arms and repulsing the invasion with the means and in the spirit of the Year II. Caulaincourt was alarmed at such language. He maintained gently that the Emperor should try to come to an agreement with the Members. Maret and Cambacérès seconded him. Fouché, calm as ever, objected to dissolution – he had too great an interest in saving the Assembly in session. Fearing that the proposal of dissolution, which would have been the end of him, might be carried, Fouché hurried pencilled notes from the Council Hall itself to his henchmen in the Assembly – Manuel, Jay, Dupin – to warn them and fend off the danger.

D'Angély, one of Napoleon's oldest friends, who, however, was being worked upon by Fouché, was the first to propose a regency. The Members, he thought, would accept one.

Napoleon's lips narrowed to a thin line.

"Speak plainly!" he said, "What they want is my abdication?"

"I fear so, sire."

And he added, astounded at his own boldness – but Waterloo justified anything:

"It might well be that should Your Majesty decide not to offer your abdication the Assembly would make so bold as to ask for it."

Lucien drew himself up:

"If the Assembly will not stand by the Emperor, he will get along without its assistance. Let him declare martial law throughout France and call all patriots to her defence!"

Napoleon then took the floor with his old assurance:

"The presence of the enemy on French soil will, I trust, bring the Members to a sense of their duty. I do not fear them. Whatever they do I shall always be the idol of the people and the army. I would only have to say the word and they would all be knocked on the head."

In a resurgence of genius he drew a lucid picture of the danger the country was in, of its last resources, of the chances it still had to win. The army was assembling at Laon. Grouchy, untouched, was marching on Givet. The arsenals had reserves. Vincennes and La Fère could provide five hundred pieces. Napoleon guaranteed that by rapid mobilisation of the reserves he could have a hundred and thirty thousand men in line within a fortnight – more than the Anglo-Prussians, so sorely taxed at Waterloo, could meet him with. The Russians and the Austrians were far away. Before they could come up, their Allies would be vanquished. Paris sat fortified and guarded. A hundred and sixty thousand men coming up from the last conscription with guns on their shoulders would fall into line beside their elder comrades.

His imagination rode rough-shod over obstacles, magnified numbers, stifled doubts. The magnetism of his voice, low at first then gradually rising till it filled the room, once more exerted its spell upon those old acquaintances, many of whom were weary, several of whom had betrayed him, and all of whom were thinking of themselves. But for fifteen years they had seen him so much the master of events that they could readily believe that he was about to work a new miracle. At the end he said with a pathos that gave them a shudder:

"I would have understood had they turned me back when I landed at Cannes. To-day I am bound up with the nation. To sacrifice me would be to hold out its hands for chains."

Then almost all of them felt ready to follow that amazing man who had lost, it was true, but who, to-morrow, alone against all Europe, might again find himself the conqueror.

Under the spur of the master they went on to actual business. Davout would be Commandant in Paris and the city would be placed under martial law. Clauzel would be Minister of War. The government would be transferred to Tours. The Federal Guard would be armed and combined with the National Guard. The Emperor would inform the Assembly of all that. How should he dress in appearing before them? In full ceremonial attire, or in his field uniform still splashed with mud? Preferences were for the uniform.

But just then the door opened and a message from the Assembly was handed to Napoleon. There was a sudden silence. He read it aloud:

"The Assembly declares itself in permanent session. Any attempt to dissolve it is a crime of high treason. Any person who shall be guilty of such an attempt will be a traitor to his country and immediately tried as such."

Check to the Emperor! The Liberals had not wasted any time!

"I should have disbanded those fellows before I left," he said bitterly. "This is the end. They will be the ruin of France."

His brief illusion shattered, he relapsed into his hesitancy again. The minds around him lost their bearings. Davout began to talk of legality. Napoleon dismissed the meeting with a phrase that brought a gleam of blissfulness to Fouché's face:

"I see that Regnault was not deceiving me. I shall abdicate if necessary."

Leave the city? It was too late. Napoleon saw himself at the mercy of propertied Jacobins, of disguised aristocrats who hated him and were afraid of losing the titles, land grants and salaries which he had bestowed on them, if he clung to power. However, he decided to wait before making up his mind. He was still hoping against hope.

He sent D'Angély to the Members and Carnot to the Peers to announce that he was "busying himself with those measures of public safety that circumstances might demand." The dragging afternoon shook his self-confidence still more while the Assembly plucked up greater and greater boldness. Aroused by Fouché and Lafayette, it suddenly voted to call upon the ministers to appear before it. Claiming that the Emperor had threatened them the Members summoned the National Guard to their aid. Napoleon passed those hours in the gardens of the Elyseé discussing the situation with Caulaincourt, Maret, Savary and Lucien. The Brumaire "President", who had been shouldered out of the blessings of the Empire, was the only one in the general collapse to try to rouse Napoleon to the energy of the old days. He implored him to make a clean sweep of the Members.

"It is not a matter of a *coup d'etat*, but of a constitutional decree. You have the right to do it."

"The Assembly will resist," Napoleon replied. "We shall have to use force. And as for that, where is the force? There are no soldiers, even in Paris. At the very least Davout would have to rush a few troops in from the reserve depots of the Somme. He has been ordered to. We are obliged to wait."

"You are deliberating when you should be acting. The Members are acting – they are!"

"What can they do? They are a lot of talkers."

"Public opinion is with them. They will vote deposition."

"Deposition! They will not dare!"

"They will dare anything."

"Let's see Davout!"

Napoleon went indoors. Lucien did not follow him. In his exasperation the Emperor's brother dared exclaim out loud in the presence of two members of the Council:

"He is hesitating – he is temporising. The smoke of Mont Saint-Jean has gone to his head. He is a ruined man."[196]

On June 22 Napoleon signed his second abdication. At first he thought of sailing to the United States. But, disliking the idea of an undignified escape, he decided instead to appeal to the English for their hospitality, and he wrote to the Prince Regent.[197] *He left the Atlantic port of Rochefort, to which he had retreated from Paris and went on board the French brig, the* Épervier, *and then transferred voluntarily to the British ship, the* Bellerophon, *commanded by Captain Maitland. Maitland sent a longboat to the* Épervier.

The longboat drew alongside. The executive officer of the *Bellerophon* came on board. He greeted the Emperor in English.

Napoleon looked around. Bertrand and Mme de Montholon turned deathly pale. The officer lowered his eyes. There was not a sound on the whole deck – a pin-drop could have been heard.

Napoleon broke the anguished tension. He asked the two ladies if they felt inclined to enter the longboat. They nodded.

"Very well! Let us be off!"

The English officer offered his arm to Countess Bertrand. The Emperor's companions followed. The officers and crew of the *Épervier* gathered around Napoleon. He addressed a brief word of thanks to them. Then he went down into the boat.

As soon as he was seated the boat shoved away from the brig. The French sailors, leaning far out over the rail, broke into a long and mighty cheer: "Hurrah for the Emperor! Long live the Emperor!" Napoleon bent over, dipped a hand in the sea, gathered a little water in his palm and sprinkled it on the hull of the *Épervier.*

Maitland stood watching the boat as it advanced towards his ship. At first he was unable to distinguish the Emperor. He passed his glass about among his officers. Finally they recognised him. They were all a-tremble with excitement. The prey was there, drawing nearer with every dip of the oars!

It was six o'clock when the longboat came alongside. Maitland did not deign to go to the bottom of the ladder to receive Napoleon. Bertrand went up on deck.

"The Emperor is in the boat," he said to the captain.

Maitland appeared not to understand. He waited on the quarter-deck with his staff grouped about him.

Napoleon came up the steps in his turn, panting a little. He passed in front of a line of sailors, but they did not present arms. Maitland was to excuse himself for this discourtesy by saying that it was not customary aboard English warships to pay honours before the flag was hoisted. That took place at eight o'clock in the morning.

Napoleon advanced slowly towards the group of British officers. Las Cases came to meet him and called Maitland's name. Napoleon raised his hat and said in a loud distinct tone:

"Commander, I have come to place myself under the protection of your prince and your laws."

Maitland saluted, addressed him as "sir." He led him to the large room on the bridge. The Emperor looked about:

"What a fine room!"

"Such as it is, sir, it is at your service while you remain on board the ship I command."

The Emperor asked to be introduced to the officers, then he visited the whole ship, escorted by Maitland.

At nine o'clock breakfast was announced. Napoleon sat at the commander's table, eating little – the dishes were cold and he was accustomed to having things hot.

The breeze had freshened offshore and the *Superb* gathered speed. She dropped anchor at half past ten. Maitland took leave of Napoleon and hurried aboard to report to his Admiral.

"Tell him, I beg of you, that I wish to see him."

Hotham came in the afternoon and called on the Emperor. Napoleon showed him his field library and chatted about service in the navy, asking a number of questions to which the Admiral replied in a deferential tone.

Dinner was served at five o'clock, with the Emperor's own plate and by his own people. Napoleon entered the dining-room first and seated himself at the middle of the table, inviting Sir Henry Hotham to take a seat at his right. Countess Bertrand was at his left.

After coffee he rose and led his guests into the large room, where the conversation was friendly and intimate in tone. He retired early after having accepted an invitation to breakfast the next day, Sunday, on the flagship.

-

On leaving his room to board the *Superb* the Emperor found a line of soldiers drawn up to do him honour. He stopped, then reviewed them and inspected their arms. With Maitland serving as interpreter, he ordered them to fix bayonets. Finding the movement awkwardly executed, he seized a musket and showed amid general surprise, how the thing was done in the French army.

His entire suite, women and children included, were to go with him. As he was getting into the boat he noted that Las Cases had appeared in naval uniform, as a commander.

"What, Las Cases?" he cried, jesting. "You, a soldier? I have never seen you in uniform!"

"Excuse me, sire! I was a commander in the navy before the Revolution. I have concluded that a uniform gets one more consideration outside one's country. I have gone back to mine."

On the *Superb* the band was playing. A tent, with a large English flag for a ceiling, had been pitched over a considerable section of the deck, and a table set beneath it. Removing his cap, Admiral Hotham greeted Napoleon with the greatest courtesy and deference. He expressed the hope that the Emperor would remain on his vessel. Not wishing to mortify Maitland, Napoleon declined the invitation, returning to the *Bellerophon* at noon.

Shortly afterwards the veteran of Aboukir, her old planks groaning under a load of fresh paint, entered the Gut of Antioch on a beat to windward. She was followed by the *Myrmidon* on which the less important members of Napoleon's suite had been accommodated. There was so little wind that by sunset the *Bellerophon* had not yet reached open water. Napoleon was seated on deck to starboard and watched the low, grey coast of France grow dim through a drapery of golden mist.[198]

Napoleon, however, was not to be allowed to live in retirement in England. He was still the symbol of the Revolution, and the Tory government – committed, in any event, to the support of the Bourbons – felt that his presence would be exploited by the Whig and Radical opposition. Napoleon protested against what he termed this violation of his "most sacred rights."[199] *But it was politically impossible to harbor him in England. Admiral Lord Keith broke the bitter news to him that he was to be exiled to St. Helena, not as the ex-Emperor but as General Bonaparte.*

12

The Price of Failure

Napoleon's failure to achieve final victory, and through it a peace, not only profitable to France but also acceptable to her opponents, may be traced to three radical defects in his conduct of war. The first, a military one, was overcentralization of command; the second, a political one, was his unrealistic policy; and his third a grand-strategical one, that the means he relied upon to accomplish his policy could at best only lead to an armistice…

Some historians have held that the Emperor's lack of success in his later campaigns was due to ill-health or physical degeneracy; there is little to support this. The truth is, that it was his activity, not his lethargy, which was as much the cause of his fall as of his rise, for it led him to believe that in his person he could combine the duties of commander-in-chief and chief of staff, and when skilled staff officers were needed they were not to be found. Caulaincourt informs us that in 1812, "The staff foresaw nothing, but on the other hand, as the Emperor wanted to do everything himself, and give every order, no one, not even the general staff, dared to assume the responsibility of giving the most trifling order." D'Odeleben says that in 1813 the staff was even less efficient than the year before, and "As a whole, the army in this campaign was a too complicated and imperfect machine to allow of coordination being established … the multiplicity of movements … gave place to difficulties which all the authority of Napoleon could not always surmount."

Napoleon's marshals had not been brought up to command, solely to obey, they were followers and not leaders, vassal princes, many of whom had been raised in rank for dynastic, political and personal reasons.

Throughout, his dominant adversary was England who, by subsidizing her continental allies, raised coalition after coalition against him. The struggle with her was not one of right against wrong, but between two survival values that arose out of the early Industrial Revolution. To remain prosperous and powerful, England had to export her manufactured goods; and to become prosperous, and thereby sustain her power, France had to protect her infant industries. As Metternich said: "Everyone knew that England could not give way on this question [the maritime problem,] which to her was a matter of life and death." And it was because Napoleon realized this that he devised what is known as his Continental System, the closing of all continental ports to English shipping, so that England's trade would be strangled and her credit undermined, without which she would be unable to raise enemies against him.

"The power of the English," he said, "… rests only upon the monopoly they exercise over other nations, and can be maintained only by that. Why should they alone reap the benefits which millions of others could reap as well?" And again: "The good of that Europe which seems to envelop her with goodwill counts for nothing with the merchants of London. They would sacrifice every State in Europe, even the whole world, to further one of their speculations. If their debt were not so large they might be more reasonable. It is the necessity of paying this, of maintaining their credit, that drives them on…"

In his struggle with England, he saw "the basic solution of all the questions" that were "agitating the world and even individuals." Therefore, as he told Caulaincourt, England was his sole enemy: "He was working against England alone", and "since their trade had ramifications everywhere he had to pursue them everywhere." It was out of this pursuit that his idea of universal empire arose. From a weapon with which to destroy England, the Continental System became an instrument whereby a new world conception would be realized – the vision of Europe united in concord…

A federated Europe was anathema to England, because in face of it she could not survive as the dominant maritime power; therefore the clash between her and France was to the death; a struggle in which, no sooner had Napoleon destroyed one of her coalitions, than another arose from its ashes. To accomplish his aim, it was necessary to subjugate England without antagonizing the continental powers; for were they antagonized, they would the more readily coalesce with England. This is what his Continental System led to, because, not only did it deprive the continental nations of goods, which England alone could supply, but it involved one and all in his war with England. His grand strategy, therefore, was at fault; it was no more than a make-shift substitute for the fleet he had lost at Trafalgar in 1805.

Immediately after the battle of Jena, the Emperor initiated his continental blockade by his Berlin Decree, and England retaliated with an Order in Council which prohibited neutral trade with France and her allies.

Thus an economic war was launched, and after the defeat of the Russians at Friedland, on 7th July 1807, Russia and Prussia agreed to take common action with France against England. With this success to his credit, Napoleon extended his blockade to Denmark, Portugal and Spain, and later to Holland. In March 1809, he placed his brother Joseph on the Spanish throne, and the result was the outbreak of the Peninsular War. War with Austria followed, and soon after her defeats at Echmühl and Wagram the Russian alliance with France began to weaken, and in 1810 Tzar Alexander allowed English merchantmen to enter Russian ports. The situation then deteriorated so rapidly that Napoleon remarked to Caulaincourt: "War will occur in spite of me, in spite of the Emperor Alexander, in spite of the interests of France and the interests of Russia. I have so often seen this that it is my experience of the past which unveils the future to me… It is all a scene of the opera and the English control the machinery." When at St. Helena, he said to Las Cases: "Russia was the last resource of England. The peace of the whole world rested with Russia. Alas! English gold proved more powerful than my plans."

Napoleon's disastrous Russian campaign followed; in 1813 he was decisively defeated by Russia, Austria, Prussia and Sweden at Leipzig, and on 11th April 1814, he abdicated his throne. Thus, both his policy and grand strategy utterly failed. So long as England was in the field, though he could overrun Europe, he could not bind Europe to his throne, because in conquering her he sold his birthright to her peoples.

In 1792, the spirit of French nationalism, awakened by the Revolution, became the soul of the French armies, and had this not been so there would never have been a Napoleon. Then, after Jena, he began to squander his heritage, and his exactions awoke, first in Spain, then in Austria, then in Prussia, and lastly in all Europe the selfsame spirit that had propelled his armies across that continent. In Spain, the Spanish guerrillas, as much so as Wellington's small army, pinned down scores of thousands of his troops; in 1809 Austria adopted conscription, and when on 13th March 1813, Prussia, in alliance with Russia, declared war on him, a *levée en masse* was forthwith proclaimed. Every man not acting in the regular army or *Landwehr* was to support the army by acting against the enemy's communications and rear. The people were to fight to the death and with every means in their power. The enemy was to be harassed, his supplies, cut off and his stragglers massacred. No uniforms were to be worn, and on the enemy's approach, after all food stocks had been destroyed, and mills, bridges, and boats burnt, the villages were to be abandoned and refuge sought in the woods and hills. "Such," writes Fain, "are the new means that the … enemies of Napoleon propose to employ against him." It was to be a repetition of 1792.

Thus Napoleon, like a missionary – indeed he was one with cannon and sword – preached the gospel of the Nation in Arms throughout the length and breadth of Europe, and in time it became the military creed of all her troublesome peoples. Spiritually linked with this is what Stanislas Girardin, in his Memoirs, relates on Napoleon's visit to the tomb of Rousseau. In reply to a question of Girardin's he said: "Well, the future will show whether it would not have been better for the repose of the world that neither I nor Rousseau had existed."[200]

The last fling of his ambition had to be paid for, like the earlier ones, by France; not only in the loss of life and the expense of war but in a severer treaty of peace. France was reduced to the frontiers of 1789, with the additional loss of one or two small areas for strategic reasons, the most important being the Saar, its future economic importance not yet suspected. An indemnity of 700 million francs was extorted. The works of art looted from Europe were to be returned. The fortresses of the North and East were to be occupied by 150,000 allied troops for a period of from three to five years. The price of the Hundred Days in the terms of a treaty can easily be stated: its price in terms of the subsequent history of France remains undefinable.[201]

The treaty of peace was not, however, as severe as it might have been and as many had hoped it would be.

Waterloo was the last act of a tragedy, the end of one age and the beginning of another.

It is much to the credit of British statesmanship that when, after the Hundred Days, a new arrangement had to be made with France, the vanquished country was still treated with moderation. If Prussia had had her way, Alsace and Lorraine would have been among the sacrifices required from the restored government of Louis XVIII. Wellington and Castlereagh, however, saw that nothing would be more certainly calculated to undermine the authority of the Bourbons than a crippling loss of territory. It was to the interest of England, as it was to the advantage of Europe, that the old dynasty, despite the tremendous handicap of its estrangement from the military glories of the Napoleonic period, should nevertheless be helped to reconquer and retain the loyalty of the French people. This, it was rightly judged, would have been a hopeless task if the full Prussian programme of spoliation had been sanctioned. France was, indeed, condemned to lose the Duchy of Bouillon and part of the Ardennes to the Netherlands, to hand over the forts of Saarlouis and Landau to Germany, to pay seven hundred million francs as an indemnity, to submit to an army of occupation for a period of five or three years, and to restore the art treasures which she was permitted under the earlier peace to retain. In these stipulations there was nothing intolerable to French pride, but the apprehensions of Alexander I, who doubted the wisdom of restoring the Bourbon House to France, were justified in the event. The plant of legitimacy failed to flourish upon soil still covered by the lava of revolution. The concert of Europe could neither save France from convulsions, nor prevent the return of Bonapartist ideas and the creation of a Second Empire. But with all its shortcomings it gave to Europe forty years of comparative peace.[202]

13

The Legend

If we ask, as the Greeks would have done, what was the end of the Napoleonic state, the answer must be war. In war it had begun, war remained its *raison d'être*, and by war it was to end.[203]

The art of the period represented this militaristic spirit and preoccupation in a highly romantic light.

Napoleon himself was represented *ad nauseam*, the hero leading the charge across the bridge at Lodi, presenting the Eagles to his legions, riding his chariot in a Roman triumph or apotheosized as a classical deity, sparing the conquered on the battlefield or subjecting the proud, visiting the victims of plague, rousing by his very presence the spirit of devotion in the wounded and dying. It is quite clear that the French painters of the period and Goya – of course, a painter on a different scale of magnitude – were not illustrating the same war. But it would be a mistake to judge the political success of Napoleon's artists by their artistic merits. Their influence in the formation of the Napoleonic legend and in creating and perpetuating a romantic attitude to war is not to be underestimated.[204]

Later influences on the formation of the Napoleonic legend have been analyzed by the Dutch historian, Professor Pieter Geyl:

The first to provide a portrait in which there was nought but unblemished beauty, endearing humanity, greatness and virtue, was Napoleon himself. On St. Helena he set about the task of shaping his reputation for posterity. The *Mémorial*, in which the Marquis Las Cases noted his conversations, a book which had an immeasurable influence in France, and which was the first and foremost source of what is called the Napoleonic legend, was peculiarly suited to become a popular classic. Anecdotes and reminiscences chosen at random from the whole miraculous life are interwoven with speculations, the whole within the framework of the Longwood tragedy and the bitter struggle with Sir Hudson Lowe, which Las Cases describes from day to day. This plan gives the book its human note. It catches the emotions as well as the interest of innumerable readers. It presents Napoleon not just as the aloof, mighty Emperor, but as somebody who, for all his incomparable cleverness, greatness and luck, is nevertheless accessible, one of ourselves.

From this living, variegated backcloth emerges the political Napoleon. He is before everything else the son of the Revolution, the man who consolidated the possession of equality, and made good his country's escape from feudalism by restoring order, by ridding France of those factions which had practically dissipated the fruits of the Revolution, and by wresting peace from the monarchs who hated France and the Revolution. That peace (Lunéville, 1801, Amiens, 1802, when Bonaparte had only just become First Consul) was a breathing space, which brought sudden overwhelming popularity to the victorious young hero. There was nothing Napoleon liked better to recall after his downfall, and the fact could hardly be denied, but how brief was that respite! How endless, bitter and bloody were the campaigns which followed, up to the disasters and the final collapse! It was all the fault, so the Napoleon of the *Mémorial* would have us believe, of those self-same monarchs, and of envious Britain. His conquests had adorned the name of France with undying fame – *gloire*, that word dear to the Frenchmen of the period – but they had been forced upon him. He had been obliged to conquer Europe in self-defence. And even this conquest was fraught with benefits. After the French it was the turn of the Dutch, the Swiss, the Germans, the Italians, the Spanish, to receive the blessings of the codes of laws and other revolutionary reforms. Had he been allowed to go his own way, or had he remained victorious, Europe would have become a federation of free peoples, grouped round enlightened and fortunate France in an eternal peace. It was the hatred of the monarchs and the envy of England, the mischief-maker, the pirate swayed only by low, materalistic motives, which had destroyed this noble future for France and for Europe.

Such is Napoleon's apology. But I would give an incomplete outline of the *Mémorial*, and would fail to account for the impression it made, were I to omit to add that not only is this apology embedded among anecdotes, reminiscences and daily particulars of the mournful exile, but that no sense of inconsistency prevents the fallen Emperor from enlarging with inexhaustible complacency on his military achievements. The whole work glows with the glory which surrounds Napoleon even in his fall, and which the people of France share with him. The glory of

France is the thought to which he constantly returns; and what he did, he did for France...

–

The Napoleonic legend was enriched from many sources, and it may well be said that the most important was Napoleon's own downfall. Was it not easier to glorify him, when he was no longer there to oppress men, and when his insatiable demands had no longer to be satisfied? Chateaubriand says something of the sort in his *Mémoires d'Outre-Tombe.* Here, though he repeats all his indictments, he allows free rein to admiration which obsessed him and which forced him to compare his own career, from his birth in the same year, with that of the All-Powerful, to compare, to contrast, to extol, in particular in connection with his own opposition.

"It is the fashion of the day," he writes, "to magnify Bonaparte's victories. Gone are the sufferers, and the victims' curses, their cries of pain, their howls of anguish are heard no more; exhausted France no longer offers the spectacle of women ploughing her soil; no more are parents imprisoned as hostages for their sons, nor a whole village punished for the desertion of a conscript. No longer are the conscription lists stuck up at street corners, no longer do the passers-by crowd round long lists of death sentences to con them anxiously for the names of their children, their brothers, their friends, their neighbours. It is forgotten that everyone used to lament those victories, forgotten that the people, the Court, the generals, the intimates of Napoleon were all weary of his oppression and of his conquests, that they had had enough of a game which, when won, had to be played all over again, enough of that existence which, because there was nowhere to stop, was put to the hazard each morning."

Indeed it was all forgotten. People were forgetting their dislike of despotism, now that they were faced with the Bourbons, their Court of *émigrés* and their priests, and now that France would harvest no new glory. They were forgetting it as they saw the famous soldiers neglected by a despicable government. The opposition, the men of 1789, listened with emotion when General Foy voiced their complaints in the Chamber of Deputies, and praised them, and in them their dead leader. Take the case of Beyle – Stendhal – who had been grumbling about trampled liberty while Napoleon lived and who only now came truly under his spell. The young people in his novels idolize Napoleon. Fabrice in *La Chartreuse de Parme* is an Italian, and in Stendhal's own view the French conquest of Italy meant an altogether desirable liberation from government by priests and obscurantism, while after Napoleon's fall stupidity, senility and cruelty set the tone once more. In *Le Rouge et le Noir*, the action of which takes place in France, Stendhal proclaims his old dislikes through the mouth of an embittered republican, to whom Napoleon is merely the man who has restored all that monarchical nonsense and put the Church back on its pedestal again. But for Julien, the young Frenchman, Napoleon is a god, and the *Mémorial* "the only book in the world, the guide of his life, and object of ecstatic admiration." And yet he wants to be a priest! But the lesson he gets from the book is that one must be accommodating, that with will power you can achieve anything in life. The world no longer belongs to the man with the sword, courageous and gay, but to the soft-voiced, ruthless dissembler, in his cassock.

That was a lesson indeed. Not everyone dared to learn it, and so perplexity, a sense of powerlessness, of being crippled, overcame a generation "begotten between two battles." It was De Musset, speaking with the melancholy voice of the romantics, who voiced their woes. He did not see in Napoleon that *professeur d'énergie*, proclaimed, as we shall see, to the French youth of a later age, nor did he know what to make of the advice "*faites-vous prêtre*" which, according to him too, was addressed to his youthful contemporaries from all sides. But among the dreary ruins of his day, what an impression the figure of the Emperor made on his imagination, how overwhelmingly mighty, inspiring a sense of oppression and of admiration alike! …

"One asks oneself," says Chateaubriand, "by what sleight of hand Bonaparte, who was so much the aristocrat, who hated the people so cordially, has been able to obtain the popularity which he enjoys. For there is no gainsaying the fact that this subjugator has remained popular with a nation which once made it a point of honour to raise altars to independence and equality. Here is the solution:

"It is a matter of daily observation that the Frenchman's instinct is to strive after power; he cares not for liberty; equality is his idol. Now there is a hidden connection between equality and despotism. In both these respects Napoleon had a pull over the hearts of the French, who have a military liking for power and are democratically fond of seeing everything levelled. When he mounted the throne, he took the people with him. A proletarian king, he humiliated kings and noblemen in his anterooms. He levelled the ranks, not down but up. To have dragged them down to plebeian depths would have flattered the envy of the lowest; the higher level was more pleasing to their pride. French vanity, too, enjoyed the superiority which Bonaparte gave us over the rest of Europe. Another cause of Napoleon's popularity is the affliction of his latter days. After his death, as his sufferings on St. Helena became better known, people's hearts began to soften; his tyranny was forgotten; it was remembered how, having vanquished our enemies and subsequently having brought them into France, he defended our soil against them; we fancy that if he were alive today he would save us from ignominy in which we are living. His misfortunes have revived his name among us, his glory has fed on his wretchedness.

"The miracles wrought by his arms have bewitched our youth, and have taught us to worship brute force. The most insolent ambition is spurred on by his unique career to aspire to the heights which he attained."

But Chateaubriand's sombre warning was the voice of the past – or of the future. His contemporaries took refuge in illusion. So did Victor Hugo, who, in a manner quite different from that of Stendhal or Balzac or Beranger, found in the figure of the Emperor an outlet for his romantic longing for greatness, which was mysteriously combined with a love of freedom. In his "Ode to the Column" – the triumphal column in the Place Vendôme from the top of which on March 31st, 1814, the day of the Allies' entry into Paris, a group of royalist noblemen with their plebeian hirelings had removed the statue of the Emperor – the poet, writing in 1830, dedicated to Napoleon "his youthful muse, singing nascent freedom", and promised the departed hero that this generation, which, though it had not known him as master, honoured him as a god, would come and fetch him from his island grave. And what transports there are when ten years later his mortal remains actually return to Paris. "The blessed poets shall kneel before you; the clouds which obscured your glory have passed, and nothing will ever dim its true lustre again."

> Sainte-Hélène, leçon! chute! exemple! agonie!
> L'Angleterre, à la haine épuisant son génie,
> Se mit à dévorer ce grand homme en plein jour.
> Jadis, quand vous vouliez conquérir une ville,
> Ratisbonne, ou Madrid, Varsovie ou Séville,
> Vienne l'austère, ou Naple au soleil radieux,
> Vous fronciez le sourcil, ô figure idéale!
> Alors tout était dit. La garde impériale
> Faisait trois pas comme les dieux.
> Tu voulais, versant notre sève
> Aux peuples trop lents à mûrir,
> Faire conquérir par le glaive
> Ce que l'esprit doit conquérir.
> Tu prétendais, vaste espérance!
> Remplacer Rome par la France
> Régnant du Tage à la Néva;
> Mais de tels projets Dieu se venge.
> Duel effrayant! guerre étrange!
> Jacob ne luttait qu'avec l'ange,
> Tu luttais avec Jéhovah!

Here are elements which we shall meet with in the writings of historians right down to our own time. Here you have pity for the hero's personal fate, dislike for cold-blooded England, unregenerate pleasure in military power, and at the same time an attempt to give spiritual life to the great struggle by linking it to the spread of French thought all over Europe, to liberty, to world peace, so that the spectacle of the catastrophe may be lifted on to a higher plane.

Victor Hugo voiced the spirit of the time in his poems, while Chateaubriand's was an isolated, independent view. This is true. Yet amid the chorus of adulation there were other discordant notes. One poem has remained famous; in it the Napoleonic legend is challenged and assailed with vivid force at the very moment of its clamorous emergence. It is all the more remarkable for the fact that the writer was a young man and spoke, not in the name of religion or of monarchy, but of liberty and republicanism. The young man was Auguste Barbier, and the poem *L'Idole* (1831).

Everyone knows the lines:

O Corse à cheveux plats! que la France était belle
Au grand soleil de messidor!
C'était une cavale indomptable et rebelle,
Sans frein d'acier ni rênes d'or.

The Corsican succeeded in controlling that marvellous animal, and rode it without pity, spurring it till the blood ran, pulling at the bit till its teeth broke, till it sank down dying – and crushed its rider. Certainly, cries Barbier (and here he is obviously aiming at Hugo), I too suffer from the memory of that humiliating day when they pulled down the statue under the eyes of the foreigner, the day when French women bared their breasts to the Cossacks, but I heap my curses on one man only: "Be thou cursed, O Napoleon." But the unholy image is set up again.

Grâce aux flatteurs mélodieux,
Aux poètes menteurs, aux sonneurs de louanges,
César est mis au rang des dieux.

Ah, ends the poet, good princes, wise men who lighten the peoples' chains:

Le peuple perdra votre nom;
Car il ne se souvient que de l'homme qui tue
Avec le sabre et le canon.

The masses honour those who force them to carry stones to build their pyramids; the masses are like a street girl who gives her love only to the man who beats her.[205]

Acknowledgements

The author wishes to thank the following for permission to reprint extracts from the following publications.

Wellington's Army by Professor C. W. C. Oman. Edward Arnold (Publishers) Ltd., London.

Waterloo by John Naylor. B. T. Batsford Ltd., London.

The Personality of Napoleon by J. Holland Rose. G. Bell & Sons Ltd., London.

Le Retour de L'Isle d'Elba by Henry Houssaye, translated by T. C. Macaulay. John Bellows Ltd., Gloucester.

Wellington by John Fortescue. Curtis Brown Ltd.

Napoleon for and Against by Pieter Geyl, translated by Olive Renier. Jonathon Cape Ltd., London and Yale University Press, New Haven, Conn. USA.

The Rise of General Bonaparte by Spencer Wilkinson. The Clarendon Press, Oxford.

The History of a Conscript of 1813 by Erckmann-Chatrian, translated by G. D. Gillman. J. M. Dent & Sons, London and E. P. Dutton & Co., Inc., New York.

Napoleon by Herbert Butterfield. Gerald Duckworth & Co., Ltd., London.

A History of Europe by H. A. L. Fisher. Eyre & Spottiswoode (Publishers) Ltd., London.

The Trial of Marshal Ney by Harold Kurtz. Hamish Hamilton Ltd., London and Alfred A. Knopf Inc., New York.

Napoleon by Octave Aubrey, translated by Margaret Crosland and Sinclair Road. Paul Hamlyn Ltd., London.

Wellington by Philip Guedalla. Harper & Row, Publishers Inc., New York.

The Conduct of War by Major General J. F. C. Fuller. David Higham Associates Ltd., London and Eyre & Spottiswoode (Publishers) Ltd., London and Rutgers University Press, New Brunswick, USA.

The Duke by Philip Guedalla. Hodder and Stoughton Ltd., London.

Napoleon in 1915: The Second Reign Harold Kurtz (from an article in History Today).

The Hundred Days by Edith Saunders. Longmans, Green & Co. Ltd., Essex, UK and W. W. Norton & Company, Inc., New York.

The Hundred Days edited by Antony Brett-James. Macmillan & Co. Ltd., London.

Napoleon in his Time by Jean Savant, translated by Katherine John. Thomas Nelson & Sons, Camden, NJ, USA and Putnam & Company Ltd., London.

Napoleon by Felix Markham. The New American Library Inc., New York.

The Congress of Vienna by Harold Nicholson. Harcourt Brace & Co. Inc., New York and Constable & Co. Ltd., London History of Modern France by Alfred Cobban. Penguin Books Ltd., UK.

The Years of Victory and *The Age of Elegance* by Sir Arthur Bryant. A. D. Peters & Co. and Collins Sons & Co., Ltd., London and Harper & Brothers, New York.

Blücher and the Uprising of Prussia Against Napoleon 1806–15 by Ernest F. Henderson. G. P. Putnam's Sons, New York.

Napoleon and Waterloo by A. F. Becke. Routledge & Kegan Paul Ltd., London.

France by Albert Guérard. University of Michigan Press, Ann Arbor, Mich,. Copyright © University of Michigan.

Notes

1. B. H. Liddell Hart, *The Ghost of Napoléon* (London: Faber, 1934).
2. Felix Markham, *Napoleon*. London: George Weidenfeld and Nicolson Ltd.; New York: The New American Library Inc., 1963.
3. Louis-Antoine Fauvelet de Bourrienne, *Mémoires*. (English translation edited by R. W. Phipps, London, 1885.)
4. Markham, *op. cit.*
5. Herbert Butterfield, *Napoleon*. London: Gerald Duckworth & Co. Ltd., 1939.
6. Albert Guérard, *France*. Ann Arbor, Mich.: University of Michigan Press, 1959.
7. Markham, *op. cit.*
8. Spencer Wilkinson, *The Rise of General Bonaparte*. Oxford, England: The Clarendon Press, 1930.
9. Markham, *op. cit.*
10. Guérard, op. cit.
11. Claud-François, Baron de Méneval, *Mémoires pour servir à l'histoire de Napoleon 1er*. Paris. (English translation by Robert H. Sherard, London, 1894.)
12. Alfred Cobban, *History of Modern France*. Middlesex, England: Penguin Books Ltd., 1961.
13. Guérard, *op. cit.*

. Pieter Geyl, *Napoleon For and Against.* (English translation by Olive Renier. New Haven, Conn.: Yale University Press, 1949; London: Jonathan Cape Ltd., 1957.)

15. Major General J. F. C. Fuller, *The Conduct of War, 1789–1961*. London: Eyre & Spottiswoode (Publishers) Ltd.; New Brunswick, N. J.: Rutgers University Press, 1961.

16. Theodore Ayrault Dodge, *Napoleon*. Vol. IV. Cambridge, Mass., 1907.

17. *Ibid.*

18. Baron Odeleben, *Relation de la Campagne de 1813*. Paris, 1817. Quoted by Jean Savant, *Napoleon in His Time*, translated by Katherine John. London: Putnam & Company Ltd.; Camden, N. J.: Thomas Nelson & Sons, 1958.

19. Markham, *op. cit.*

20. General Thiard, *Souvenirs militaires et diplomatiques*. Quoted by Savant, *op. cit.*

21. Earl of Stanhope, *Notes of Conversations with the Duke of Wellington*. London, 1888.

22. J. Holland Rose, *The Personality of Napoleon*. London: G. Bell & Sons Ltd., 1912.

23. *Ibid.*

24. Markham, *op. cit.*

25. Cobban, *op. cit.*

26. Markham, *op. cit.*

27. Louis Constant, *Mémoires de Constant, Premier Valet de Chambre de l'Empereur.* Paris, 1830. Quoted by Savant, *op. cit.*

28. *Mémoires du Général Baron Thiébault*. Paris, 1895. Quoted by Savant, *op. cit.*

29. Général de Ricard, *Autour de Bonaparte*. Paris, 1891. Quoted by Savant, *op. cit.*

30. Markham, *op. cit.*

31. Guérard, *op. cit.*

32. H. A. L. Fisher was writing in 1936.

33. H. A. L. Fisher, *A History of Europe.* London: Eyre & Spottiswoode (Publishers) Ltd.; Boston: Houghton, Mifflin Co., 1936.

34. Harold Nicolson, *The Congress of Vienna*, New York: Harcourt, Brace & Co., Inc.; London: Constable & Co. Ltd., 1946.

35. Fisher, *op. cit.*

36. Octave Aubry, *Napoléon.* Paris: Flammarion, 1961. (English translation by Margaret Crosland and Sinclair Road. London: Paul Hamlyn Ltd., 1964.)

37. Erckmann-Chatrian, *The History of a Conscript of 1813.* (English translation by G. D. Gillman. New York: E. P. Dutton & Co., Inc., 1909.)

38. Aubry, *op. cit.*

39. Fleury de Chaboulon, *Mémoires pour servir d l'histoire de la vie privée, du retour et du règne de Napoléon en 1815.* London, 1819–1820. Quoted by Jean Savant, *Napoleon and His Time*, translated by Katherine John. London: Putnam & Company Ltd.; Camden, N. J.: Thomas Nelson & Sons, 1958.

40. Aubry, *op. cit.*

41. Henry Houssaye, *Le Retour de l'Isle d'Elba.* Paris, 1893 (English translation by T. C. Macauly. Gloucester, England: John Bellows Ltd., 1934.)

42. Houssaye, *op. cit.*

43. *Ibid.*

44. Ney had been created Prince de la Moskowa after the battle of Borodino.

45. Houssaye, *op. cit.*

46. *Ibid.*

7. *Ibid.*

48. Antoine-Marie Chamans, Comte de Lavallette, *Mémoires et Souvenirs.* Paris, 1831.

49. Duc de Broglie, *Souvenirs.* Paris, 1886.

50. Lavallette, *op. cit.*

51. *Ibid.*

52. Jean Rapp, *Mémoires de Général Rapp, aide-de-camp de Napoléon, écrits par lui-même.* 2nd ed. Paris, 1823. Quoted by Jean Savant, *Napoleon in His Time*, translated by Katherine John. London: Putnam & Company Ltd.; Camden, N. J.: Thomas Nelson & Sons, 1958.

53. Harold Kurtz, "Napoleon in 1815: The Second Reign." In *History Today*, XV: 10, October, 1965.

54. *Ibid.*

55. *Mémoires du General Baron Thiébault.* Quoted by Savant, *op. cit.*

56. Duc de Broglie, *Souvenirs.* Paris, 1886.

57. Octave Aubry, *Napoleon.* Paris: Flammarion, 1961. (English translation by Margaret Crosland and Sinclair Road. London: Paul Hamlyn Ltd., 1964.)

58. Thiébault, *op. cit.*

59. *Ibid.*

60. H. A. L. Fisher, *A History of Europe.* London: Eyre & Spottiswoode (Publishers) Ltd.; Boston: Houghton, Mifflin Co., 1936.

61. Aubry, *op. cit.*

62. G. R. Gleig, *The Life of the Duke of Wellington.* London, 1858–60.

63. C. W. C. Oman, *Wellington's Army.* London: Edward Arnold (Publishers) Ltd., 1912.

64. Sir Arthur Bryant, *The Years of Victory.* London: Collins Sons & Co. Ltd.; New York: Harper & Brothers, 1944.

65. Philip Guedalla, *The Duke*. London: Hodder and Stoughton Limited, 1931. Published in the United States under the title *Wellington*. New York: Harper & Brothers, 1931.

66. Gleig, *op. cit.*

67. John Fortescue, *Wellington*. London: Williams & Norgate, Ltd., 1935.

68. *Ibid.*

69. Oman, *op. cit.*

70. Fortescue, *op. cit.*

71. Oman, *op. cit.*

72. *The Principles of Military Movements, chiefly applicable to Infantry.* Sir David Dundas succeeded the Duke of York as Commander-in-Chief in 1809.

73. Second son of George Ill, the Duke of York was appointed Commander-in-Chief in 1798.

74. Oman, *op. cit.*

75. Fortescue, *op. cit.*

76. John Naylor, *Waterloo.* London: B. T. Batsford Ltd.; New York: The Macmillan Company, 1960.

77. *Ibid.*

78. Earl of Stanhope, *Notes of Conversations with the Duke of Wellington.* London, 1888.

79. General Count Gneisenau, *Blücher.* Berlin, 1815.

80. Ernest F. Henderson. *Blücher and the Uprising of Prussia against Napoleon, 1806–1815*. New York: G. P. Putnam's Sons, 1911.

81. *Ibid.*

82. *Ibid.*

83. *Ibid.*

Ibid.

5. *Ibid.*

86. *Ibid.*

87. Friedrich M. Kircheisen, *Napoleon I.* Munich and Leipzig, 1914. (English translation by Henry St. Lawrence. London: Gerald Howe Ltd., 1931; New York: Harcourt, Brace & Co., 1932.)

88. Captain A. F. Becke, *Napoleon and Waterloo: The Emperor's Campaign with the Armée du Nord, 1815; A strategical and tactical study*. London: Routledge & Kegan Paul Ltd.; New York: E. P. Dutton & Co., 1914.

89. *Ibid.*

90. For the strength and organization of this army, see A. F. Becke, *Napoleon and Waterloo*, (London, 1914) ii, pp. 245–255; also, Edith Saunders, *The Hundred Days* (London: Longmans, 1964), pp. 294–298.

91. For the full text of this proclamation see *Correspondance de Napoléon I* (Paris, 1858–1869), 22,052.

92. Henry Houssaye, *1815: Waterloo*. Paris, 1893. (English translation by Arthur Emile Mann, 1900.)

93. John Naylor, *Waterloo*. London: B. T. Batsford Ltd.; New York: The Macmillan Company, 1960.

94. For the final numbers and organization of the Prussian army, see F. de Bas, *La Campagne de 1815 (Paris, 1908–1909)*. For those of the Anglo-Allied army, see Captain W. Siborne, *History of the War in France and Belgium in 1815* (London, 1844). Also, Becke, *op. cit.*, ii, pp. 256–262, and Saunders, *op. cit.*, pp. 287–294.

95. Philip Guedalla, *The Duke*. London: Hodder and Stoughton Limited, 1931. Published in the United States under the title *Wellington*. New York: Harper & Brothers, 1931.

96. The Emperor's Order of the Day, dated Avesnes, June 13, is given in *Correspondance de Napoléon I*, 22,049.

97. Houssaye, *op. cit.*

98. Theodore Ayrault Dodge, *Napoleon*. Vol. IV. Cambridge, Mass., 1907.

99. Becke, *op. cit.*

100. Houssaye, *op. cit.*

101. Naylor, *op. cit.*

102. Houssaye, *op. cit.*

103. For full text, see Becke, *op. cit.*, ii, p. 282.

104. For full text see *Correspondance de Napoleon I*, 22,058; 22,059.

105. Houssaye, *op. cit.*

106. Prussian generals having the same surname were distinguished from each other by the addition of Roman numerals. Major-General von Pirch I commanded the II Corps; his younger brother, von Pirch II, commanded a brigade in von Zieten's I Corps.

107. Houssaye, *op. cit.*

108. Antony Brett-James, ed., *The Hundred Days.* London: Macmillan & Co. Ltd.; New York: St. Martin's Press, Inc., 1964.

109. *Ibid.*

110. *A Series of Letters of the First Earl of Malmesbury*, edited by his grandson. London, 1870.

111. Houssaye, *op. cit.*

112. Earl of Stanhope, *Notes of Conversations with the Duke of Wellington.* London, 1888.

113. Becke, *op. cit.*

114. Houssaye, *op. cit.*

115. Naylor, *op. cit.*

116. Brett-James, *op. cit.*

117. For the text of Ney's rather more sanguine account, see Alberto Pollio, *Waterloo* (Paris, 1909), pp. 248–249.

118. Naylor, *op. cit.*

119. Harold Kurtz, *The Trial of Marshal Ney*. London: Hamish Hamilton Ltd.; New York: Alfred A. Knopf, Inc., 1957.

120. Francis Lieber, *Reminiscences, Addresses and Essays*. Philadelphia, Pa., 1881.

121. Brett-James, *op. cit.*

122. Houssaye, *op. cit.*

123. *Ibid.*

124. General Count Gneisenau, *Blücher*. Berlin, 1815.

125. Brett-James, *op. cit.*

126. Henry Houssaye, *1815: Waterloo*. Paris, 1893. (English translation by Arthur Emile Mann, 1900.)

127. For the text of these instructions, see Becke, ii, App. 24.

128. Henry Houssaye, *1815: Waterloo*. Paris, 1893.

129. Baron von Müffling, *Passages from My Life*. London, 1853.

130. Houssaye, *op. cit.*

131. General Cavalié Mercer, *Journal of the Waterloo Campaign*. London, 1870.

132. Commandant Henry Lachouque, *Le Secret de Waterloo*. Paris: Amiot-Dumont, 1952.

133. Captain A. F. Becke, *Napoleon and Waterloo: The Emperor's Campaign with the Armée du Nord, 1815; A strategical and tactical study*. London: Routledge & Kegan Paul Ltd.; New York: E. P. Dutton & Co., 1914.

134. Antony Brett-James, ed., *The Hundred Days*. London: Macmillan & Co. Ltd.; New York: St Martin's Press, Inc., 1964.

135. Houssaye, *op. cit.*

136. Becke, *op. cit.*

137. Major R. D. Gibney, ed., *Eight Years Ago, or The Recollections of an Old Army Doctor – Dr. Gibney of Cheltenham*. London, 1896.

138. Mercer, *op. cit.*

139. Capitaine Hippolyte de Manduit, *Les Derniers Jours de la Grande Armée. Documents et correspondence inédite de Napoléon en 1814 et 1815*. Paris, 1847. Quoted by Brett-James, *op. cit.*

140. For full text of this dispatch, see Becke, ii, p. 292.

141. Edward Cotton, *A Voice from Waterloo*. London, 1849.

142. Henry Houssaye, *1815: Waterloo*. Paris, 1893. (English translation by Arthur Emile Mann, 1900.)

143. Theodore Ayrault Dodge, *Napoleon*. Vol. IV. Cambridge, Mass., 1907.

144. *Ibid.*

145. Captain A. F. Becke, *Napoleon and Waterloo: The Emperor's Campaign with the Armée du Nord, 1815; A strategical and tactical study*. London: Routledge & Kegan Paul Ltd.; New York: E. P. Dutton & Co., 1914.

146. General Brialmont, *Wellington*. Paris, 1856–57.

147. Captain Sir J. Kincaid, *Adventures in the Rifle Brigade*. London: Peter Davies Ltd.; New York: Robert M. McBride Company, 1929.

148. Houssaye, *op. cit.*

149. *Ibid.*

150. For full text of this letter, see Becke, ii, p. 293.

151. Houssaye, *op. cit.*

152. *Ibid.*

153. General Baron Jomini, *The Campaign of Waterloo*. (English translation by S. V. Benét. New York, 1853.)

154. John Naylor, *Waterloo*. London: B. T. Batsford Ltd.; New York: The Macmillan Company, 1960.

For the text of Soult's order to Ney confirming this, see William O'Connor Morris, *Waterloo* (London, 1900), p. 387.

156. For Napoleon's order of attack issued to each corps commander at 11 A.M., see *Correspondance de Napoléon I*, 22,060.

157. For the full text of this letter, see Becke, ii, pp. 293–294.

158. For the full text, see Becke, ii, p. 294.

159. Houssaye, *op. cit.*

160. *Les Mémoires du Capitaine Duthilt.* Lille, France, 1909. Quoted by Antony Brett-James, ed., *The Hundred Days.* London: Macmillan & Co. Ltd.; New York: St. Martin's Press, Inc., 1964.

161. Brett-James, *op. cit.*

162. *Ibid.*

163. *Ibid.*

164. Sir Arthur Bryant, *The Age of Elegance.* London: Collins Sons & Co. Ltd.; New York: Harper & Brothers, 1950.

165. General Cavalié Mercer, *Journal of the Waterloo Campaign.* London, 1870.

166. Bryant, *op. cit.*

167. Sergeant Thomas Morris, *Recollections of Military Service in 1813, 1814, and 1815. London*, 1845.

168. *The Reminiscences and Recollections of Captain Gronow.* London, 1862–66.

169. Bryant, *op. cit.*

170. General Baron Auguste Pétiet, *Souvenirs militaires de l'histoire contemporaine.* Paris, 1844.

171. Bryant, *op. cit.*

172. Edith Saunders, *The Hundred Days.* London: Longmans, Green & Co. Ltd.; New York: W. W. Norton & Co., 1964.

173. Christopher Hibbert, ed., *The Wheatley Diary.* London: Longmans, Green & Co. Ltd., 1964.

174. Houssaye refers to Sir John Shaw Kennedy's *Notes on the Battle of Waterloo* (1865).

175. Henry Houssaye, *1815: Waterloo.* Paris, 1893. (English translation by Arthur Emile Mann, 1900.)

176. Bryant, *op. cit.*

177. Antony Brett-James, ed., *The Hundred Days.* London: Macmillan & Co. Ltd.; New York: St. Martin's Press, 1964.

178. John Naylor, *Waterloo.* London: B. T. Batsford Ltd.; New York: The Macmillan Company, 1960.

179. Saunders, *op. cit.*

180. Bryant, *op. cit.*

181. Saunders, *op. cit.*

182. Mercer, *op. cit.*

183. Saunders, *op. cit.*

184. Earl of Stanhope, *Notes of Conversations with the Duke of Wellington.* London, 1888.

185. Ernest F. Henderson, *Blücher and the Uprising of Prussia against Napoleon, 1806–1815.* New York: G. P. Putnam's Sons, 1911.

186. Houssaye, *op. cit.*

187. General Baron Jomini, *The Campaign of Waterloo.* (English translation by S. V. Benet. New York, 1853.)

188. For Grouchy's self-exculpatory report, pp. 306–307. see Becke, op. cit., ii, pp 306–307.

189. Captain A. F. Becke, *Napoleon and Waterloo: The Emperor's Campaign with the Armée du Nord, 1815; A strategical and tactical study.* London: Routledge & Kegan Paul Ltd.; New York: E. P. Dutton & Co., 1914.

190. Theodore Ayrault Dodge, *Napoleon*. Vol. IV. Cambridge, Mass., 1907.

191. G. R. Gleig, *The Life of the Duke of Wellington*. London, 1858–60.

192. For the text of Gneisenau's letter giving the Prussian view, see E. F. Henderson, *Blücher and the Uprising of Prussia against Napoleon* (New York, 1911), p. 315.

193. For the conditions demanded by the Prussians for a truce, and their reasons for wanting Napoleon executed, see Gneisenau's letter to Müffling, in Müffling's Memoirs, pp. 272–274.

194. Earl of Stanhope, *Notes of Conversations with the Duke of Wellington*. London, 1888.

195. For the text of this *communiqué*, see *Correspondance de Napoléon I*, 22,061. It may be compared with Wellington's dispatch in Ourwood's *Selections from the Dispatches of the Duke of Wellington*, no. 951. For Napoleon's subsequent version, dictated on St. Helena, see *Mémoires pour servir à l'histoire de France en 1815* (Paris, 1820).

196. Octave Aubry, *St. Helena*. (English translation by Arthur Livingston. London: Victor GoUancz Ltd., 1937; Philadelphia: J. B. Lippincott Co., 1938.)

197. For the text of this letter, see *Correspondance de Napoléon I*, 22,066.

198. Octave Aubry, *St. Helena*. (English translation by Arthur Livingston. London: Victor GoUancz Ltd., 1937; Philadelphia: J. B. Lippincott Co., 1938.)

199. For the text of this protest, see *Correspondance de Napoléon I*, 22,067.

200. Major General J. F. C. Fuller, *The Conduct of War, 1789–1961*. London: Eyre & Spottiswoode (Publishers) Ltd.; New Brunswick, N. J.: Rutgers University Press, 1961.

201. Albert Guérard, *France*. Ann Arbor, Mich.: University of Michigan Press, 1959.

202. H. A. L. Fisher, *A History of Europe*. London: Eyre & Spottiswoode (Publishers) Ltd.; Boston: Houghton, Mifflin Co., 1936.

203. Alfred Cobban, *History of Modern France.* Middlesex, England: Penguin Books Ltd., 1961.

204. *Ibid.*

205. Pieter Geyl, *Napoleon For and Against.* (English translation by Olive Renier. New Haven, Conn.: Yale University Press, 1949; London: Jonathan Cape Ltd., 1957.)